Trade secrets of a property expert

PROPERTY UNCOVERED

Louisa Fletcher

 Harriman House

Contents

HARRIMAN HOUSE LTD
18 College Street
Petersfield
Hampshire
GU31 4AD
GREAT BRITAIN
Tel: +44 (0)1730 233870
Email: enquiries@harriman-house.com
Website: www.harriman-house.com

First published in Great Britain in 2014
Copyright © Harriman House
Cover image (c) Stewart Williams

The right of Louisa Fletcher to be identified as the Author has been asserted in accordance with the Copyright, Designs and Patents Act 1988.

ISBN: 9780857194336

British Library Cataloguing in Publication Data

A CIP catalogue record for this book can be obtained from the British Library.

Typeset by e-Digital Design Ltd.

Design by Harriman House/C.A.W.P.

To JD – Because before I met you, I knew a lot about houses, but you've taught me what it takes to build a home.

To Mumsie – Thank you for instilling in me that nothing is out of reach if you work hard enough, and for being such an amazing support over the years. I wouldn't be here without you (quite literally).

About the Author

Louisa Fletcher is a property expert, businesswoman, author and broadcast journalist. With over fifteen years' experience in the property industry, Louisa has consulted at board level to the biggest estate agents, new home builders and property websites in the UK, as well as launching and successfully exiting her own critically acclaimed property valuation website and software business.

Louisa has also advised celebrities, public figures and high net worth individuals on their property assets and portfolios, as well as managing commercial and residential re-development projects, both for her clients and herself. Through her media work on television and in the national press, she regularly provides down-to-earth advice to millions of consumers about buying, selling, renting and letting, as well as neighbour disputes, property values, the housing market and practical elements such as property maintenance and improvements.

Louisa lives in the New Forest in Hampshire with her husband John.

www.louisafletcher.com

Acknowledgements

This entire adventure would not have been possible without my friend Murray Lyndon-Harkin who convinced me that I could actually write a book in the first place, much to my protestations to the contrary. Thank you for believing in me and making me do this.

I'm similarly indebted to Myles Hunt and his team at Harriman House, especially my 'editor extraordinaire' Suzanne Tull who has gone far beyond the call of duty to assist me as a fledgling author. This book has been a long time in the making, but thank you guys for sticking with me.

I owe Lucy Heather copious amounts of fizz for her stirling support and ability to keep calm in a crisis. Additionally, massive thanks are due to Stewart Williams, the hugely talented photographer, and marvellous make-up artist Sherrie Warwick who created the shot used on the cover.

As I go about my daily routine I often get talking to people, taxi drivers for example, and it inevitably comes up in conversation that I'm in the property business. Once that happens, I'm usually asked, "Well...don't suppose you know anything about...?" If in the time it takes to get from Marble Arch to the South Bank I can give them a nugget of advice that might save them a few hundred (or thousand) pounds then that really makes my day. It's my belief that *everyone*, regardless of their financial circumstances, should have easy access to straightforward unbiased knowledge around homes and property and that's what inspired me to write this book.

Whilst there is a wealth of information available for free on the internet, most of the time people 'don't know what they don't know', or for that matter, where to look to find out more. I know there will be folk who say some of what I've written in this book is stating the bleedin' obvious. Well that's great, because if they know this stuff already then clearly they don't need my help. But for those who are dealing with a problem for the first time, and just can't see the wood for the trees or don't know where to go for help, it can be scary and confusing and, crucially, can lead to costly mistakes.

That's when you need someone to point you in the right direction, which hopefully is where this book will help. I'm not saying any of this is rocket science, but what I *have* attempted to do is compile a 'roadmap' to provide you with all the basic information in one handy place so you can dip into the various chapters when you need them. I'm a big believer in taking advantage of any free resources, so where relevant I've tried to steer you towards where you can get more information and expert guidance that won't cost you a penny.

With over twenty years' worth of wisdom to draw on, I've based much of *Property Uncovered* on my own experiences, both as a property professional but also from the perspective of being a flatmate, tenant, buyer, seller, landlord and home owner. I've worked on the basis that if it's happened to *me*, it could happen to *you*, therefore you get to benefit from my having had to learn the hard way.

So, as you read this book, picture you and me sat down over a nice cup of tea, chatting about a load of stuff that you need to understand, but don't quite know where to start. I'll try not to make it too boring for you, but we'll cover all the important things to make sure you're properly clued up. It's a conversation rather than a 'how to' manual; I want you to feel that I'm going through this with you, that you're not on your own and that help is at hand should you need it.

Now, go and put the kettle on, and we'll get started...

Louisa

PS: None of the companies or organisations referred to throughout this book have paid any commission or fee to be included. I've simply recommended them to you as they are sites or companies I use myself, and have always found their services or content to be extremely useful or helpful, or they have been a valued contributor to this book.

1.
Fantastic Flatmates

In an ideal world, we'd all be able to afford our own pad – a bijoux space that reflects our personality and offers us a sanctuary from the rest of the world. Or for the more pragmatic, a facilitation point for dressing/sleeping/watching TV and, when lucky, the occasional romantic encounter. A place where neat-freak tendencies can be indulged, or for others of a less orderly persuasion, somewhere to leave all their worldly possessions strewn everywhere with no fear of nagging.

However, the stark reality these days is that it can take a while to get a foothold on the property ladder, and therefore compromises must be made in the short term. Becoming a flatmate or, conversely, letting out a spare room to bolster cash flow so that the mortgage or rent can be paid, are ideal alternatives to living with your parents. Or squatting.

In fact, chances are, if you're reading this, are under thirty and live in one of the UK's major cities, it's highly likely that you are living in a house or flat share set-up. In fact, according to **www.spareroom.co.uk**, one in eight flat sharers is actually over forty. Given the rise in rents and property prices over the last ten years, there has been a startling increase in 'professional renters' – people who need to balance the career advantages of living in a city with the sky-high costs of urban housing. At the same time, there's been a proliferation in property owners with crippling mortgages who need to rent out a room or two for a period of time to boost their income. So let's get it straight now: house or flat shares are not just for students.

In fact, it's estimated that by 2020 two out of five of all private households will enter into private sharing arrangements: households made up of people living together who are not related or in a relationship.

So, whether you're a student or a professional sharer, there are rules to be observed – some official, some unofficial. And there is truth in the old saying *"You don't know anyone properly until you've lived with them."* From experience, I can tell you that having a mate who is great fun to go shopping or out on the town with is one thing, but sharing a property together is quite another, especially if you have different approaches to domestic bliss.

One of my earliest experiences of sharing was with a friend who, on the face of it, was ideal flatmate material. Always perfectly dressed with an immaculate manicure and blow-dry, I assumed she'd have a similar approach to housekeeping.

How wrong could I be?

Like a one-woman Hurricane Winnie, she could decimate a room in ten minutes. I haven't seen such a talent before or since. Yes, she was a joy to be around, but her penchant for noisy nocturnal activities became a little too much – and that was only in the first week. By month two, she had developed her own 'code' for when she was entertaining at home: a bra hung on the front door. If I saw the lingerie on display, then I knew there was a fair chance I'd find her and some beau *in flagrante delicto*, either over the kitchen counter or on the lounge floor. Not quite the warm welcome I was expecting.

Clearly, when looking for a house share or advertising a room for rent it's reasonable to outline a few ground rules to make sure all parties are on the same page. Otherwise, like me, you may just find yourself in a situation where you have to have *that* uncomfortable chat with your flatmate about her handcuffs being left on the dining table. Not great when my mother decided to drop in for an impromptu visit. And yes, dear reader, that really did happen.

If approached well, sharing a house or flat can be great – someone to go halves on the chores and split the bills with, and perhaps, if you're lucky enough, to lend you clothing/money/a shoulder to cry on in a crisis.

So, how does one go about finding that elusive perfect flatmate? What are the golden dos and don'ts?

1. Where to look

Back in the good old days, finding a flat or house share usually meant scouring the classified section of your local paper or looking on the notice board in the local Post Office or newsagent. Trying to ascertain from a forty-word advert where exactly the property was, if it was habitable, and if you would actually want to share with the individual in question was a little tricky. Much time could be wasted visiting hovels that didn't meet your expectations.

Now, however, life is easier. A plethora of websites – not dissimilar to online dating, one might suggest – are available that provide full details and photographs of countless properties, along with descriptions of potential flatmates. Those seeking a room can also post their profile and property criteria and await automatic matching.

The main sites, including **www.spareroom.co.uk**, **www.easyroommate.com** and **www.flatmaterooms.co.uk** all work in a slightly different way, but generally it's free to join, then you pay to upgrade in order to either enhance your profile (as a lodger) or property listing (as a landlord), as well as to access any advanced features. Expect to spend between twenty to forty quid, depending on how long you run your ad for. As it means that you are likely to find your next abode or lodger without leaving the comfort of your duvet or desk, I'd suggest it's probably money well spent.

One thing I would mention though – don't forget that everyone will be trying to portray themselves in the best light. So, for example, if someone's profile says that they are a "light smoker", on meeting them qualify exactly what that means. If you can't stand the whiff of Marlboro Lights and think that two a week is an excessive habit, yet your potential flatmate has just cut down from seventy a day to fifty, that slight difference of opinion is going to become a wide gulf very quickly indeed.

By all means be honest about what you can and can't tolerate – just be polite about it and don't come across as judgemental. Also, be truthful about your budget in your profile; if you can afford to pay £500 a month, but that has to include all bills, say so. Better to be upfront so that you only look at rooms you can afford, rather than falling for a great room with someone you think you could really get on with, only to realise that you can't afford it.

If you are placing an advert for a room that is available, above all make sure the photos you use are an honest representation to avoid wasting everyone's time. No Photoshop or quirky Instagram filters here, thank you. If the room has an en-suite, or comes with secure off-road parking or any other unusual features such as a private balcony or a river view, take pictures of that as well.

If you employ a cleaner, and the rent covers a contribution towards the costs, that's worth mentioning too. Most sites have features that show the location of the property in relation to transport links, as well as a form you can complete that shows how much the bills are etc.

Should this particular route feel a little too clinical (or scary) don't forget the good old-fashioned 'word of mouth' method – for that read 'Facebook'. Even a friend of a friend of a friend could have some kind of recommendation, and it's some comfort, even if small, to know that the individual in question isn't a complete stranger.

Better still, if they are on the worlds' largest social network, you can even (within reason) have a bit of an online stalk to find out who else they know and what they get up to in their spare time. Don't forget, though, the reverse also applies.

Top tip: Unless you know the person exceptionally well and socialise with them regularly, avoid sharing with someone you work with. Everyone needs time apart, and having to deal with the person who used all the hot water or bog roll that morning in the office doesn't exactly make for a good professional relationship.

Also, the temptation to gossip to your co-workers about your flatmate's bad habits or love life may prove irresistible, particularly if they've really hacked you off and you need to moan to someone. I speak from experience. Likewise, it's not a great idea to take 'humorous' pictures of your flatmate in compromising positions and post them for all to see on Twitter or Instagram, nor make cryptic comments in Facebook posts about their lack of cleanliness/loud music/habit of emptying the fridge.

In other words, don't air your dirty linen in (virtual) public.

---

2. *The interview*

So, you've done your research, been online and found a couple of suitable contenders for lodger of the year or potential rooms in the right area. You now need to take the plunge and meet with the other party/parties. This is easy if it's you who's renting out the room – you'll be on home turf and therefore a lot more confident. Invite the individual round for a cuppa (or alcoholic beverage if their profile suggests it's appropriate) so you can get an idea of how they might fit in, if they have any perceptible unpleasant body odour or sociopathic tendencies and, crucially, if you think you can trust them in your home when you're not there.

Remember, *this is not a CIA interrogation, so no polygraph is required.* Mind your manners and don't pry too deeply about relationships, religion, political tendencies or ethnic background. Any information volunteered is great, and with a few intelligent questions you should be able to glean enough to arrive at a reasonable verdict. For everything else you may want to know it's pretty easy to find someone's digital footprint these days with the click or two of a mouse.

Don't think you need to make a decision straightaway – no matter how suitable you think the person is, explain that you are seeing other people and that you'll get back to them in a day or so. Try not to leave it any longer, or else they may decide to go elsewhere. You can then invite them round again, perhaps even with a friend present who can offer an alternative opinion afterwards.

If, on the other hand, you are the candidate, do bear in mind that you will be under close scrutiny. Yes, you need to be yourself, but remember to be polite and treat the situation a bit like a job interview. Ultimately, *you are selling yourself and the ability to be trusted with the front door key to someone else's home.*

However, don't be so intimidated that you don't ask questions yourself. You absolutely need to know if you will feel comfortable in the property and with the other person. Is this somewhere you can flop on the sofa and unwind without feeling like you're intruding? Is there the possibility that a strict cleaning rota or house rules will be enforced? You should be able to relax in your home environment, so trust your gut feeling. If you want to see the place a couple of times before committing, mention that you're looking at other options and that you'd like to come back in a couple of days' time.

Whichever side you are approaching the situation from, *don't forget to ask for references* – you need to feel safe about the new arrangement, particularly if the other party is of the opposite sex.

At the very least, find out where the person works and what they do, so that you know they are in full-time employment and are (reasonably) trustworthy. If you're a gal and you'd like some more tips on personal safety, a good resource is **www.suzylamplugh.org.**

Also, always follow your instinct; it really is your best self-preservation device. If someone gives you the creeps, no matter how nice they seem, or how well their references check out, find somewhere or someone else.

3. The paperwork

For some people, a casual, verbal agreement to pay each month is enough (although I wouldn't recommend it). For others, particularly those with a hefty mortgage, a more formal written contract with their lodger could be a good idea. This will outline responsibilities for both parties, the amount of rent and contribution towards bills that will be paid each month, and crucially, how much notice needs to be given on both sides in order to extricate yourself from the arrangement.

In other words, what you need is a Lodger Agreement.

Most solicitors can draw something like this up for you, and it should cost no more than a couple of hundred pounds. Or you can download a standard contract (for example, **www.spareroom.co.uk** have a Lodger Agreement template you can purchase for a very reasonable £7.50).

If you go the solicitor route, I'd suggest it's reasonable that the cost of doing so is split equally between you. However, whichever way you go, do remember that this is a *binding* agreement – you will be held to it once you've signed it. You are, in effect, both safeguarding yourself and giving the other party a leg to stand on. So don't go into it lightly, especially if your circumstances are such that you may need the option of a quick 'get out' clause.

The main areas any agreement should cover are as follows:

- The names of the people entering into the agreement, in other words the landlord and the lodger.

- The address of the property, details of the room that will be let out and which other parts of the property can be used by the lodger.

- The amount that the lodger will pay the landlord per month for their room.

- Which bills are included in the amount paid per month, or if not, what the lodger's contribution towards the bills will be.

- The day of the month that the money is payable on, or by what date each month the money should be in the landlord's account.

- The date the agreement has been made and how long the agreement is in place for (best to use dates, so for example 'agreement to end on 31.12.15').

- The notice period, i.e. how much notice needs to be served by either party to end the agreement.

- If the landlord owns the property, it's a good idea to include in the agreement a notice documenting that the lodger, whilst paying the landlord rent, has no rights in terms of any property claim or any right to the property.

- Details of any deposit taken by the landlord.

That level of detail should be sufficient, and to be honest, it's not like you're getting married and looking for a pre-nup, so short and sweet is good.

Get two copies and ensure there is a landlord and lodger signature on both. That way you've each got a copy for your records. It may not be a bad idea to scan and keep an electronic copy as well. Fingers crossed, you'll never have to refer to it, but hey, better safe than sorry.

If, however, you're moving into a rented property and will be going on the lease, then you won't need a Lodger Agreement. Instead you'll need to enter into a **Joint Tenancy Agreement**, which normally takes the form of an **Assured Shorthold Tenancy** agreement or **AST** (see Section 2, 'Understanding your lease' under 'The Realities of Renting' chapter, for more information on ASTs).

If there's a letting agent involved, they will need to check your credit and employment history, for which there may be a fee. (Ask how much it's going to cost in order to avoid a nasty surprise.) They may also charge a fee to draw up a new Tenancy Agreement on which you will be named. Make sure they are doing this, and of course get a copy, as well as asking how much you're going to be charged for the privilege.

Now, whilst we're on the subject of paperwork, a word about deposits. There are basically two scenarios to consider.

- If you're renting a room directly from the landlord and they own and live in the property, you'll probably need to give them a deposit against you trashing the place. As you won't have a Tenancy Agreement (e.g. an Assured Shorthold Tenancy) this money *won't* go into a **Client Money Protection Scheme**, so get in writing what you've paid as a deposit and also that, unless there are unpaid damages when you move out, you'll get your deposit back.

- If you're flat sharing with someone else in a rented property under a Joint Tenancy Agreement which *is* an Assured Shorthold Tenancy, your deposit should be lodged with a **Client Money Protection Scheme**, and by law you should be told where your money is being held. For more on Client Money Protection Schemes, how they work and how to safeguard your deposit, see Section 3, 'Deposits' under the 'Realities of Renting' chapter.

In the second scenario, it's best if you can pay your deposit directly to the letting agent (if there is one involved) or the landlord. This way you can track where your money is, and it's very clear what you've paid. If you're replacing someone who's moving out, I really wouldn't recommend you giving them money for their deposit to 'save on paperwork'. It can get messy and lead to problems in the future.

4. To tax or not to tax?

If you own a property and are renting out a room, you are liable to pay income tax on the rent paid to you. Yes, the government wants a cut of that dosh as well.

The good news is that you are allowed to receive up to £4,250 tax-free from a lodger under the government's 'Rent a Room' scheme. To be eligible for this, you have to rent the room *furnished* (a bed and a wardrobe will suffice) and you need to live in the property as your main residence. Any income over the £4,250 threshold and you'll have to declare it in your tax return.

For details about what you can and can't do check out: **www.gov.uk/rent-room-in-your-home/the-rent-a-room-scheme**

I know, I know, your lodger may be paying you in cash and you may, just may, get away with it, but trust me, it's not worth playing games with HM Revenue & Customs.

However, if you are living together in the biblical sense (as happened to some friends of mine: she started off as his lodger, but six months later became his girlfriend and married him shortly afterwards) then the rules are different and the tax thing is an irrelevance. This does not, however, give you *carte blanche* to sexually harass your lodger.

Another party you need to inform should you be acting as landlord is your mortgage company – chances are they'd never find out, but it is your duty as the borrower to inform your **lender** of any changes to your personal circumstances.

5. Get permission

If you are *renting* a property and decide that you want to have a lodger, you'll need to get your landlord's permission. Why? Well, this is classed as **subletting** and in most standard Assured Shorthold Tenancy agreements it's not permitted. However, you can change the tenancy and put it into joint names (which is called a **Joint Tenancy Agreement**) – again, with the landlord's permission.

If you do this, just be mindful of the fact that this gives the other person *the same rights to the property as you*. So, if you don't get on, you can't just give them two weeks' notice to remove themselves and their *Twilight* DVD collection. You'll have to go through the rigmarole of both of you giving notice to the landlord to change the agreement. Worst case, if they won't move out, you'll have to.

Also, bear in mind that if you put the tenancy in joint names (or multiple names if you're sharing with more than one person) it means you are **jointly and severally liable** – in other words, if they don't pay the rent, you'll have to pick up the whole tab, not just your share.

Lastly, if you do enter into a Tenancy Agreement in joint names and then decide it's not working out, the landlord has the right to decide who stays and who goes. Brutal, but them's the breaks. This decision can be based on income levels (so who the landlord believes will be the most able to keep up the rent payments), credit score and previous tenancy references. The letting agency (if there is one) may also get involved at this point to review individuals' situations to assess who is best placed to continue the tenancy.

This actually happened to me once when I was renting an apartment with another girl who turned out to be very difficult to live with. Although she found the apartment first and had lived there for quite some time before I moved in, we entered into an Assured Shorthold Tenancy on which we were both named when I took up residence. When we fell out (following ongoing issues with her borrowing my clothes/shoes/cash and not returning them, as well as paying the rent and bills late) she tried to throw me out – pretty forcibly, as I recall. However, the letting agency informed me that we both had equal rights as it was a Joint Tenancy Agreement. Seeing as my 'delightful' flatmate wasn't employed at the time (and hadn't been for a while), and because I had a good job which I'd been in for a couple of years, they felt I was a more suitable candidate to stay.

The moral of the story? *Be aware of what you're signing and what your rights are.* No one else is going to figure it out for you.

6. Cover yourself

I appreciate it's really dull, but if you are in a flat or house share, you'll need to consider some kind of **contents insurance** for your possessions. Yep, it's not sexy, but better to consider it now rather than after something horrific has happened.

If you're the lodger, think about it: how much would it cost to replace your clothes/hi-fi/stock of rare Japanese comics should your housemate decide to leave a load of candles unattended and burn the place down? Exactly, more than a fiver. As a tenant, insuring your own personal effects and possessions is your responsibility – you're unlikely to be covered on the landlord's contents insurance – so if you're renting a pad with a mate on a Joint Tenancy Agreement or a lodger in someone's property, *don't for one minute assume that you will be covered any other way.*

Most general household insurers do offer policies specifically for flats or house sharers, which normally cover up to £10,000 worth of 'stuff' – including items away from the home (so if your bike or handbag gets nicked whilst you're out and about, that would be insured too). Expect to pay between £50 to £100 per year for a decent policy. Perhaps start by looking on the normal comparison sites, and before long you'll find something to suit your requirements. Make sure you read the small print as some policies have some pretty kooky clauses about what they will and won't cover you for or may require a lock on your bedroom door in order to insure your personal possessions, particularly if you're sharing a property with more than one person.

If you're the landlord and renting out a room, you need to tell your buildings and contents insurer. Chances are it won't put the price up on your premium, but you have to inform them about any changes to your circumstances so that they can note it on your policy. And here's the thing: if you don't tell your insurers that you have a lodger, and *do* end up having to make a claim, you may well find that your policy is invalid. Not good.

So for the price of a phone call, it's a no brainer.

7. Guys 'n' gals

Sharing a place platonically with a member of the opposite sex can have its upsides: if you do end up fancying each other, you can forget your Tinder app, and downsides: girls tend to be very fussy about cleanliness and blow small things out of proportion, whilst boys seldom see 'a bit of dirt' and their used socks hanging around the place as an issue.

Another potential benefit is if your flatmate does have an active social life, then chances are if there isn't any attraction between the two of you, they may well have a fit friend who visits occasionally.

Bear in mind though ladies, if you are sharing with a guy and there is absolutely no way, not on this earth, ever-in-a-million-years that you would consider any horizontal liaison, don't parade around in just your underwear or a towel. It might lead to a drunken amorous manoeuvre from the other party at some stage and that's just awkward for everyone.

On a similar note, it's a girl thing to be a bit territorial when another woman comes to visit. So if he brings a lady friend back, be nice. Don't make catty comments, regardless of how unsuitable you think she is, and turn a blind eye if she steals a bit of your shampoo. Remember, you're going to want to do some entertaining yourself, and you won't want him sat there watching *Match of the Day* and farting whilst you try to create a romantic atmosphere. *Treat as you would be treated.*

8. Sharing is caring

Along with housework (or lack of it), other major flashpoints in a shared-abode set up are viewing habits and provisions.

With regards to the TV thing, in my experience, most guys would watch tiddlywinks if it were televised, so in an all-male household, there are rarely going to be any complaints about football, cricket or golf being on. The whole weekend.

Therefore (sexist comment alert) if your housemate is a bloke and you're female, *forget any rights you may think you have regarding the remote control*. Won't happen. Safest way forward, if finances allow, is to get your own telly for your bedroom or acquaint yourself with the joys of catch-up services.

In terms of supplies, always try to be generous and pool resources. Unless absolutely necessary, separate cupboards and shelves in the fridge are very divisive. Get into the habit of writing a shopping list together every week and then each contribute financially, taking it in turns to do the supermarket run. Of course, it's fair to lay claim to any 'special purchases' or ingredients for a particular meal you're cooking, so do ask before you take anything that you think may have a specific purpose.

The idea is that you can trust each other – so marking a line on the bottle of wine in the fridge to ensure it's not being snaffled behind your back isn't really on. *If you use the last of the toilet paper or milk, replace it. Don't think about it, just do it.*

9. *Entertaining etiquette*

It's perfectly reasonable to want to bring friends or suitors back to your pad, but it's also important to check that it's okay with your flatmate and, if the occasion is appropriate, to ask if they would like to join you. If it's not convenient, then offer to reorganise – there's nothing worse than trying to get an early night because you have to be up at the crack of dawn, to find that your home is full of party animals enjoying an all-night bender, with accompanying Pacha inspired soundtrack. Been there, done that (as in I was the one who had to get up at 5am) and I wasn't a happy camper.

It's also very important to discuss with your flatmates the partner situation. In other words, how many nights is it OK to have your boyfriend or girlfriend to stay. Most people would say three nights a week is the maximum. This is important, because unless you agree otherwise, no one wants to take in a flatmate or lodger and then end up sharing with a couple.

Remember, if you agree in writing to a maximum number of 'conjugal visits' per week and exceed them, you will be in breach of your Lodger Agreement, as well as royally hack off your landlord or flatmates in the process.

Another thing: besides your beloved, it's okay to have people to stay over, but do ask first. *Never – and I mean, **ever** – offer out your housemate's bed to anyone without checking and getting agreement first then changing the bedsheets afterwards.* Rather than invading their space you should sleep on the sofa or floor and let your guest use your bed.

One last thing on this – if you are renting a room from the owner of the property, their word is the last word, regardless of the situation. No arguments.

10. The long goodbye

Inevitably, at some point, you'll want to move on. Either you'll somehow find the dosh to buy a place, or meet the love of your life and want to give cohabiting a go. Or you may just decide that the situation isn't working out, and opt to make alternative arrangements. Whilst that's all great for you, don't forget, you're now throwing the other party's domestic arrangements into turmoil. So treat the situation with the seriousness it deserves.

Sit them down and explain what you are going to do, and give them a reasonable amount of time to replace you (yes, I know no one is going to be as wonderful a flatmate as you've been but hey, they're going to have to try). A minimum of a month's notice will suffice, particularly if the relationship between you has broken down and neither of you can bear the sight of each other, but ideally, two months is better if you can afford to do so. Or, if you did draw up paperwork in the form of a Lodger Agreement, check the notice period and go from there.

If you are on a Joint Tenancy Agreement, check to find out when the break clause is (a specific date that's been agreed when you can serve notice to vacate the property) so you're not in breach of your lease. If you want to move out *before* the break clause, speak to the landlord or letting agency and ask if you can amend the agreement once your flatmate has found a new house-buddy. Chances are, if you're happy to pay the fee involved (normally about £100 to change an agreement) and the new party checks out with references etc., you won't have a problem. But do ask the appropriate questions.

Remember to inform your utility companies that you're moving on if any accounts are in joint names (don't forget your Council Tax either). Make sure you're up to date with your share of the bills too, particularly if you are not parting on amicable terms.

No matter how unpleasant the situation is, leaving loose ends with regard to finances will somehow come back to haunt you in the long run. It may even negatively impact your credit score, which isn't what you want, so as boring and potentially aggravational as it is, get it sorted and make a clean break.

Conclusion

For many, flat or house sharing is an effective solution to a short or mid-term problem. If you're a lodger, it means you can afford to live in a much nicer property than you would be able to on your own. If you're a landlord, it makes that monthly mortgage payment a bit easier to manage.

I've made some very good friends from sharing in my earlier days, and if you get it right, hopefully you will too. I saved a fortune on rent when I was starting out on the career ladder in London, and lived in some great places with some lovely people who ended up as close friends that I otherwise wouldn't have met. Apart from the odd glitch, at the time it was the best thing I could have done.

Just don't use up the last of the loo roll without replacing it, OK?

2.
The Realities
of Renting

I remember the first place I rented really well. On the face of it, it was quite likeable. The landlord had taken a Victorian semi and converted it into two flats, so everything was shiny and new; basic but clean. Lots of wood-chip wallpaper and the sort of grey carpet you'd expect to find in an office. Being young and naive, as I waltzed around the day I got the keys, I never stopped to query where the radiators were.

It was August, I was eighteen and heating wasn't really on my list of priorities. Unfortunately, when I *did* eventually ask the question (after I'd signed my lease), it turned out that the flat didn't have any heating other than a tiny electric fan in the bathroom. As the landlord put it,

> *"Tenants always seem to have trouble with boilers, so I thought, no boiler, no problems!"*

Let me tell you, it was one of the coldest winters of my life – and it taught me a very valuable lesson about being 100% sure about important facts before singing on the dotted line.

For many, renting is a convenient option. Over the years, I've rented a few times when I've been between properties I've been developing, in the 'try before you buy' stages of a relationship, or settling in a new area with a new job and trying to work out what I wanted to do. There is an old but true adage:

> *"If you're buying, you're gambling on the market going up, if you're renting, you're gambling on it going down."*

Some people say that renting is dead money – well, you're certainly paying someone else's mortgage for them. But, as it's now getting harder and harder to buy, more people are finding there aren't any other options. Rental property isn't the 'stop gap' for many that it used to be, and rather than choosing to step off the property ladder, rent for a while and then buy when the time is right, private renting is, for many, the only realistic long-term housing route.

As it stands, of the 23 million or so households in the UK, current figures suggest that over 4 million households are privately rented. We don't know how many of those people would like to buy but are unable, or are renting due to relocation or a change in circumstances. But whichever way you look at it, that number is only going to increase over the next few years.

In my case, when an ex and I ended up going our separate ways after nearly a year, whilst we'd spent a fair bit in rent over that time, it was nothing compared with the amount of money we would have shelled out had we bought somewhere together then had to go through the awful process of splitting assets and getting ourselves out of a joint mortgage. (See Chapter 7, 'Breaking Up is Hard to Do' to *really* put you off living together.)

By contrast, arranging for him to move out and for me to take over the lease was, whilst traumatic in its own way, a walk in the park compared to how it would have been if we'd owned the place.

Compared to buying a property, renting is a lot easier – there's less paperwork to deal with and the process is much quicker. Finding the pad of your dreams to getting the keys normally takes between two to four weeks, rather than the long and torturous process of buying somewhere. You don't have to find a huge deposit – usually it's between four to eight weeks of rent. And, of course, if something goes wrong you just call the landlord or letting agency. Someone not only comes out to fix it, but the landlord (usually) pays for it too. Happy days.

Now for the reality check. Because more and more people are renting, in some areas of the country we are beginning to see rents increasing and more competition in terms of numbers of tenants applying for the same properties. Which basically means that in some towns and cities, it's a landlord's market. Great news if you're a Buy To Let investor, but not so great if you're looking for a decent place to live which is affordable.

The other thing is that, where there is an increased rental demand, the possibility of dealing with unscrupulous landlords or letting agents is greater. No happy endings there then.

On the lower end of the Armageddon scale, you're always in a position whereby it's not your home so your landlord can give you notice to move out (subject to your lease agreement, of course). And you need to get permission for putting up pictures, decorating or keeping pets.

So, in this chapter, we're going to look at the process of renting from a *tenant's* perspective: how to protect yourself as best as possible against rogue landlords, how to get your deposit back when it's time to move on, and how to best avoid getting evicted.

1. Be fussy about letting agents and landlords

If you want to rent with as few problems as possible, make sure that the letting agent you deal with is a member of one of the professional bodies for the lettings industry.

The good guys will be members of either ARLA (Association of Residential Letting Agents), RICS (Royal Institution of Chartered Surveyors), NALS (National Approved Lettings Scheme), UKALA

(UK Association of Letting Agents) or the NAEA (National Association of Estate Agents). If you're in London, make sure that the letting agent is accredited with Boris' new scheme, the London Rental Standard.

As with estate agents, there is currently no mandatory regulation process – don't get me started on that one – but members of these organisations will have:

- Signed up to a strict code of conduct regulated by a redress scheme. The good news is that by the end of 2014, this is going to change from being voluntary to mandatory and all letting agents will have to sign up to one of the three redress schemes available – The Property Ombudsman, Ombudsman Services or the Property Redress Scheme. For the time being though, this isn't law, so your best bet is to use a letting agent who is a member of one of the industry bodies as they each have their own processes for dealing with complaints.

- Undertaken training and exams to make sure that they have a thorough understanding of the law surrounding residential lettings (which is actually quite complicated) and committed to keeping that knowledge up to date with ongoing specialist education. The only exception to this is UKALA, who offer training for their members, but whose exams aren't mandatory.

- Registered to administer deposits and rents via a **Client Money Protection Scheme**. In other words, providing you've not trashed the place or owe any rent, the landlord will have to prove that deductions from your deposit are required, and even then, the process is managed completely independently.

My personal preference would be to always rent a property through an agent who belongs to a professional body. Knowing that the person I'm dealing with has had the correct training and really knows what they are talking about has always given me peace of mind.

So once you've finished looking on **www.rightmove.co.uk** or **www.zoopla.co.uk** for the perfect rental property and found a few possibilities, check to make sure the agents are registered with ARLA, RICS, NALS, UKALA, NAEA or the London Rental Standard. You can get a list of members in your area by going to the various websites:

- ARLA – **www.arla.co.uk**
- NALS – **www.nalscheme.co.uk**
- UKALA – **www.ukala.org.uk**
- RICS – **www.rics.org/uk**
- NAEA – **www.naea.co.uk**
- London Rental Standard – **www.london.gov.uk/priorities/ housing-land/renting-home/london-rental-standard**

It's also worth checking out sooner rather than later what fees you'll be charged as a tenant. Letting agents have to publish these upfront and seeing as they can be pricey it's good to know in advance what you might be getting yourself into.

Also, find out what you'll be charged for renewing your lease if you decide to stay put longer, and what fees you'll be charged when you leave the property.

That all said, do bear in mind that increasingly many landlords are letting their properties directly and aren't using letting agents. For you, dear tenant-to-be, that can cause an issue.

If your prospective landlord is a professional investor, they *may* know what they are doing. On the other hand, they may not. The law surrounding lettings and tenancy agreements is complex, and things can get tricky quite quickly if a landlord isn't fully aware of their responsibilities. Let's face it, downloading an Assured Shorthold Tenancy agreement for a fiver and filling in the blanks does not a professional landlord make. Not only that, if your landlord is technically a resident overseas, you may have to deduct income tax from any rental payments you make. And you really, *really* don't want to go down that road.

Also, look at it another way. If a landlord doesn't want to pay a few hundred pounds to a letting agent to find a tenant and administer the deposit and agreement correctly, let alone a small percentage to professionally manage the property each month, what do you think your chances are of that landlord being swift to send out a plumber or electrician if you need them? Exactly.

Worse still is the overseas landlord who only deals directly with tenants and doesn't use a letting agent. Try tracking him down when you've got boiler issues.

I'm not saying that you should never deal direct. I appreciate that in some circumstances, you may not have the luxury of choice, and the fees that you'll spend on applying to rent via a letting agent are not cheap. So I can see why both sides might prefer this option. But all I would say is, *if you **can** rent your property via a reputable agent who is a member of a professional body, then do so* as you will have a degree of protection and redress should you have any problems.

OK, so whether you are renting via a letting agent or dealing with the landlord directly, there are a couple of important things you should check regardless.

I know what I'm about to say might make you think I'm being a) overly cynical or b) anally retentive, but I'm trying to look out for your best interests here, so take my word for it. There are two really, really important questions you need to ask before you sign on the dotted line.

1. **Make sure that the landlord *actually* owns the property that you want to rent.** Sounds obvious right? Think again. Sad but true, there is a rising trend of landlords who are renting properties

long term, then subletting them to tenants at a profit without permission, causing a world of pain around Tenancy Agreements, safety and property maintenance, not to mention putting the tenants who are unintentionally subletting at risk of being evicted with little or no notice if the real owner finds out. It's easy to check that the landlord is who is they say they are. Just go on the Land Registry website (**www.gov.uk/government/organisations/land-registry**) and for £3 you can download the deeds to the property to check the owner's details. Perfectly legal, and for the sake of £3, I'd say it's worth doing.

2. **Make sure that the landlord has permission from their mortgage lender to let their property.** If you have done what I've just suggested, if there is an outstanding mortgage on the property it will be noted on the deeds so you can see which lender the landlord's mortgage is with. Once you know there is a mortgage in place, ask to see the **Letter of Consent** from the lender or **proof of a Buy To Let mortgage**. Why? Well, if the landlord is being sneaky and hasn't told their lender that they are letting out their property – probably because it may mean that they would have to switch to a Buy To Let deal, which may be more expensive, or their lender might impose a slightly higher interest rate on their current mortgage deal – then should they default on their mortgage, your Tenancy Agreement *isn't* enforceable on the lender. This is called an **Unauthorised Tenancy** in technical speak. In this situation, you could find yourself being served with a few days' notice to vacate the property, even if you've rented through a letting agent and have a proper Tenancy Agreement in place. Not good.

So, to protect yourself, you need to check that your landlord has informed their lender and got permission. The lender will have either provided confirmation in writing that they are aware that the property is going to be rented out (called a **Letter of Consent**) or the property will be financed on a Buy To Let mortgage, in which case the landlord can then provide a letter from the lender to prove everything is above board.

Either way, that's good for you because that makes you an **Authorised Tenant** (give yourself a gold star) which means if your landlord does decide he wants to spend the rent you're paying him on a Lamborghini rather than paying back his mortgage, you're covered should the property get repossessed. Don't just take the letting agent's word for it – insist that you see this information. If they are a reputable agent, they will have this on file anyway, so it should be a no-brainer for them. If they stall you, make excuses or make you feel silly for asking, then explain why you want these details and that it will give you peace of mind. If further arguments are made for not providing you with the details, I strongly suggest you walk away. Briskly.

Whilst we're on this subject, if this happens to you (and I hope it doesn't) and Billy the Bailiff *does* turn up on a Saturday morning and serve you an eviction notice, then it's helpful for you to know that, as an Unauthorised Tenant, you do have *some* rights available to you. The Mortgage Repossessions (Tenant Protection) Act 2010 means that you can attend the possession hearing and plead your case that you need longer than a few days or a couple of weeks to find somewhere else to live, but *only* if you are up to date on your rent payments and not in arrears. Once you've made an application, the court can, if it sees fit, postpone the repossession of the property by up to two months.

Yes, I know it still means you have to move out, but at least two months gives you time to find somewhere and get everything organised properly. For more information about what to do in the event that your landlord does default on their mortgage, I'd suggest you visit Shelter's website (**www.shelter.org.uk**), which has an excellent section about this very topic.

Just bear in mind that in most cases the tenant finds out late in the process that the property is being repossessed, which means you may not get the chance to attend the possession hearing because it could already have taken place. So, if you ever get an official looking letter from a court addressed to 'The Occupier' *always open it*. This is the early warning sign that the wheels have fallen off and you need to take action.

2. *Understanding your lease*

There are three types of tenancy, and I have to say, legislation surrounding renting property is, at best, a wee bit confusing. I'll try to give you a basic outline here so you know, broadly speaking, what you're getting yourself into, but to be honest, I could write a whole book just on this subject alone (although it may be somewhat dull and I don't know how many people would read it). Anyway, the bottom line is that there are three types of Tenancy Agreement:

- **Assured Shorthold Tenancy**
- **Non-Housing Act** or **Common Law Tenancy**
- **Assured Tenancy**

The most common is an **Assured Shorthold Tenancy** agreement. These types of agreements form the majority of rental contracts and are the most likely form you will encounter. However, I'll mention the other two just in case.

A **Non-Housing Act** or **Common Law Tenancy** agreement normally only applies if the total rent for the property exceeds £100,000 a year or if the property you are living in is self-contained but your landlord lives in the same building. So think a large house, converted into separate units with their own bathrooms and kitchens, where you rent one apartment, but your landlord lives in another one. Common Law Tenancies are generally for a fixed term, although you can extend them.

Assured Tenancies are quite rare these days as they have mostly been superseded by Assured Shorthold Tenancy agreements. If you have an Assured Tenancy, your landlord will have had to provide you with a written notice before your tenancy started to tell you that you had an Assured Tenancy and *not* an Assured Shorthold Tenancy.

The difference between the two is this: if you have an Assured Shorthold Tenancy, the landlord can regain possession of the property at the end of the fixed term of the agreement, provided they give you two months' notice, no matter how exemplary a tenant you've been. On the other hand, with an Assured Tenancy you have the right to stay in the property even after the duration of the agreement *unless* the landlord can prove to a court that they've got grounds to get you out (for example, if you're running a crack den or not paying your rent).

Needless to say, the overwhelming majority of landlords opt to let their properties on an Assured Shorthold Tenancy basis, and it's quite common to be offered a twelve-month lease with a six-month break clause so that either of you can get out of the agreement if required. It's also worth knowing that, due to government legislation introduced in 1996, all new tenancies these days are automatically Assured Shorthold Tenancy agreements unless you specifically negotiate otherwise.

Assuming, then, that it's likely you'll end up with an Assured Shorthold Tenancy (AST), you should also be aware of the difference between a **fixed term** and **periodic** agreement. All ASTs start as a fixed-term agreement, which is pretty Ronseal (does what it says on the tin), lasting for a pre-determined amount of time (normally six or twelve months) whereby neither party can give notice to the other during the term to break the tenancy, unless a break clause is specifically negotiated.

At the end of the initial fixed tenancy term, you may have the option of either continuing the lease as a fixed-term arrangement, or allowing it to become periodic. Once a tenancy has become periodic, the tenant can give one month's notice to leave the property, and likewise, the landlord must give two months' notice to ask you to vacate. But be aware: assuming you pay your rent monthly, if your rent is due at the beginning of a month, and you give notice midway through a month, it's likely that you will actually have to pay rent up until the end of the *following* month (see 'Giving Notice' later on in this chapter).

The majority of rental arrangements move to a periodic agreement after the initial fixed term has elapsed as it gives both parties more flexibility. That said, it's ultimately down to your landlord or the letting agent to decide if they will let the agreement 'roll over' into a periodic agreement, or if they will request that you sign into another fixed-term tenancy. It's worth raising this when you're about six weeks or so away from the end of your initial fixed tenancy term, so that you can agree with the landlord or letting agent what sort of agreement you'll be under for the rest of the tenancy.

Do take the time to read your lease agreement through, particularly as there may be a number of things that you are specifically not allowed to do. For example, many landlords specify no children/ pets/smokers when advertising a property, and also include these caveats in the lease agreement. Remember: *if you breach your lease (albeit inadvertently), you could end up evicted* at any point in your tenancy, regardless of how long you've been there.

Also, be aware that if you are renting with another party and put the lease in joint names, you will be jointly and severally liable for the rent. In other words, if one of you can't or won't pay their share of the rent, you'll need to cover it yourself, otherwise you'll be in arrears with the rent and, again, liable to eviction.

3. Deposits

Depending on the type of property you're renting, you're likely to be asked to put down somewhere between one and two months' worth of rent as a deposit, which will be held as security against you wrecking the joint, not paying your rent or breaching your agreement whilst you live there.

The law around the holding of deposits changed in 2007, in a way that makes things a lot fairer to the tenant than before. You see, previously, the deposit could be held by either the letting agent, or the landlord himself. Which was fine, until there was a problem when the tenant moved out, and there was the possibility of money having to be docked from the deposit. The landlord (or letting agent, if they were acting on behalf of the landlord) was allowed to withhold a 'reasonable' amount to cover any damages or unpaid rent. But you try defining reasonable without going to court.

To combat the problem of some unethical landlords profiteering from tenants' deposits, the government introduced the **Tenancy Deposit Protection Scheme**. Under this legislation, any deposit for an Assured Shorthold Tenancy *must* be protected by a government-backed deposit protection scheme. The three they will be able to use are:

- Deposit Protection Service (**www.depositprotection.com**)
- Tenancy Deposit Scheme (**www.tds.gb.com**)
- My Deposits (**www.mydeposits.co.uk**)

There are two types of scheme – **custodial** and **insured**. The **custodial** scheme, run by the **Deposit Protection Service**, involves the letting agent or landlord physically handing over the deposit for safe-keeping. Here, the deposit can't be released at the end of a tenancy unless both parties agree on the amount that is being returned.

Insured schemes, which are the **Tenancy Deposit Scheme** and **My Deposits**, and also the **Deposit Protection Service** (which is both custodial *and* insured), are where the letting agent or landlord pays a fee for protecting the deposit, but in return they get to keep control of the money. You still have the same rights at the end of tenancy, in that if you are not happy with the letting agent or landlord retaining any of the deposit you can raise it with the scheme and use their free dispute resolution service. An independent adjudicator will decide who is entitled to the deposit, and if the agent or landlord doesn't pay the money then the scheme's insurance company will.

All of these websites have a helpful 'check online' function so that you can make sure your deposit is covered where it should be. Goes without saying that I'd highly recommend you make sure your money is with the Tenancy Deposit Protection Scheme you've been told it's lodged with. Your landlord has 30 days from the time you hand your deposit over to protect your money with one of these schemes, and if they don't they are liable to a fine of up to three times the value of your deposit. All the schemes will send you confirmation that your deposit has been protected, so when you get the paperwork through, stash it somewhere safe.

If there is an issue at the end of the tenancy, the landlord has to prove to the dispute resolution service, which all schemes operate, why they need to withhold an amount of money, rather than just doing it. It's a better, fairer way of approaching things.

Should the landlord not provide you with details of where your deposit is held within 30 days (although this should be in your Assured Shorthold Tenancy Agreement) as well as the potential of a fine they also may not be allowed to give you notice to leave the property at the end of your agreement.

As well as protecting your deposit in a scheme, landlords and letting agents also have to serve something called **Prescribed Information**. This is really just basic information about the tenancy and the process for reclaiming your deposit at the end of it, but it's a legal requirement and failure to serve it carries the same fines as non-protection. I highly recommend you read it, or at least file it somewhere so you can refer to it later should you need to.

Best advice I can give you? Before you part with your hard-earned dosh, ask the letting agent or landlord to highlight for you the note in your tenancy agreement that documents which Tenancy Deposit Protection Scheme they will use to administer your deposit. By being clear about this from the get-go, you can be sure that you are protected.

You may be asked to put down a **holding deposit** when you find the place you want to rent, in order to secure it whilst your references are being checked and the paperwork drawn up. Again, this can range from between a couple of hundred pounds to half of the first month's rent.

Generally, the amount you pay as a holding deposit is deducted from your first month's rent, but get everything in writing upfront before you part with a penny so there aren't any surprises further down the line. If you've taken my previous advice and checked out in advance what fees you are liable to pay then it won't come as a shock, but if you haven't, it's worth mentioning that it's also likely that you'll be charged a fee by the letting agent to draw up the lease agreement, run your credit check and arrange an inventory check in. Again, get the amount you're going to be billed in writing, when it's due, and how much it's all going to add up to.

4. Important questions to ask

I know it's really easy to get excited and carried away when you've found the perfect place and want to make sure that no one else beats you to it, but as with most things in life, it's best to just take a step back and make sure you're fully aware of what you're getting yourself into before you sign on the dotted line.

A few things to ask your letting agent or landlord about the property before you put down that holding deposit might include:

• *Can I get satellite/cable/broadband?*

Check with relevant suppliers before you sign the lease if this is a deal breaker for you and the letting agent or landlord isn't sure. You'll need the full address and postcode of the property to do so, then you can look on your provider's website. You can also find out about the available broadband speed on U-Switch (**www.uswitch.com/broadband/speedtest**).

• *What's the mobile phone reception like?*

Turn your phone on and walk around the place to check you can get a signal in all the rooms. You'd be surprised how many people don't do this. Then complain later on.

• *Can I keep pets?*

If Rover is coming with you, this is a very important one to ask, because many flats don't allow animals in the building, regardless of whether you own or rent. So if the answer comes back as a no, then don't think about smuggling your pooch in and hoping no one will notice. They will, and you'll get evicted as you'll be in breach of your lease.

• *Which one is my parking space?*

If the property comes with allocated parking, make sure you know which space(s) is yours.

• *Can I use the garage/shed?*

Some landlords use the garage or shed belonging to a property as additional storage for themselves, which means you can't. Check whether you're going to be able to use it, and make sure you get it confirmed in writing that it will be clear and ready for you to use the day you move in if the answer is affirmative.

• *Can I keep my bike in the bike shed/rack?*

Again, always ask. There may be a reason why not, and it's better to know upfront rather than upsetting your neighbours and/or landlord.

• *Is it okay to hang pictures on the wall?*

This is one you absolutely need to get written permission for. It will have a bearing on getting your deposit returned, so before you get hammer-happy, ask the letting agent or landlord to write to you (email is fine) to confirm permission.

• *Is it OK to smoke?*

You'd be amazed at the amount of tenants who rent a property claiming to be a non-smoker, then suddenly develop a 30-a-day habit as soon as they move in. By all means, lie if you want to about your nicotine addiction, but know that it will likely lose you your deposit and get you evicted into the bargain if you've signed a tenancy agreement which forbids smoking. The smell of cigarettes (worse still, cigars) together with nicotine stains on walls and fabrics are expensive to remove without totally redecorating and replacing soft furnishings, and that will all be at your expense, my friend. Some landlords are OK with smokers, so don't think you'll never find a place to live. But always, always ask the question.

I guess *the point I'm trying to make here is: assume nothing.* If something is important to you, ask the landlord or letting agent verbally, then put it in writing (email is fine) and make sure you get a response in writing. If you're happy with the answers, then fine, go ahead and put down your holding fee.

You need to make sure you go into this with your eyes wide open, as trying to get out of a lease agreement is pretty tricky, not to mention expensive, unless you wait until your break clause comes up.

In addition to asking about what you can and can't do, it's also important to ask a few questions to make sure that the landlord has complied with their legal obligations to you as a tenant. So, for example, you are quite within your rights to ask to see:

- The Landlord's **Gas Safety Certificate:** Under the Gas Safety (Installation and Use) Regulations 1998, landlords have to do a gas safety check every twelve months. This has to be carried out by a qualified gas engineer registered with the Gas Safe Register (**www.gassaferegister.co.uk**), and a copy of the certificate for the check needs to be given to the tenant. Why do landlords need to do this? Well, boilers that aren't functioning correctly can emit carbon monoxide, a highly poisonous substance produced when a boiler doesn't completely burn gas. It can be fatal if you're exposed to it, and it's called the silent killer for a good reason, because there isn't really a detectable smell or sound. The only way to make sure you don't fall victim to a dangerous boiler is to ensure that the landlord has the boiler checked and serviced regularly.

Top Tip: If you *do* find yourself experiencing flu-like symptoms and regular headaches after you've moved into the property, as well as shortness of breath and difficulty breathing (and only when you're at home), it may be worth checking the carbon monoxide levels in your property. You can do this very simply with a carbon monoxide detector, which you can buy in DIY stores like B&Q or even on Amazon. You can pick one up for around £10, and it's worth doing if you are at all concerned. Failing that, if you have the slightest doubt that your boiler is misbehaving, get your landlord or letting agent to send a gas engineer out to have it checked asap.

- **Energy Performance Certificate (EPC):** The letting agent or landlord (if you're dealing direct) will have to prepare an EPC in order to advertise the property to let – you can usually find an electronic copy on property websites along with the property description and photos. I don't know anyone who looks at them, but they're law (it's a Brussels thing) and you'll also be provided with another copy of the EPC as part of the paperwork you'll receive with your tenancy agreement. Basically, an EPC provides information on a property's energy usage and typical energy costs, which are graded from A to G (A being super-efficient and G being rubbish and expensive) along with recommendations and suggestions on how you can reduce energy use and save money. Regardless of whether you read it or not, you have to receive this by law.

5. Safeguard yourself

Okay, so you've sorted out all the paperwork, sailed through your credit check, paid your deposit, signed your agreement and, finally, the day that you get the keys to your new pad has arrived. Your next challenge is to get through the **check in** procedure. At its simplest and quickest, you show up, scan your eyes over the paperwork, scribble a signature, grab the keys and get on with your move.

But I wouldn't recommend you do that. First, you need to make sure you are absolutely on top of something called an **inventory**.

This is a very detailed document (normally it contains photographs and sometimes even video footage), which notes every mark, scratch, scuff and stain in the place on the day you move in. It will also include meter readings for all the utilities. This document is prepared by a specialist **inventory clerk** tasked with noting the condition of the property, fixtures, fittings and furniture (if you're renting somewhere furnished). And it's important that you pay close attention because this is the document that is going to be used at the end of your tenancy to check the condition of the place, and basically work out if any damages need to be deducted from your deposit.

Think of it like the paperwork that you have to sign off when you rent a car – you look to see whether it has any dents, scrutinise it for scratches, and check the alloys for scuffs so that you don't get hammered when you bring it back, right? Same principle.

So, take an hour or so out of your life, and go round the property with the inventory clerk, checking everything he or she is writing down. If you spot something that they haven't, speak up – now's not the time to be shy. Make a list of anything you're not sure of.

Top tip: Take a photo of that day's newspaper next to any problem areas during your check in, to prove that they were there on the day that you say they were.

Photograph anything that you're not sure about, then send your list with any pictures to your letting agent within 24 hours of your check in with a note explaining what you've seen and why you want it documented if for any reason it's not included on the inventory. You're protecting yourself here, so take your time and check everything thoroughly.

You're allowed what's called **reasonable wear and tear** during the time you live in the property – I mean, the landlord doesn't expect you to levitate over the carpet or never use the shower. But be warned: if you're only in the place for six months, the amount of wear and tear that's expected is significantly less than you'd think. You get more leeway the longer your tenancy is.

The cleanliness of the property is also noted on the inventory, so if the place has been professionally cleaned before you move in (including the carpets and curtains) then you'll need to vacate the property in the same condition. Conversely, if the place is a bit grubby then get it noted on the inventory because that means you shouldn't have to cough up to get the place spick and span when you move out.

Once you've been checked in by the inventory clerk and they've made all their notes, a week or so later you should receive a copy of the updated inventory (which will also be sent to the landlord). Check it through and return it as soon as you can – within a week is ideal – with any changes you need to make. Then I suggest you keep that in a safe place, because you'll need it when you check out. But I'll come back to that bit later.

You should also take out a specialist tenant's accidental damage insurance policy, which will cover you for any spills or accidents to any of the fixtures and fittings in the property. Your letting agent should be able to sort this out for you, and it's not horrifically expensive, at around £80 to £100 per year. Alternatively, if you are taking contents cover, you may find this is included on your policy. Make sure you check with your insurer.

LIST OF THINGS TO CHECK AT INVENTORY

- **State of walls, glosswork and any wallpaper – look for any scuffs, marks or cracks.** It's also a good idea to check the ceilings for tell-tale brown stains that indicate a water leak.

- **Carpet and flooring** – scrutinise for any stains, scuffs or marks or missing carpet/flooring. Also look out for any loose or badly fitted carpet or floor covering which could cause a trip hazard.

- **Kitchen** – marks or damage to work surfaces, cupboard doors, floor, sink, taps. Check the white goods to make sure they work, open the freezer (if there is one) to make sure it's defrosted. Run the taps and shut them off to make sure they don't drip or leak. Check under the sink to make sure nothing is leaking.

- **Bathroom** – marks or damage to tiles, grouting, sanitary ware (bath, shower and loo). Check for signs of damp/mould and any water escapes, make sure the extractor fan works, run the taps and shut them off to make sure they don't drip or leak. Likewise check the shower to make sure the shower head functions correctly and there's no limescale build-up or other issues.

- **Furniture** – if you're renting the place furnished, it pays to check the inventory against the condition of what furniture is there whilst the inventory clerk is with you. Yes, I know this means another hour of your life that you won't get back, but it's worth it in the long run. You need to note down any staining, marks, wear and tear that is evident, holes or rips and again, ensure that the inventory is updated otherwise you'll get the blame – and the bill – for it when you move out.

- **Electrics** – make sure all the lights work, and if renting furnished, that any electrical equipment such as lamps, TVs or microwaves are also functioning. If any light bulbs are blown, note that down as well. Check light switches and power sockets to ensure they are secure on the wall.

- **Curtains/blinds** – draw them to make sure they shut correctly, and check if they have any marks or stains on either side. Wooden and roman blinds in particular can be temperamental so these should always be checked to ensure they're working properly.

- **External areas** – if you're renting a house, expect your inventory to cover outside the building, as well as inside. That means you need to check and note the state of the garden (including any flowerbeds or ponds), the rainwater goods (that's drains, hoppers, downpipes and guttering to you), the windows, as well as the condition of any gates or fences. Be clear about what your obligations are in respect of garden maintenance. If you are responsible for the upkeep of the garden, you need to understand what you are required to do, e.g. keep the grass cut and the pond clean. Many a deposit has been lost because of issues around this subject. Again, take pictures and bear in mind the time of year you move into the property and the state of the garden. These sorts of details are crucial in the event of a deposit dispute.

- **Smoke detectors** – Have they been installed? If so, test to see if they are working. They may be hardwired into the mains or battery operated, so it's a good idea to work out which ones they are then, if they do need batteries, you can make a mental note to change them regularly as it will be your responsibility.

6. *Paying your rent on time*

The single most common reason for landlords starting the eviction process is late or non-payment of rent. This is so easy to avoid by setting up either a standing order or a direct debit. You can even ask your letting agent to help you with this when you're setting up the lease agreement.

I can't express to you strongly enough how important it is that you do pay your rent promptly, because if one month you do forget (and it's easily done, trust me) and you are late by even a few days, it gives your landlord the automatic right to start proceedings. And you don't want to end up kipping in a cardboard box now, do you?

If you do find yourself in a position where you know that your rent payment will reach the letting agent or landlord later than it should, tell them straightaway. Explain the reason, and let them know the date when they will receive it. Then stick to it.

One transgression of this nature can, in the grand scheme of things, be overlooked (if the reason is good enough, of course).

If it becomes a habit, that's different. But as with everything, be honest. The sooner you tell the landlord or the letting agent that there is an issue, the sooner you can work together to find a resolution. And don't forget – be apologetic. Now is not the time to be recalcitrant. Launch as much of a remorse-filled charm offensive as you can. Unless you relish the prospect of an eviction notice, of course.

7. Inspections

Not that they don't trust you, but at some stage during your tenancy (usually once every three or six months, depending on how paranoid the landlord is and/or how proactive the letting agent is) you'll be notified that the agent or landlord will be visiting the property to make sure all is OK and that you've not turned it into a doss house.

By law, they need to give you **reasonable notice**, whether you are going to be at home for the inspection or not. Generally, forty-eight hours is deemed acceptable, although the reality is, if you've got a good relationship with your landlord or agent, they may give you up to a week's notice.

For your own sake, and I hate to point out the obvious here, it makes sense to get the place in pristine condition for your inspection. Make sure everything is clean, neat and tidy, and that you've not left a load of dirty washing on the bedroom floor that morning. The idea here is that you prove to whoever is checking the place that you're an upstanding and reliable tenant, who's looking after the place and generally very responsible. Which you are, of course.

If for any reason the landlord or agent finds a problem, they will notify you in writing – or possibly, depending on the severity of the issue, by phone as well – and discuss with you how it can be rectified. If it's a matter of the property being damaged in some way (and you are responsible for the problem) then you may be given a certain time frame within which to get the repairs made. If, however, you're in breach of your lease – for example, your agreement says no pets, but you've decided to adopt a Rottweiler – then you will be made aware of the issue in writing, and given a time frame by which to resolve the situation.

In both examples, you need to be mindful of the fact that if you choose to ignore your landlord's request to comply you could end up getting yourself evicted (and being forced to pay for the privilege), which isn't really the right way to go.

Wherever possible, *I would recommend that you arrange to be at home for your inspection.* This shows that you're taking the process seriously, and also, if you have spotted any problems, you can then talk the agent or landlord through them first-hand. Offering to make the agent or landlord a cup of tea, smiling and being polite will also help establish you as their favourite tenant.

As with everything in life, if people like you, they will be more accommodating when you need some help. And bear in mind that one day you will wish to move on, so any goodwill you can generate during your tenancy will stand you in good stead once you do decide to hand in your notice.

8. Giving notice

So, you've decided for whatever reason that you want to move out. Surely it's just a case of ringing the landlord or agent and letting them know, right? Wrong. Depending on what sort of lease you have, you'll either need to wait until the **break clause** – a specific date that's been agreed when you can serve notice to vacate the property – or, if you're now into a periodic agreement, you'll need to give your landlord one month's notice.

Bear in mind: if you pay your rent monthly in advance, if you give notice in the middle of the month, your move date won't be a calendar month from the day you give notice but would be at the end of the following month.

In other words, if you pay your rent on the first of every month, and give notice on 15th May that you want to move out in June because you need to give a month's notice, you would actually end up moving out on 30th June. Confused? Yeah, I know it's not exactly crystal clear, so that's why you need to put everything in writing and double check that everyone agrees what's going on, so you don't get any nasty surprises on your final rent bill.

You will need to write to your agent or landlord to confirm that you're giving notice. This doesn't need to be Shakespeare, just a couple of lines explaining that you're giving notice on X date, with the intention to move out on Y date, and that you will liaise with them nearer the time regarding the check out procedure and return of the deposit.

As with everything else, make sure you keep a copy of the letter or email for your records. If you don't have the best of relationships with your landlord or letting agency, make sure you can prove that you've actually served them with notice to leave the property. This is why emailing the letter and then sending it by registered post may be a good idea. Otherwise, they may try to deny that they've received any communication from you, which could mean you're liable for a bit more rent.

9. Dealing with problem landlords and letting agents

As a tenant you have responsibilities and a long list of things you can and can't do documented in the lease agreement that you've signed, but there are also a whole load of things that *landlords* can and can't do. As legislation has tightened around the letting sector, tenants do have quite a bit of protection against naughty landlords, so it's increasingly rare to run into serious difficulties. That said, you find a few rotten apples in any barrel, so it pays to know your rights.

As I said earlier, there's so much information and detail I could go into, but I just don't have the room to cover it here. So I'll just outline some common problem areas. If you find yourself in a situation that you are unhappy with, I'd suggest you get advice from your letting agent or the Citizens Advice Bureau as soon as you can. Shelter (**www.shelter.org.uk**) have also got fantastic resources, both online and as a helpline, should you need further help.

The point is, there is free advice from experts out there. Don't sit in silence. Talk to someone who knows what they are doing. A problem shared is a problem halved and all that.

Issues that you may come across with more unscrupulous landlords include:

- Trying to serve notice on you to repossess the property without following the correct procedure.

- Not providing furniture, fixtures, fittings or fulfilling any other obligations that were agreed in writing before your tenancy commenced, and are documented in your tenancy agreement.

- Turning up at the property unannounced without giving you adequate notice (unless there is a reasonable emergency).

- Not arranging replacement/repairs to the property or items within it should they break/fail through no fault or negligence on the tenant's part, e.g. fixing or replacing the washing machine if it's broken, getting the central heating fixed if it stops working, etc.

In any of these situations, your first point of recourse is your letting agent. This is why I was banging on earlier about renting your place through a member of one of the professional bodies, as they are normally very good in terms of sorting this kind of stuff out.

You'll need to put your complaint in writing (email will suffice) and provide evidence to support your claim. This is where you'll also need copies of any correspondence you have which support your grievance, for example that the landlord agreed to replace the carpets before you moved in, if that's what was agreed but hasn't been done. If your heating has stopped working, or your fridge has broken down through no fault of your own, you should allow your landlord a reasonable amount of time to get the repairs, or if necessary a replacement, arranged.

However, if you've gone for a significant period without hot water or heating, then you are entitled to negotiate a reduction in your rent for that month, to cover the inconvenience. If the situation continues for a considerable length of time then your landlord could be in breach of their lease, in which case you need to make a decision about either withholding your rent for that month, or perhaps finding somewhere else to live.

As with all these things, the more of a paper trail you have, the better. So if you're ringing the letting agent or landlord every week to chase the repairs through, then make sure you send an email or write a letter each time, keeping a copy for your own records. Text messages aren't going to stand up in the same way, so make your complaint formal. That way, if things do get difficult, you can at least prove that you are not acting unreasonably, and that you have grounds for your actions.

If you *do* decide to withhold your rent, be aware that just because you don't think you should pay it doesn't mean it's not legally due. So, put the rent you would have paid in your savings account and leave it alone. Should things ever get to court, it's a great defence of your actions, but also if you do end up having to pay up, then at least you've got the money put aside.

Finally, if it's the letting agent who is being naughty and they *are* a member of one of the industry bodies (ARLA, RICS, NALS, UKALA, NAEA or the London Rental Standard) there will be a redress scheme and dispute resolution service in place that you can refer to. Again, don't be shy – if you feel you are being treated unfairly, then get in contact with the relevant scheme's dispute resolution service and get some help.

Currently, letting agents who aren't a member of one of the bodies don't have to belong to a redress scheme. At the time of writing, there are moves by the government to implement mandatory membership of a redress scheme for all letting agents by the end of 2014. When this finally happens, all letting agents will have to sign up to the code of practice and redress schemes run by either The Property Ombudsman, Ombudsman Services or the Property Redress Scheme. But until that happy day, you can seek advice from your local Citizens Advice Bureau (**www.citizensadvice.org.uk**) if you're struggling and need some pointers in terms of how to deal with a delinquent agent.

10. Checking out and getting your deposit back

Once you've given notice and agreed when you're vacating the property, the letting agent or landlord will arrange the **check out** with the inventory clerk, normally for the day you move out or the day after.

Basically, this is the reverse procedure of when you moved in. Once you've moved out all your furniture and personal possessions (and, if appropriate, either cleaned the place or employed a cleaner to do it for you) the inventory clerk will visit the property to assess it against the inventory you were checked in with.

Remember I said earlier that it's important to note the condition of the property once you've been through the inventory on the day you check in? That's going to pay dividends now because, if you've looked after the place, you should find that you'll get your deposit back in full, or with very few deductions.

That said, although you may have been careful, key things which are the main cause of deposits being docked are:

- Scuffs and marks on walls and paintwork
- Stains on carpets, flooring, curtains and soft furnishings
- Scratches or marks to work surfaces and furniture
- Light bulbs that have blown but not been replaced
- Picture hooks or nails/screws left in walls that haven't been made good
- Lost door/window keys or remote controls for electric gates
- General lack of cleanliness (particularly in kitchens and/or bathrooms)

- Mould and condensation caused by lack of ventilation when showering, cooking or drying laundry

The thing is, with the majority of these issues it's so easy to sort it out before the inventory clerk carries out their inspection it's worth an hour of your time going round the property fixing the odd job here or there. For marks to paintwork (emulsion or gloss) you can buy these amazing 'eraser pads' from supermarkets or places like Robert Dyas or Wilko. I've got some at home, and they really are brilliant, and not very expensive – I think I paid less than two pounds for mine, if that. You just make them slightly damp, buff them across the offending spot, and with a bit of gentle rubbing you can get most marks or scuffs off. I don't know how they work, but seriously, get some. Seeing as the alternative to get rid of marks is to repaint the wall (for which you'd be charged a hefty sum), it's worth a couple of quid and ten minutes of your time giving this a go. They also work a treat on trainers, by the way.

Places around a house where paintwork takes a battering and therefore may need some attention are:

- Inside hallways and up stairways

- Above radiators where you've put clothes or towels on them to dry

- At head height behind your sofa or bed if they've been up against a wall

- On windowsills where you may have had plants or ornaments

If you can, avoid having to touch up walls or paintwork, as the new paint will stand out a mile against the old, and sometimes this can look even more obvious than whatever it was you were trying to cover up.

Likewise, light bulbs are an easy thing to sort out, but a common reason for deposits being held up. As the tenant, it's your responsibility to make sure that you replace any bulbs that have gone before you move out. Most people forget this, which means that the return of your deposit might be delayed whilst calculations are made about how much you owe to replace the ones that need changing. Landlords can and probably will charge you for getting someone round to sort this out if you don't. Expect to pay around £15 for labour for a £1 light bulb to be replaced if they do, which is considered to be fair and the going rate. Given that you can rectify this easily before you move out for probably less than the cost of a latte, is it really worth having to wait longer to get your deposit back? Exactly. Just do it.

If you've hung pictures or mirrors around the place, you will no doubt be asked to **make good** (in other words, remove the picture hook or nail, fill the hole and daub it with a bit of paint). One word of warning here – it's worth sending a specific email to either the letting agent or landlord about this, because as we've already discussed, by using new paint on old you will get a noticeable patch, even if you're using paint from the same tin. So put in writing that you're happy to carry out the repair, but it may be slightly noticeable due to the difference between the old paint and the new, and ask the agent or landlord to confirm that this will not affect the return of your deposit.

Few tenants think to do this, so it'll show a) that you're on the ball and b) that you are aware of the potential issue and you're trying to sort it out before it happens. As with other correspondence, keep a copy of the email or letter in case you get into difficulties later on.

As far as carpets, curtains and soft furnishings are concerned, if there are any major, noticeable stains (red wine, coffee, grease, etc.) then book a professional cleaning company to come in and do the business. With any carpet or soft furnishings, you really have to do the whole room, piece of furniture or both curtains, even if the patch or mark is only in one area. This is because the chemicals that are used to get stains out tend to lighten the area they are used on, so you need to blend it in with the rest of the material or carpet, otherwise you'll end up with something that stands out as much as the original blemish. Yes, I know it's going to cost you a few quid to get it put right, but the reality is that if you don't then the letting agent will just get their own people on the job, and I guarantee you it will be more expensive if they sort it out than if you do.

On **check out** day, make sure you're there (no excuses), and that you go around each room with the inventory clerk so you're on hand to answer any questions or discuss any issues that may arise. Once that's complete, you'll then be asked to hand over all your keys. Check beforehand that you've got them all together and you know which key is used for what (front door, back door, windows, any remote controls for security gates, etc.) as there will be a list of keys in the inventory which will need to be checked off to ensure you've handed them all in. The inventory clerk will also check the meters to get a final reading for the various utilities companies so they can prepare your final bill.

Once your inventory has been processed, you'll be provided with a copy and a list of any deductions to your deposit in respect of any repairs that are required. If you don't agree with these, and unless you can reach a compromise (assisted by the letting agent if relevant), you'll need to go through the redress process in place with whichever scheme was used to protect your deposit. Or take the landlord to the small claims court.

If you find yourself in this situation and are dealing directly with the landlord, then free advice can be found on **www.shelter.org.uk** or obtained from your local Citizens Advice Bureau. If you've been renting via a letting agent, then it's worth speaking to their redress scheme if you feel you are being treated unfairly. All of these resources are available to you for free, remember, so it really is worth spending half an hour or so on the phone to understand from the experts how best to deal with the situation.

Conclusion

Renting is for some a flexible and convenient solution whilst in-between properties (or relationships) or when relocating to a new area. Or in the 'try before you buy' stage of a new liaison. For a growing number, however, it is the *only* solution for long-term housing rather than a stop gap. Either way, to ensure that you have as much security as a tenant as possible, it pays to do your research, check out your letting agent and landlord and know your rights.

I've been lucky enough to have had great relationships with my previous landlords – to the point where with one (the lovely Val) it meant that when she came round for quarterly inspections, we'd often crack open a bottle of wine or have a cuppa and put the world to rights, as well as sending each other Christmas cards. Of course, that's the exception, but there's no reason you shouldn't find your experience of renting to be a positive one as well.

Just make sure that you ask the right questions and read everything thoroughly. Time spent upfront getting everything organised correctly will pay dividends in the long run *and* help to ensure you get your deposit back.

Put it this way, if you're handing your keys back in a coffee shop rather than a courtroom, chances are you've done alright.

3.
Financially Fabulous

I'm actually not sure which of the following three situations is more terrifying:

1. Your first job interview (or any job interview, for that matter).

2. Meeting 'The Parents' for the first time.

3. Arranging your first mortgage.

They're equally pretty nerve-racking, because you know the relevant parties *will* judge you on both the first few words that come out of your mouth and what you're wearing.

Bearing all that in mind then, it's no wonder that people get themselves in a bit of a tizz when contemplating the financial aspects of buying a place. I'm not going to kid you, it *is* quite scary, particularly when you realise exactly how much you'll be paying off over the next 25 years or so, taking into account interest on the amount that you've borrowed. Mortgage statements always tend to look a bit like telephone numbers, I find.

Recently, the whole way we borrow money changed. You see, during those heady years of the property boom BCC (Before Credit Crunch) it was ridiculously easy to borrow a ridiculous amount of money. Self-certified mortgages, where you basically told the lender how much you earned and they took your word for it, meant that really, had lenders stopped to think about it for a bit, thousands of people shouldn't have been able to borrow anywhere near the amounts they were offered. Then it all went pop – lenders like Northern Rock and the Royal Bank of Scotland suddenly realised they had next to no money in the coffers and had to ask nicely if they could be bailed out by the taxpayer.

So, to make sure this couldn't happen again – rearrange these words into a well-known sentence: door, bolted, horse, shut, after – there was a massive shake up of the financial services industry in 2012, which reviewed home loans and what was deemed 'sensible' by the **Financial Conduct Authority** (FCA). This was called the **Mortgage Market Review**, and is big news for anyone who is buying a home for the first time, as well as for those who already have a mortgage.

Why? Well, simply put, the Mortgage Market Review, or MMR for short, means that it is much harder to borrow money. It's basically introducing stricter criteria to ensure more realistic lending practices. So, no more easy-to-come-by six-times-income multiples or 100% deals, and certainly no more self-certified mortgages. Those days, my friend, are long gone.

Now, responsible lending is a good thing, don't get me wrong. But here's the rub: the MMR has really cranked up the difficulty rating of getting a mortgage for most normal first-time buyers. If you're a self-employed first-time buyer, it's even more of a challenge.

Simply put, ten years ago, you chose which lender you wanted to apply to for a mortgage, and most of the time, provided you answered the questionnaire correctly, had the deposit and weren't the worst credit risk in the world, they'd say yes. These days, mortgage lenders are 'cherry picking' the best customers who they see as the least risk. And saying 'non' to everyone else.

So, what does all this mean for you? Well, I'm not a mortgage advisor, so nothing I can write here can be construed as 'financial advice' – I have to say that, otherwise my publisher will smack my bottom. But what I've tried to do in this chapter is give you a bit of a steer about the most common elements of securing a mortgage since the new legislation came into force, and explain many of the buzzwords and jargon you'll hear as you go along. Hopefully you'll then have the basics under your belt so you can ask the right questions of your mortgage broker or lender, as well as getting yourself prepared for your mortgage interview. You know what they say: "Fail to prepare, prepare to fail." Or something like that anyway.

I would also direct you to my mate Martin's website, **www.moneysavingexpert.com**, where you will find his brilliant and free Mortgage Guide. It's 56 pages long, but I urge you to download it and study it very carefully. It's a masterclass in mortgages, and goes into far more detail than I can here. Martin has written it in a way that's easy to digest and really explains the trickier points very well, using examples to break down the more complex elements into bite-sized chunks. Seriously, make yourself a cuppa and get stuck in, it's awesome.

If you only make it your business to understand one thing really well, make sure it's how your mortgage works. Believe me, it may be a bit dull listening to someone drone on about capital and interest repayment and loan to value ratios, but the more you know about it, the fewer sleepless nights you'll have in years to come. Especially when interest rates rise.

Oh yes, a word on that one as well. Since 2009, we in the UK have been enjoying the lowest interest rate (0.5%) in 200 years. That's right, *200 years*. These are not normal circumstances, and frankly, rates are only going to go one way, and it ain't down. Now, when you think that the 'average' interest rate for the ten years prior to the credit crunch was around 5%, you can see what an impact this is going to have on people once the rates start to rise. For those who aren't on a fixed rate deal, their monthly payments are going to go up. This is why, like I say, you need to understand what you are signing up for, and make sure that when interest rates do increase – which they will, it's a certainty – that you can *still* afford to make your monthly payment. Think carefully before you commit to a mortgage, and *always* get the advice of a **qualified financial advisor** before you sign on the dotted line. Although the new Mortgage Market Review legislation is more geared to protecting borrowers than previously, ultimately *you* are the only person who is really going to look out for *your* best interests.

Before I get into the nitty-gritty though, let's just set the scene. By and large, the way most banks and building societies work is to borrow money themselves (either from their savings customers or on the money markets) which they then loan out to their mortgage customers. The smaller, provincial building societies generally operate on the more traditional model of offering savers a good rate to entice them to deposit their money, which is then recycled to lend out to people looking for a mortgage at a profit to the building society.

The larger companies – which have the capacity to write a higher volume of lending business – need more funds than they will generate from their savers, so they go out to the money markets to borrow the dosh themselves, and then charge a premium (profit) on that money to lend it out to mortgage customers. With it so far? Good.

What *can* be a bit confusing is how the lenders borrow money between themselves. You see, like any other commodity, the more demand there is for mortgage funding, the more it costs to buy and sell it. So although we have the **Bank of England (BOE) base rate**, which most people are aware of – this is the one that Mark Carney, Governor of the Bank of England, is in charge of – there is another rate called LIBOR (**London Interbank Offered Rate**) which is what reflects how much the banks and building societies charge to lend money to *each other*. Although the BOE base rate does have a bearing on things, the real determining factor of how much that mortgage is going to cost is the LIBOR rate.

Alright, lesson in macroeconomics over, let's talk in a bit more detail about the types of mortgages you may be offered, what to look out for and how to protect both yourself and your biggest asset as best you can.

1. Product placement

There are literally thousands of mortgage products available at any one time, so it's impossible to give you a thorough briefing here. However, broadly speaking, most commonly available mortgages fall into one of the following types:

STANDARD VARIABLE RATE

The first thing to be aware of as you navigate your way through the mortgage maze is each lender's own **standard variable rate** (SVR), which the bank or building society sets itself. Normally, the SVR isn't something offered to a new customer. The SVR usually comes into play when an existing mortgage, like a fixed rate or tracker, comes to an end, at which point you would automatically go onto the lender's SVR until you apply to go onto another product.

You need to be aware of a lender's SVR because at some point it's likely you will be moved onto it, and the historic SVR will give you a good idea of the lender's track record, as in how quickly they reduced it when interest rates went down, and how often they increased it when rates moved upwards. Although given that rates have been static since 2009, you need to check their performance over the last ten years or so to get the real picture.

Also, as you compare mortgage products when you're deciding which lender to apply to, you will see that the current SVR is quoted in terms of what you will pay when the deal ends, so it's worth paying attention as this will also give you a good indication of how you'll be treated in the longer term.

BASE RATE TRACKER

This type of mortgage follows any changes in the Bank of England (BOE) base rate, so if that goes up or down, your mortgage will too. For example, you may be offered a tracker rate of something like 1.35% above the BOE base rate for a predetermined period – maybe two or three years – after which the rate you'll pay will return to your lender's SVR.

Now, the good bit about a **base rate tracker** is that it's pretty easy to understand, and you know that the only way your mortgage payments are going to change is if the BOE base rate goes up. But that's the thing, because it is highly likely to be doing just that very soon. So if you go with this option, you need to be sure that you will be able to make your monthly payments as that upward movement occurs.

Base rate trackers are a good bet for those who have a larger deposit (therefore require a lower loan to value mortgage) and have more flexibility in their monthly budget to act as a cushion as rates do rise.

FIXED RATE

Obvious by anyone's standards, a **fixed rate** mortgage does exactly what it says. You sign up for a pre-determined amount of time to an interest rate which your lender guarantees won't change during that period. So regardless of what interest rates are doing, you'll pay the same amount each month.

There are a lot of permutations on this in terms of rates available and the amount of time you can fix for, so it's really down to how long you want to be tied in for. This is something to consider because, in return for the security of knowing what your monthly repayments are going to be, the lender may lump you with hefty redemption penalties should you decide to chop in your mortgage before the end of its term. Whilst you get redemption penalties with most mortgages, they tend to be highest on fixed rate deals, so be aware of this when you're doing your research.

Also be aware that sometimes the tie-in lasts beyond the period of the fixed rate – again, read the small print to find out what the situation is with the particular product you're looking at. If you think that you may move within the term of the fixed rate deal, then make sure you can move your product without paying a penalty. This is called **porting** your mortgage (see the 'Other stuff you need to know' bit at the end of this section).

On the plus side, however, you'll know exactly what your outgoings are, so for the term of the fix it'll be easier for you to budget each month. One last thing to consider – arrangement fees for the lowest fixed rate mortgages can run into thousands of pounds, which you'll usually need to pay upfront to get the deal, so make sure you factor that into your calculations before you start.

However, given that, as I keep saying, interest rates are only going to go up, a fixed rate will ensure that your payment doesn't budge. If you are of a nervous disposition, then it *may* be a good bet.

CAPPED RATE

Not so readily available these days, although some lenders do still offer them. Basically, one of these will offer you pretty much the best of both worlds, as it's a halfway house between a variable and a fixed rate. As the name suggests, with a capped rate you sign up to a deal where the interest rate is capped at a certain level (for an agreed amount of time, say two to three years), which means that if interest rates rise above that point, the rate you pay won't increase. However, if interest rates drop, you'll get the benefit as your payment will *reduce* to take the change into account.

Ascertain whether the capped deal you're being offered is based on the BOE base rate, LIBOR or the lender's own SVR. Yes, I know it sounds like I'm playing buzzword bingo, but you'll thank me for this later. The fee to sign up for one of these varies from lender to lender and redemption penalties can be punchy, so make sure the whole package works out to your best advantage before you sign on the dotted line.

DISCOUNTED VARIABLE RATE

This is a cheaper alternative to the lender's standard variable rate. Here, the bank or building society will offer you a mortgage which is at a discounted rate off their normal SVR, fixed at a certain percentage, e.g. 1.5% less than the SVR. So whilst your mortgage will still go up or down, you'll always pay less than the lender's SVR.

Again, maybe not the best thing to go for if you're looking for a degree of certainty about what your monthly payment will be, because as interest rates change so will your mortgage. But you'll probably pay less of an arrangement fee, so if that bothers you, this could be worth considering.

If interest rates remain low for a bit longer, you'll be on to a winner as in the short term, the rate you'll pay will be competitive without having had to fork out for a fixed rate deal. Just remember to make sure you have a cushion in your budget each month so that *when* the interest rate rises and your payments *do* go up, you can still afford your repayments.

Also worth bearing in mind is that the rate you pay is linked to the lender's SVR, which it can change at any time. In the last couple of years, some people have seen their discounted variable rate mortgage payments rise, not because the interest rate has moved but because the lender just decided to increase its SVR. Forewarned is forearmed, as they say.

OFFSET

Now, this ain't sexy, and it's not exactly the easiest product to get your head around, but if you can and are good with money, then this type of mortgage can potentially save you a fair amount of cash. So bear with me.

In theory, the way they work is relatively simple. Most people have a current account and a savings account, and then have a separate mortgage, the monthly payments on which gradually reduce the amount they owe until they pay it off. With an offset account, the money you have in your current and savings accounts are balanced (or 'offset') against the amount you owe on your mortgage. Whilst you don't earn any interest on the money in your current or savings account, you don't pay any interest on the outstanding element of your mortgage either (once it's calculated against the funds you have got in credit in your current and savings accounts). Just remember when you're looking around, offset mortgages do sometimes tend to attract a slightly higher interest rate.

I know that doesn't exactly sound like a great deal, but here's the clever bit. You see, you're likely to be paying more interest on your mortgage than you'll earn in interest on your savings or the money in your current account, so because you are offsetting that amount each month, you'll be reducing the amount of interest you owe on your mortgage. Which means you can either pay a smaller amount each month over the term of your mortgage (called **paying net**), or you can keep paying the same amount (called **paying gross**), but you'll just pay back the loan a lot faster because you are effectively overpaying, thus saving yourself money into the bargain.

So if this option appeals to you, all I'd say is think about how good you are at controlling your dosh. It's not for everyone, but if you are able to manage it, then you could potentially save yourself thousands.

OTHER STUFF

A few other terms that you may hear or read when you're getting clued-up about mortgages:

- **Porting**: This means that if you decide to move home during the term of a mortgage deal (for example, a fixed rate product) you can take your existing mortgage with you to the next property. Different lenders have different rules on how much you can **port** to the next property and what you need to do to top up the amount if you need to borrow more, so always check to see what the details are and what would apply to you.

- **Payment holidays**: A few mortgages allow what's called a **payment holiday** – in other words, an agreed period of time, normally up to three months, where you don't have to make the monthly mortgage payments. The amount that you won't have paid back during your payment holiday is just extended onto the overall term of the loan, so remember you will have to pay it back at some stage and it's not 'free money'. Not many lenders offer this, so if it is something that you think you might need at some stage in the future it's worth asking early doors when talking to your mortgage advisor so he or she can make sure that the product you apply for has this flexibility built in. Also bear in mind your lender may require you to have made overpayments before you qualify for a payment holiday, so check the conditions thoroughly.

- **Overpayment**: Pretty straightforward, this means that you can, if you have the funds available, pay off more than your monthly mortgage payment in order to reduce the overall amount that you owe. Unsurprisingly, lenders love it when their customers do this, as it reduces the risk on the mortgage on that property. Also unsurprisingly, not many people can afford to do it or indeed want to. However, overpaying will clear your mortgage quicker and increase the difference between your outstanding mortgage and the amount of capital you have in the property, which is a great buffer to have against negative equity if you live in an area where prices have been static for a while. If you think you may want to be able to make overpayments to your mortgage, check with your mortgage advisor at the time you apply to make sure that the products you're looking at incorporate this facility.

- **Early repayment charges:** So, whilst lenders like you to overpay your mortgage (see above), they aren't *quite* so keen for you to pay it off completely during the term of your mortgage with them – whether you've won the lottery or want just to move your home loan to a better deal elsewhere. Do this, and you're likely to be hit with early repayment charges (also known as tie-ins or redemption penalties) which can cost thousands. These vary enormously depending on the lender, the deal you're on (they are almost certain to apply if you take out a fixed rate or discount deal, for example) and how much you borrowed, so always check before you sign up what you would have to pay in the event you decide to move your home loan elsewhere.

It's probably also a good idea to mention at this point the difference between repayment and interest only mortgages. A **repayment mortgage** takes into account the capital (the chunk of money that you borrowed) plus the interest, which together is calculated to give you a monthly payment that will reduce the overall amount that you owe. By the end of the term, you'll have paid everything off.

An **interest only mortgage** is just that – you are only servicing the interest that you owe, and not paying back any of the capital, which makes them a lot cheaper in terms of monthly repayments. These used to be commonplace and easy to apply for, but now since the Mortgage Market Review it's become exceptionally difficult to get an interest only mortgage with many lenders withdrawing them altogether for new applicants.

2. Where can I get a mortgage?

These days, there are a variety of ways to fix yourself up with 25 years of excruciating debt. However, since the credit crunch, the amount of mortgages (or products) available has greatly reduced, with many lenders now requesting a minimum 10% deposit. To snag yourself one of the better deals, you'll probably need at least a 20%, or even bigger, down payment. Lenders are basically looking for customers who represent the least amount of risk. That's why it's so crucial that you get the best possible advice to suit your individual circumstances to make sure that your application is one of the successful ones.

DIRECT TO LENDER

First up, there are a plethora of **banks** and **building societies** that will deal with you directly – all you need to do is make an appointment with their mortgage advisor and away you go. The upside here is that you can potentially get a good product that you won't get anywhere else (for example, not through an independent financial advisor or mortgage broker). The downside is that they will only offer you their own products, so you'll have to do all the research and market comparisons to make sure it's the best deal for you.

INDEPENDENT FINANCIAL ADVISORS AND MORTGAGE BROKERS

Next are **independent financial advisors** (IFAs) and **mortgage brokers**. Essentially, both do the same thing, which is look at a number of available mortgage products before making their recommendation about what product(s) may be most suitable for your circumstances. This method takes a lot of the legwork out of the whole situation, as they do all the research and just present you with a few options.

Things to consider here are how much they charge you for their advice, and how many products they review before they recommend something to you. Make sure you ask your IFA or broker whether they are **panel** or **whole of market** – it makes a big difference.

Why?

Because a **whole of market** IFA or broker will look at every single product available to get you the best deal, which at any one time could be hundreds or even thousands. A **panel** IFA or broker will only look at a certain number of lenders that they have a relationship with, so while it could mean they still look at a lot of products for you, it's limited to those particular banks or building societies they deal with, so you may not get the best rate available.

The IFA or broker will also factor in fees and lending criteria to get the right fit for you, as well as making sure you get the best advice to suit your individual circumstances.

Finally, to make sure that you're entrusting your financial future to the right person, make sure they are a bona fide, qualified professional by checking the Financial Conduct Authority (FCA) register at **www.fca.org.uk**.

ONLINE

Your third option is to use one of the price comparison sites, which offer you an easy way to look at what's around, before applying for the product online. Again, you need to make sure that the website you're dealing with is whole of market, not panel-based, and also be aware of the fact that you won't get the advice that you'll get by dealing either with the lender directly, a broker or an IFA.

So, in other words, *you need to be confident that you have a good grasp of how mortgages work.* And you have to take the time to go through all the terms and conditions so that you know exactly what you're getting yourself into.

I'd suggest that for the first-time buyer, the more advice you can get the better, so perhaps use the internet just for research purposes, and get a professional to walk you through everything. When you come to move next time (or remortgage), and you're a bit more confident about the whole process, maybe then you can think about a DIY online mortgage application.

3. How much can I borrow?

There are two factors:

1. The overall amount you can afford to borrow.

2. How much you can afford to pay each month.

These two are *not* mutually exclusive. Lenders use a series of processes to work out how much they will lend you, and these are all pretty much the same:

- First, they will look at your basic salary (if you're an employee) or your yearly earnings (if you're self-employed).

- Then they will take into account any additional income you may have earned in the past, such as commission, bonuses or overtime.

- When they've added all that up, they will then deduct any loans or outstanding debt you may have, together with any credit card or finance repayments you regularly make or any other financial responsibilities you may have, such as nursery or school fees, together with outgoings such as utility bills, any child support payments, food, car or travel costs and any regular savings you make.

- They will then multiply that figure by a certain amount, which is called an **income multiple**. This varies depending on the lender, how much you earn in the first place and how big your deposit is.

If you're applying for a joint mortgage, the process is nearly identical, but the **income multiples** (the bit where they take your income net of debts etc. and times it by a certain factor to ascertain the total amount you can borrow) may vary. Again, each lender has slightly different criteria in terms of how they approach this.

The next step is 'stress testing'. No, that doesn't mean reciting your twelve times table backwards whilst standing on one leg. As part of your mortgage interview process, the advisor will walk you through how much your mortgage payments would be if interest rates were to go up by 3% over the current rates, to make sure you'll still be able to afford it. Now, whilst this may sound a bit daunting, they are doing it to make sure that you can still afford to buy food and get the train to work. So take it in the spirit it's meant.

At the end of all of this, a number will be spat out of the computer which, by the lender's calculations, is what they believe you are able to repay.

Now, in most cases, it's pretty non-negotiable but, depending on your circumstances and the evidence you can supply, with some lenders it is possible that your case may be sent a bit further up the food-chain for the **underwriters** to review it. In this position, *sometimes* you can borrow a little bit more, but I wouldn't bank on it (no pun intended). This procedure is more for those who are self-employed or where secondary income needs to be taken into account.

Now, even up until the beginning of 2014, the way that mortgage interviews were conducted had been pretty similar for a long time. But in April 2014 a lot changed under the Mortgage Market Review, which introduced certain practices for lenders to ensure that they are not entering into what could be termed 'predatory lending practices' – in other words letting people who've got no chance at all of paying a big mortgage back borrow far more than they should do.

The practical implications of this are that these days, people applying for mortgages are asked for much more detailed information at interview, because the lender wants to make sure that they can afford the monthly repayments both in the short term and the longer term. All well and good, you might say, and of course I support responsible lending, but it has made it tougher for a lot of people to secure a mortgage which, even just a few months ago, would have been a lot easier to come by.

Lenders are also looking for borrowers to put down bigger deposits, which is a way to safeguard against negative equity should prices cool over a period. Again, whilst this is designed to ensure that fewer people get into difficulties with their mortgage and to provide a 'buffer', having to find a 15 or 20% deposit rather than the 5 or 10% that was the previous standard is having an impact.

However, when all is said and done, you need to be cognisant of how much you can actually afford to pay each month, not just the big number you can convince someone to lend you. Your mortgage payment shouldn't be any more than 30% of your take-home earnings each month, so do the maths and figure out what that comes to, and go from there. Nothing is worth getting yourself into financial difficulties over, so it may be better to hold fire for a few months and build up a bigger deposit, or perhaps it's worth just hanging on and waiting until your circumstances change to ensure that you're more comfortable financially before you commit yourself to that amount of debt for the next 25 years.

4. Co-buying with friends/siblings ... and getting parents involved

In the last few years, an increasing number of first-time buyers have ended up co-buying with either a friend or sibling, leading to a growing rise in what's been termed 'mates mortgages'. And it can be a very effective way to go, particularly when you consider that, if you were renting a gaff together, you'd probably be paying the same amount each month, so why not convert that into a mortgage payment?

If you are considering going down this route, there are a few things to bear in mind. Firstly, you will obviously need to agree finances in terms of who's putting what into the deal towards the deposit, legal fees, etc., and how much each of you is going to contribute towards the mortgage.

When buying property with someone who isn't your husband or wife, you also need to get everything documented legally to ensure you don't have any problems later on. It's a good idea to get a **Deed of Trust** drawn up by a solicitor (you can read all about this and other legal stuff in Chapter 7, 'Breaking Up is Hard to Do', most of which is as relevant to co-buying with your best mate as it is with your romantic partner).

In terms of getting a mortgage together with friends or siblings, you don't need to get a specific product, but you do need to be aware that the maximum number of people that can be listed on the **deeds** of a property is *four*, which limits the amount of you that can hold a joint mortgage.

Other than that, the actual process of applying for a mortgage is pretty much the same. You will need to take individual advice about how the property is held, for example if you will be noted on the deeds as **Joint Tenants** or **Tenants in Common**. There are factors to consider which may make a difference to which way you decide to go. Again, this can all be dealt with by the solicitor acting for you during the purchase, so it's all very straightforward to get everyone's interest in the property noted correctly so you're safeguarded in the future.

If you don't have siblings or a friend to buy with but can't stretch to a mortgage on your own income, then all is not lost. Over the last couple of years **Guarantor mortgages** have become increasingly popular with first-time buyers who have a parent or grandparent (or even a friend, you don't have to be related) who is willing to effectively underwrite their mortgage.

In this scenario, your **Guarantor** also has to go through an assessment process by the lender to ensure that if you default on your mortgage payment they can afford to step in and pay it on your behalf. Depending on the lender, they may also look for further guarantees, such as a charge on the Guarantor's property in the event that both of you default on the mortgage payments.

Clearly then, not to be undertaken lightly, but at least for some this does provide another option. Not all lenders offer this type of home loan though, so if it's something that you are interested in pursuing, then best to let your mortgage advisor know early doors so they can correctly guide you through the application process.

5. Gifted deposits

If you're lucky enough to have generous parents or other family members who are giving you a chunk of cash to get you started (or to get you out from underneath their feet), there are a few things to bear in mind. First of all, you'll need a letter from the person giving you the money stating that you're going to use it as a deposit and that it's been 'gifted'. In other words, that it's not a loan, you don't have to pay it back, and that they have no interest in the property.

On the other hand, if your folks are offering to provide you with a deposit on the basis that, as and when you sell the property later on, they will get their money back and a percentage of the proceeds to boot (or even that you pay them back a chunk each month, albeit interest-free) many lenders won't go for it because that also constitutes a loan of your deposit. You'll need to flag this up as early in the application process as possible with the lender to see if they will agree to it and what special terms they may apply.

The reason for all this is that your mortgage lender will have **first charge** on the property, which means that should you get repossessed, they have first dibs on recovering the debt that you owe. If they *aren't* the only interested party (for example, if you've borrowed your deposit) the person who leant you the deposit could have a claim on the property. Which makes things rather complicated.

Don't be put off, though, it's a relatively easy thing to sort out. You just need to be upfront with your financial advisor or lender about the situation so that they can tell you what you need to put in place legally to make it all work – and what you can or can't do. Your solicitor will also be able to help you out and advise the best way to deal with it, and raise the necessary paperwork.

6. The small print/big fee situation

So you've figured out how much you can afford, done your homework and sorted out a rate and product that works for you. You're nearly there, but there are some pretty important bits and pieces that you need to be aware of to make sure that, once you've signed your life away, you know exactly what you've got yourself involved in.

If you haven't already asked the question, find out what **redemption penalties** are chargeable if you decide to redeem your mortgage before the end of the product term (you will normally have to cough up a percentage of the amount you've borrowed). Depending on exactly what deal you're taking out, you may find that redemption penalties are chargeable after the tie-in too.

Another cheeky little expense that some lenders impose are **Higher Lending Charges** (HLC). These are applied if you are borrowing more than a certain amount of the property's value (for example, over 90%). In which case, the lender will want to protect themselves against you defaulting on your mortgage, so they will effectively take out an insurance policy which covers them for that potentially happening. Each lender has a different threshold for HLCs and a different scale of charges, so you need to find out what the deal is with your prospective lender early on; the likelihood is you'll have to pay the HLC upfront, which will add to the cost of applying for your mortgage.

Application fees are also something you need to look out for – you can almost guarantee that the cheaper the mortgage rate, the higher the application fee. As with everything else, find out what you're in for, and factor it in to the overall cost of the exercise.

7. How to apply for a mortgage

No, it's not just as easy as filling in a few forms and keeping your fingers crossed. You're going to need to get together some key bits of paperwork to support your application.

Broadly speaking, if you're an employee (e.g. you pay your tax through PAYE and get wage slips each month) you will need:

- Three months of recent payslips.

- Your last P60.

- Three months of recent bank statements.

- Two utility bills to prove your current address.

- Your passport (or if you don't have one, your birth certificate).

- A bank or savings account statement to show your deposit amount, or a letter if this is being gifted or provided by a third party.

If you're self-employed, you'll need a slightly different set of bits and pieces:

- Three years' worth of audited accounts, signed off by a qualified accountant (some lenders will accept two years, but check before you go to the interview to make sure).

- Three years of your SA302 – this is a document issued from HMRC to prove how much tax you've paid, thus supporting your earnings claim.

- Three months of recent bank statements.

- Two utility bills to prove your current address.

- Your birth certificate or passport.

- A bank or savings account statement to show your deposit amount, or a letter if this is being gifted or provided by a third party.

Resign yourself to the fact that it's going to take you an evening to hunt around and get it all together, then just get on with it. Take photocopies of everything, so you've got copies of the originals to hand should you need to run through stuff with anyone on the phone. It'll make life a bit easier as you can both see what you're discussing. If you have to send original documents in the post, for goodness' sake send them registered so at least you know they'll get there okay and you can trace them.

The forms that you're going to have to fill in do look a bit daunting, so if you're not sure about anything, play it safe and ask. You won't look stupid, don't worry – everyone wants to make sure you get this bit right, because *one in four mortgages are rejected first time around due to incorrect paperwork*.

Whilst we're at it, this is not the right time to be elastic with the truth about how much you earn or any debts you may have. Someone is going to go through your application with a fine-tooth comb (well, they *are* considering lending you an obscene amount of money), which means any 'anomalies' are going to be looked at long and hard.

By the time you've completed your application forms and supplied them with the supporting paperwork, the lender is going to know pretty much everything about you, apart from your inside leg measurement and the name of your first pet. If you fib, they *will* find out and are likely to turn down your application, so don't even go there. Quite apart from the fact that obtaining a mortgage fraudulently is against the law, and therefore, not exactly recommended. Unless you fancy a rent-free stint at Belmarsh, that is.

8. Help to Buy

So much has been written about the two Help to Buy schemes in the press recently that I felt it was important to include information on them in this book, but I just wasn't sure where to put it. Well, I think this chapter is about as good a place as any, so here goes.

Help to Buy is a government initiative to assist those who want to purchase a property, and can afford the monthly mortgage repayments, but are struggling to find the higher deposit required these days to secure a home loan. There are currently over 4 million people in private rented accommodation in the UK, and many of these people are paying more in rent each month than it would cost to service a mortgage. So, Help to Buy is designed to assist exactly these folk to effectively convert their rent payments into mortgage payments.

Help to Buy can *also* be used by *existing* home owners who need to move, can afford the increased monthly payments, but again lack the larger deposit now required.

In brief, here's how it works. There are two schemes, the **equity loan** and the **mortgage guarantee**.

With the **equity loan** scheme, which is for new build homes only, the buyer puts in their deposit, which can be as little as 5%, then the government will lend up to 20% of the value of the new build property through an equity loan (in other words, the money is secured against a chunk of the property) to make the total deposit up to 25%. Then, the buyer raises a 75% mortgage through one of the lenders which is part of the scheme.

The loan from the government for the deposit is interest-free for the first five years, and then a fee of 1.75% will be charged from year six, rising annually by RPI inflation plus 1%. The equity loan can be repaid at any time within 25 years, or on sale of the property. The initial loan is repaid, plus a proportion of any growth in the property value. You'll need to apply for this part of the scheme via a **Help to Buy Agent**, and you can find out the nearest branch by taking a look on the Help to Buy website: **www.helptobuy.org.uk**

If, however, you want to buy a 'second-hand' property rather than a new build, then there is another option available under Help to Buy: the **mortgage guarantee** scheme.

This differs from the equity loan because not only can you use it to purchase any property (so new *or* existing), but the way it's structured is more of an indemnity policy for the lender rather than a deposit loan to you.

With this scheme, a few of the high street mortgage lenders have agreed to offer mortgages for those with smaller deposits (5% minimum) on the basis that the government underwrites a proportion of the mortgage they lend, to avoid the need for a bigger deposit.

From the buyer's perspective, it's pretty simple; the mortgage you take out works exactly the same way as any other normal mortgage, but under this scheme the government offers lenders the option to purchase a 'guarantee' on the mortgage. So if, for example, you're putting in a 5% deposit and have secured a mortgage via one of the lenders offering Help to Buy home loans, you will still need a 95% home loan which you will pay back in the normal way. The difference is, because a lower deposit mortgage is seen as higher risk, the lender is getting an insurance policy, for want of a better description, from the government.

So, worst-case scenario, if you took out a home loan using the mortgage guarantee scheme, got into financial difficulties and your home ended up getting repossessed, the government would cover part of the loss suffered by the lender.

Not every lender offers home loans under the Help to Buy mortgage guarantee scheme, so I thought I'd include a list for you of the ones who do. That way, you can have a look on their websites and familiarise yourself with what's on offer:

- Aldermore

- Bank of Ireland (Northern Ireland only)

- Bank of Scotland

- Barclays

- Halifax

- HSBC

- Lloyds

- NatWest

- Post Office Mortgages

- RBS

- Santander

- Virgin Money

This list is changing all the time, so make sure you check to see what's available at the time you apply.

As with the equity loan option, the mortgage guarantee scheme is available to movers as well as first-time buyers. With both schemes, providing you can get the mortgage and have the required deposit, you can purchase a property of up to a maximum value of £600,000 (at the time of writing).

Now, as you can imagine, there are quite a few T&Cs attached to both the options under the Help to Buy scheme in terms of who can apply and things you can and can't do, so if this is something that interests you, there's a load more information on the Help to Buy website (**www.helptobuy.org.uk**). Also, it's worth remembering that the Help to Buy schemes available vary between England, Northern Ireland, Scotland and Wales, so do check to see what will apply in your local area.

Bottom line, it's still a mortgage and whichever option you go for, you still have to keep up your repayments as you would with any other home loan. But if it means that you can buy rather than rent without having to save for the next decade, it's probably well worth a look.

9. Intelligent insurance

Now, I'm going to let you into a bit of an industry secret here. By the time you've waded your way through all those forms and everything is ready to go, you'll be so stressed and frazzled that when your mortgage advisor asks:

"Have you got buildings and contents insurance arranged?"

You'll want to deck them. No, of course you haven't thought about insurance. You've not slept for two weeks, and whether or not the place burns down is the last thing on your mind. Your advisor, who by now might be sniffing a golden opportunity to make a few more quid, will then say:

"Well, I can offer you a very reasonable policy which will only be… "

You won't hear any more because the offer of someone else to sort out this mundane yet essential task will be so welcome, you'd sign your own grandmother away right now if it meant you didn't have to see one more bloody form.

And that, my friend, is where you're about to go wrong.

Over the lifetime of your mortgage, you *could* end up spending thousands more than you have to on buildings and contents cover, not to mention life insurance. You see, you don't *have* to take the products offered to you by your lender or advisor, and they aren't necessarily the most competitive around.

This is one thing you can and should shop around for on your own. It's not difficult – ask your lender for the rebuild figure they want you to insure for, and get on the internet. Use the price comparison websites – that's what they are there for. You'll need:

• **Buildings insurance**

Unless you're buying a flat, in which case check with your solicitor because chances are, if it's a **leasehold** property, the buildings cover will be included in your service charge. If this is the case, you don't need to worry about it.

• **Contents insurance**

Your mortgage lender won't require you to have this, but you should get it, based on the Sod's Law principle that if you don't, chances are you'll set fire to the sofa or get burgled.

• **Life assurance**

Not the nicest thing to have to consider, but if you do kick the bucket you'll need a basic policy in place to pay out and cover the mortgage. Again, you don't need to spend a fortune on this. Check with your lender to make sure you're covering yourself for the right amount.

If you're happy to spend the extra, it's well worth considering critical illness and redundancy cover too. These come into play if you're seriously ill and can't work or if you lose your job, and either way can't pay your mortgage. Definitely worth bearing in mind if you're able to afford it. As with anything else, make sure you understand the policy so you know what you're signing up to, and if you're not sure, get expert advice.

10. *What to do if you get into difficulties with your mortgage*

If you're having trouble paying your mortgage, the sooner you talk to your lender the better. Do not bury your head in the sand. This is because the minute you miss a payment you're in arrears and your bank or building society can (and probably will) start repossession proceedings.

By having a dialogue with them early on about why you're having trouble, you're giving them the opportunity to help you. Believe me, lenders don't like repossessing properties – it's expensive and time-consuming, as they have to go through a lengthy legal process to get a court order to evict you.

To get that eviction order, the lender will also have to prove to the court that they have done everything possible to give you the opportunity to stay in your home. Which means if you're prepared to do everything you can to help yourself, you've got a good chance of hanging on to your property.

It's likely you'll be asked to fill out a form showing all your monthly expenditure, so that a specialist advisor from your lender can then assess how much you can afford to pay back each month. Once that's done, the bank or building society have a few options in terms of how they may decide to help you:

- **By changing your repayment mortgage to interest only**

This reduces your monthly payments, and is generally only used as a short-term solution because you won't be paying any capital off the loan, so at some stage your payments will go up again. But this would be an easy way to assist you if, for example, you've lost your job. As soon as you have got yourself back into employment, your mortgage would revert to your normal repayments.

- **By increasing the term of the loan**

In other words, if you're five years into a 20-year mortgage, and are still reasonably young, the lender may offer you the chance to extend the loan to 25 – or even, depending on your age, 30 years – which will reduce the monthly payments considerably. Be aware, though, you will need to make overpayments as and when you can afford to in order to pay off the capital, or else you'll be saddled with a mortgage well into your sixties.

- **By allowing you a payment holiday**

Usually the last resort, and really only available to those with a considerable amount of equity in the property. But, if your lender thinks you're a suitable case, they will assess your assets and then potentially allow you some time off making your mortgage payments. Remember, this will extend the mortgage amount, meaning that you may have to pay back more of any equity of the property to your lender should you sell it in the future. Get legal advice from a solicitor if this is the route you're going to go, just to make sure you totally understand what you're signing up to and why.

The point is banks and building societies are very adept at sorting the 'can't pays' from the 'won't pays'. If you're blagging it you *will* get found out, and the penalties are severe. However, if you're really up against it, just be honest, and bend over backwards to give the lender as much information as you can. Help them to help you.

If you need advice or debt counselling, a great website to look at is **www.stepchange.org**. It's a debt advice and counselling charity that helps people avoid getting into debt, or assists those in financial difficulties. It's well worth a look to pick up tips on how to avoid getting yourself in the sticky stuff, or as a first port of call if you find yourself approaching financial meltdown. They have a great free helpline which is open six days a week, so it's worth giving them a call to get some impartial advice and tips to help you broach the subject with your lender.

Of course, there are other options open to you that can help to pay the mortgage if you find yourself in a tricky situation. You could take in a lodger, which can earn you up to £4,250 tax-free per year which could really help out with the monthly repayments. Have a read of Chapter 1, 'Fantastic Flatmates' to find out more about making money from your spare room.

Or, you may decide that it's better to move out and let the property for a year until your situation stabilises. In which case, take a look at Chapter 6, 'Virgin Landlords' for an introduction into letting out your property.

I guess what I'm trying to say is that you've got a few options, so please don't panic (easy to say, harder to do, I know). But take it from me, the sooner you sit down and talk to someone about your predicament, the sooner you can work out what's best for you and safeguard your home.

Conclusion

If you find the prospect of applying for your first mortgage scarier than taking your driving test, don't worry – it all sounds far worse than it is. With the right preparation and research, providing you are truthful about what you earn and realistic about how much you want to borrow, chances are there is a home loan out there with your name on it.

Just try to remember when you are being questioned about everything from what you spend on petrol each month to the cost of your gym membership, *the lender isn't being nosey*. They just want to make sure you can afford to pay back the money they're going to lend you. So smile, be nice and answer as best you can. This is for your benefit. The mortgage advisor doesn't care what you spend your money on, he just needs to do the best he can to make sure that you don't borrow too much and end up getting your home repossessed.

Also, bear in mind that once you've worked through all those forms, answered all those difficult questions and provided photocopies of every important document you forgot you ever had, you will (fingers crossed) get that magical piece of paper with your mortgage offer in principle confirmed, which will absolutely make you forget any trauma you've suffered in the proceeding weeks within seconds.

Why?

Well, because now you're on to the next, far more exciting stage: house shopping.

4.
Buying Your First Home

It's a daunting process. Someone has just agreed to lend you more money than you will ever be able to pay back (at least, that's how it feels right now) at a rate of interest that would make you consider selling one of your vital organs if you thought it would reduce your monthly repayments. But, against all the odds, here you are, looking to take your first step on the property ladder.

Times have changed considerably since I bought my first place at the tender age of nineteen. The base rate of interest was 11% eighteen months before (it got as high as 14% in the late eighties) and the property itself cost me £47,500 (you'd be lucky to get a garage in London for that these days) and was exempt from Stamp Duty. You'd be forgiven for thinking that this was another planet, but actually this was 1993.

However, fast-forward 20-odd years and, although the property market and interest rates have changed, the way that you buy a property has, for the most part, not. It's still a complex process that requires a good solicitor, plenty of patience and nerves of steel. There's a reason why it's one of the top five most stressful things you'll ever do. Accept that from the outset, and you'll be okay. Think that you'll breeze through the process and still be able to sleep at night and you may have a bit of a shock coming.

Having said all that, you can help yourself greatly by having a good grasp of the process so that you can ask the right questions of your solicitor, mortgage lender, and the estate agent that you're buying the property through. Also, as with most things, I find that the more you understand it, the less stressful it is, because at least you know *why* things happen and *how* they take so darn long.

But first off, you need to find something that you want to buy. I'm going to assume here that you've got your mortgage sorted, as really, it's pointless looking until you've got finances agreed and you know what you can afford, especially with the recent changes to the mortgage market. Also, you'll be taken a lot more seriously if you do have a **mortgage offer in principle**. If you haven't arranged a mortgage offer yet, read through Chapter 3, 'Financially Fabulous' before you do anything else.

Now, the first thing to wrap your head around is where you, as the buyer, sit in the pecking order of the whole process. You see, unlike any other major purchase you may make, when you're buying a property you're not actually the most important person in the room. It's completely different to anything else where you're spending a huge amount of moolah (say, for example, a new car, expensive holiday, new kitchen, etc.) and the salesperson will be sucking up to you big time. In the property stakes, as far as the estate agent is concerned the **vendor** (or person selling the property) is king. This is because the vendor will be paying the estate agent's fees when the sale goes through.

Bear this in mind and be prepared when you go out looking for your first place. It's quite a shock sometimes to realise that, at least when it comes to buying property, the customer isn't always right. At best, you may be met with polite enthusiasm. At worst, downright rudeness. Most likely, a distinct touch of apathy. You need to be proactive, show that you're ready to go and that you are able to complete the transaction quickly. To an estate agent you then represent the best outcome – their commission cheque being paid swiftly.

You need to be very clear about what you're looking for in terms of type of property, what your *absolute* upper limit is (that's why you need to have been through the mortgage application process first), how many bedrooms you want, the location you're after, whether you require outside space or off-road parking, if you need to live near transport links, etc.

So, before you do anything else, sit down and work out what the absolute, got-to-have, can't-compromise things are. Then think about the nice-to-haves that you could perhaps do without if a property ticks all the other boxes.

This is particularly relevant if you're buying with someone else, be it partner, sibling or friend, as if you can't agree on these things before you start looking, just you wait until one of you has fallen in love with a place that the other wouldn't even consider fit as a rabbit hutch. At that point, having a list of criteria that you can both refer to will at least form some kind of basis for a rational discussion. Well, hopefully, anyway.

Once you've got your property brief together, start looking. Ring agents in the area you're looking to buy in, and explain exactly what you're looking for. The more specific you are, the better, or you'll spend all your evenings and weekends viewing stuff that's not relevant. And I probably don't need to tell you this, but use the internet too. The main sites to visit are **www.rightmove.co.uk** and **www.zoopla.co.uk**. There are others, but the majority of homes for sale are listed on these sites, and they are normally kept up-to-date with new properties being added every day.

In the last few years, estate agents have got really savvy at providing a good set of marketing details, so you should be able to see floor plans, colour photos of most rooms in the property, 360 degree virtual tours and maps of the local area, as well as links to Google Earth so you can check out the street view. Make sure you take advantage of this. Again, if you can get a really good idea of the place before you visit and it just doesn't tick your boxes, then don't waste your time (or anyone else's) going to see it.

Bear in mind that to find your dream home you're going to have to be proactive. Estate agents need chasing, particularly if the market is buoyant in the area you're looking in. Keep a list of the agents you've registered with and ring them each week (on a Thursday is good, so you can book your viewing at the weekend if there is something you particularly want to go and see), and ask if they have taken any properties on in the last few days which fit your criteria. Again, *don't assume that because you are the person who's buying you'll get the gold-star service.* It's up to you to make this happen.

So, you've got viewings lined up, all within your budget and meeting your criteria. The mortgage offer is eating a hole in your back pocket. What next?

Wherever you can, make sure that when you view the property the vendor isn't at home. It's so awkward walking around someone's place, trying to work out if you'd like to live there, with them following you around telling you how nice the neighbours are and that they've just spent a fortune on planting roses in the flowerbeds. If it's just you and the agent you'll get a much better feel for the property. Open up cupboards and be nosey. This is going to be the biggest purchase you've ever made, so you need to feel 100% happy and comfortable. Try to look past dodgy furniture, carpets and wallpaper, as these are things which are easily (and relatively cheaply) changed.

KEY THINGS TO THINK ABOUT

- **Outlook:** What can you see when you look out the windows? Can you cope with the view? Can anyone see in?

- The **amount of light** you get in the property: Is there plenty of natural light or is it dark? Be aware of one of the estate agent's favourite tricks, which is to put all the lights in the house on, even during the day, to make it look brighter than it is. If you see lights on, turn them off so you get a real feel for the place.

- **Size and layout of rooms:** Can you see yourself in the space? How would you use it? And will your furniture fit?

- **Use of space for storage:** If there are already built-in cupboards and wardrobes in the bedrooms and living areas, great. If not, where would you put them? Think about the amount of stuff you have and where you are going to put it.

- **Security:** How easy is it for someone to break in, particularly if you're a girl living on your own? A ground floor flat with patio doors in a busy city may be fine, but you are going to have to be on top of your security to make sure you don't end up leaving yourself wide open to burglars.

- What are the options for **car parking**? Does the property have its own private driveway or allocated parking space? Or do you have to park on the road and pay for a resident's parking permit? Or is it a free-for-all – first come, first served – in the road?

- What sort of **boiler and heating system** does the property have? Is it a combi-boiler or boiler with hot water tank? Are there radiators, underfloor heating or electric heaters?

- **White goods** in the kitchen: Are there integrated appliances like a washing machine, dishwasher, fridge, freezer and microwave, or will the owners be taking all that with them when they move?

- Is the property on **mains drainage and services**? In other words, can you use normal utilities, or, as in some rural areas, do you have to use gas tanks or oil to run the heating, and a private drainage tank that will need to be emptied?

- **Access:** Is the property near a school, offices or shops? Not a bad thing by any means (in fact, that may be what you're looking for), but just consider how much traffic there will be around the property at rush hour.

- **Trains, planes and road noise:** Is the property on a flight path, near a train line or on a busy road? If so, how much can you hear when you're inside, both with the windows shut and open? Think about it: in the summer you may want to sleep with the windows open ... so backing onto a motorway or living underneath an airport flight path might not be ideal.

If you're buying on your own, consider taking someone with you (parent, older sibling, good mate, etc.) to get a second opinion. It's amazing how much you overlook because you're so excited. Having someone with you who knows the drill and will be able to point out the achingly boring but very practical stuff is invaluable. Like where will you dry your washing, the fact that the garden is overlooked by a block of flats at the back, or perhaps that it's next door to a particularly fragrant kebab shop. Also, if you're a girl, from a safety conscious point of view, I'd avoid turning up to a viewing on your own – get a friend to go with you, even if they know nothing about property, just so you're not in a strange place with a person that you've never met before.

When you arrive at the property for the first time, take a good look at the outside of the place. In the trade, it's called **kerb appeal** – in other words how good (or not) it looks from the road. This is crucial as one day you'll probably want to move on, and therefore something that looks great before you even get inside the front door is a good potential investment.

Probably this point is as good as any for another of my 'pearls of wisdom' which is:

The first thing to think about when you're buying a property is how you're going to sell it.

Now, I know that sounds a little bit counter-intuitive, but hear me out. Sometimes, it's all too easy to fall for a quirky property, or perhaps a place that's on a busy road or backs onto a train line, because it's been priced to sell. You'll reason that, for the money, it represents great value and you can live with whatever it is that's slightly unusual (e.g. the second bedroom being off the kitchen, the noise of the busy bus route or the fact it's next to the local sewage works). And chances are, you probably can. However, when you eventually come to *sell* the property, it may be more difficult if there are things about it that are a little more 'unique' than other places. So, as you wander around your first few potential properties like a kid in a sweetie shop, just bear in mind that one day you will want to sell it. Try to think that through and avoid properties that come with what I like to call 'emotional baggage'.

OK, back to your viewing. Go armed with the ability to take photos (ask permission before you actually start snapping) so you can remind yourself of what you particularly like about the property – chances are, the photos taken by the agent won't be hugely detailed. Also, take the floorplan with you (if there is one), and the set of particulars for the place and make notes on them, so that you can easily compare properties later on when you're trying to whittle the shortlist down.

Don't forget to ask the agent about the **vendor** (that's the person selling the property). For example, have they found somewhere else to buy, or is it a couple who are divorcing and just need to sell quickly? Perhaps it's an investment property that the owner is disposing of so there isn't a chain, which means a series of people buying and selling from and to each other. Ideally, you want somewhere which is offered with **vacant possession**, which is estate agent speak for 'no one is living in it at the moment'. This means things may move along a little bit quicker. The vendor's circumstances will be something you'll need to take into account should you decide to make an offer on the place (we'll come back to that later).

View the property more than once, ideally at different times of the day. You'll need to get a feel for the area; for example, how safe and well-lit the street is at night, how much noise you will hear from other properties when the occupants are at home. Make sure you include at least one evening viewing (the agent might not be able to attend, but a keen buyer should accommodate you themselves if they really want to sell). You're looking out for stuff like being able to hear next door's TV/kids/dog/loo flushing. Sounds awful, but in some conversion apartments and terraced houses the soundproofing is so poor you can hear pretty much everything.

Ultimately, the best bit of advice I can give you is to take notice of the 'warm tummy feeling'. Research has shown that a buyer makes a decision about a property within thirty seconds of walking inside. If it doesn't feel right, no matter how good a deal it is or how many boxes it ticks, chances are you'll never be completely happy there. You need to have a good gut feeling about a place. In all the years I've bought property, the times I've had problems are when I've ignored my instincts and rationalised the purchase. However, when I've gone for a property which felt like the right thing to do, even if it wasn't the most logical choice on the face of it, I've always come out smelling of roses. Call it what you will, but it works for me.

So, after a lot of worn shoe leather and patience, you've found The One. Now what? Well, this is where you really need to listen up and pay attention, because the haggling, stress and real effort starts now.

First, you need to put in your offer. This is not just as simple as saying you'll pay whatever the price the place is on the market for (the **asking price**). Why? Well, estate agents can be a cheeky lot sometimes. They'll tell the vendor to put the place on the market for slightly more than it's worth, mainly in the hope that you'll fall head over heels in love with it and be happy to pay top whack to secure it.

Don't be fooled. Do your research. Look at other similar properties currently for sale in the area to get a good idea of what comparable properties cost. Have a quick nose online to check the values of other places that have been sold in the last few months. The more you know about the local market, the better position you'll be in to make an offer below the asking price and justify why you've done it.

There are other times when the asking price isn't the price you should pay. **Stamp Duty** plays a massive part. Stamp Duty Land Tax (to use its proper name) is the whopping great cheque you pay to the government for the privilege of buying your own home. The amount you pay (which is a percentage of the value of the property) depends on which band it falls into:

Property purchase price	Rate of Stamp Duty
Up to £125,000	0%
£125,000 to £250,000	1%
£250,000 to £500,000	3%
£500,000 to £1 million	4%
£1 million to £2 million	5%
Over £2 million	7%

As you can see, it's a pretty punchy amount by the time you've factored in that many properties these days aren't exempt from Stamp Duty. Now, the reason this is relevant to the price you pay for a property is simply because if something is on the market at, say, £265,000, and you pay the asking price for it, your contribution to the government's coffers will be £7,950, based on the fact that the property is in the 3% Stamp Duty bracket.

However, if you were to pay £250,000 for that property instead, you would be *under* the 3% band and therefore only pay £2,500 in

Stamp Duty. Big difference. Quite why estate agents and vendors don't think people will work this out is beyond me, but there you go. So, when you're off looking, remember where the thresholds are, as this does give you a degree of negotiating room.

For example, if your budget is absolutely, not-a-penny-more than £250,000, go and look at properties priced anywhere up to £275,000. That twenty-five grand difference is really aspirational profit for the vendor and extra commission for the agent.

People in the know understand it's very rare in most areas that a property will actually sell for between £265,000 and £270,000, due to the issue of additional Stamp Duty. It's a marketing price, designed to get the vendor bang on the nose a quarter of a million. Stands to reason though, doesn't it? Because if you put it on at £250,000 you know you'd only end up getting knocked down and probably accepting £240,000 or thereabouts. Of course, if the area you are trying to buy in is particularly buoyant and four people are after the same property (which at the time of writing is still the case in some areas, such as London) then yes, of course it's entirely possible that you may have to pay £265,000 or £275,000 to secure the pad of your dreams, and end up paying a lot more Stamp Duty to boot.

Negotiating your offer price is where you need to stop being a nice, considerate human being for a moment. You have to concentrate on your more avaricious side and consider the circumstances of the vendor. Remember I told you earlier to find out what their position is? That's because you're now going to use that as a negotiating tool. If they are desperate to sell, you can perhaps be a little bit more aggressive in your offer (see, I told you this is no time to be kind).

If, however, the vendor is trying to buy somewhere else, it's likely that they won't happily accept a lower offer, but they *will* be more impressed if you're a **first time buyer** and not in a chain, as it means the sale is probably going to proceed more smoothly. Which means they *might* think about at least a slight reduction in the asking price.

Don't forget, the estate agent is acting on behalf of the vendor and *not* the buyer, so expect a limited amount of information from him about the seller: it's in the agent's best interests to secure the top price for the property. You're on your own here – you just need to be confident in your knowledge, and how you present your offer, in order to get the best result.

Armed with all this information, then, and the fact that you've done your homework and have a good feel for how much the place is worth, take a deep breath, ring the estate agent and tell him that you'd like to put in an offer. Be upfront. Tell him why you think the property is worth what you're offering. The more logical the argument you can present, the more likely that your offer will at least be considered.

I always leave myself a few grand of negotiating room, so if the property is on the market for £265,000, and I know that realistically the vendor will probably accept £250,000, I'd start by offering £245,000.

Worst case, the agent comes back and asks you to up your offer, which you can then do in increments *if you can afford it*. Best case, they accept your first offer (rare, but it does happen) and you've saved yourself a few thousand pounds.

Also, with the recent changes in mortgage lending, estate agents are (mostly) more aware of the fact that people just aren't able to borrow 'a bit more' if their offer is unsuccessful. It used to be the case that the agent would know they could stretch a higher offer out of a buyer because, chances were, they could go back to their mortgage lender and squeeze out an extra few thousand pounds. Not anymore.

So these days, it's perfectly reasonable to say, "This is my limit and I can't get a bigger mortgage." That way, the vendor either has to accept that as a first time buyer you're in a strong position and accept what you're offering or take the risk that someone else will cough up more. The likelihood of either outcome is entirely dependent on the vendor's circumstances and the market in the area you're trying to buy in. You may well find that there are so many other people after the property that your offer gets rejected. But if you're trying to buy in an area where prices and demand are cooler, you *could* get lucky.

One last word on Stamp Duty (for now). The tax man doesn't care *who* pays it, just that he gets his money. So, if you end up paying just over a Stamp Duty threshold because the vendor won't haggle, you do have one option left to you. The vendor pays the difference between the Stamp Duty threshold on your behalf. Here's how it might work:

- Chris is a first-time buyer who is interested in a property that's currently on the market for £275,000. He's already got a mortgage in place, and his absolute top whack is £265,000. But he really doesn't want to pay more than £250,000 for a property because of the Stamp Duty threshold.

- Chris offers £250,000 for the property, but the vendor refuses, even though Chris can move quickly. The estate agent says that the vendor may agree to £265,000, a £10,000 reduction in the asking price. So, before he goes back, Chris does a quick bit of maths:

- Stamp Duty on purchase price of £250,000 at 1% = £2,500

- Stamp Duty on purchase price of £265,000 at 3% = £7,950

- Therefore, the difference between rates of Stamp Duty is £5,450

- Chris goes back to the estate agent and offers £265,000 on the condition that the vendor pays the difference of £5,450 in Stamp Duty. As Chris is a first-time buyer and can move quickly, the offer is accepted.

The mechanics in this example are pretty simple, but you can see how it works. The vendor has the choice of compromising on Stamp Duty or turning away a well-intentioned buyer who can move quickly. The vendor has still ended up with nearly ten grand more than he would have done if he had accepted the first offer of £250,000. Chris, on the other hand, will have a slightly bigger mortgage, but his cash outgoings at the point of purchase aren't any more than if he'd paid £250,000 for the place. So everyone wins.

Now, I've done this myself when I've bought property over the years where the asking price is close to the Stamp Duty threshold, and have advised other people to do it as well. And, depending on the vendor's position and the market at the time you're trying to buy, I'd say you've got about a 50/50 chance of pulling it off. If your position is strong and you can move quickly, it's worth a go. If you don't ask, you don't get and all that. Just remember, so long as *someone* pays the taxman the Stamp Duty, he's happy. That doesn't always have to be the person buying the property.

If this does work out for you, don't forget to tell your mortgage lender and your solicitor, so that they are both aware and whoever is doing your conveyancing can make sure that the Stamp Duty payment is made correctly.

By law, the agent has to put every offer made to the vendor in writing. Generally speaking, the minute the offer is made, the agent will ring the vendor to put forward the offer verbally and gauge a reaction (either 'tell them to where to stick it' or 'bite their hand off') and then follow up with a formal presentation of the offer afterwards.

Most people just want to get the ball rolling, so, allowing for the vendor being difficult to get hold of (e.g. out of the country or at work) you can usually count on hearing back within 24 hours. Once you've agreed the price, the real fun begins.

1. Get yourself a solicitor

As soon as the offer is accepted, you need to instruct a conveyancing solicitor (a lawyer who specialises in buying and selling property). Sounds simple, right?

Well, in theory maybe, but there are some key points to consider here:

- Other than a sense of humour (rare in conveyancing solicitors, but some are human), try to find a firm that is open early, closes late and answers the phone between 12 noon and 2pm. You'd be amazed at the amount that don't.

- Try and talk to the person who will actually be dealing with your file to see if he or she can clearly communicate with you. Don't forget, your solicitor is pretty quickly going to become the most important person in your life, if only for a short amount of time. You need to be able to talk to them and feel comfortable that they can explain the complexities of property law to you in a way that you understand.

- Beware of battle-axe legal secretaries, who seem to think they wield more power than Boadicea. Remember, *you're* the client, you're paying the bill and you deserve politeness and good service. They are there to help you. It may take a couple of tactful reminders of this, but stand firm.

- Check to make sure that the solicitor you are about to instruct is either a member of the Law Society or a Licensed

Conveyancer, and ask if they have an online service where you can track the progress of your sale. It also helps if you can correspond with them via email, so ask that question too. Again, you'd be surprised at the amount of antiquated 'local' solicitors who won't deal via email. It's changing – thank goodness – but do check.

- Don't forget, you don't necessarily have to use a solicitor in the same area as the property you are buying – a large, national conveyancing company that uses the latest technology may do the job as well (if not better and quicker than) the fusty local solicitor who was 'highly recommended' by the estate agent you're buying through. You don't have to use the law firm your estate agent advocates, so shop around to find someone you feel you can work with and whose fees you think are reasonable. Remember that estate agents who 'recommend' a solicitor will usually receive a referral fee from said solicitor. So their motives may not be altogether altruistic.

- Where possible, select a solicitor who is a member of the Conveyancing Quality Scheme. This was introduced in 2011 and is a voluntary scheme, with members vetted by the Law Society and audited once a year to ensure their work is of the highest standards. It's worth also knowing that many mortgage lenders will only use solicitors who are members of the CQS, so if you do decide to go 'off piste' and use a solicitor who isn't recommended by your mortgage lender, make sure they are a member.

- Ask if your solicitor can offer Residential Abortive Transaction Insurance, or 'after the event' insurance. This will cover the cost of your legal fees if your purchase doesn't exchange (by which point you will have racked up a pretty hefty legal bill, believe me). Expect to pay around £80, so in the grand scheme of things, if your solicitor offers this, it's really worth considering.

For a straightforward conveyancing service to buy a freehold property, expect to pay around £500 upwards. If you're buying a flat, which is likely to be leasehold, then expect to pay a little more as the paperwork is more involved. You'll probably have to make an initial 'payment on account' to your solicitor to start the process off, then pay the rest of the bill when you complete. Just make sure you've factored that into all the money you are going to have to spend so you don't lose track of what you owe.

Once you've appointed a solicitor, you'll need to tell them who your lender is, and also let your lender know which solicitor you've instructed. Your solicitor will then be sent instructions from your lender, which will contain the conditions of the mortgage and how they will require the transaction to be completed, etc. At this stage your lender will also start to arrange the **mortgage survey**, which is when they send out a **surveyor** to check the property – basically to make sure it's worth the money that you're going to pay for it, that it's structurally sound, and isn't going to fall down around your ears anytime soon. But I'll come back to that bit in a minute.

You also need to inform your estate agent who your solicitor is as quickly as possible. Your solicitor will also ask the estate agent for a copy of the **Memorandum of Sale**, which will have the details of the vendor, the basic address and details of the property, and the details of the vendor's solicitor.

At the same time, your solicitor will request the **Contract Package**, which contains the proposed **Sales Contract** drafted by the vendor's solicitor, plus any guarantees. For example, if the property was built recently it may have the remainder of the **NHBC** warranty, or if there been any building work such as a new roof, replacement boiler or windows, the guarantees for these should also be included, along with the copy of any planning permissions and building regulations that were required for any major works to the property. The Contract Package will also include a **Property Information Form** and **Fittings and Contents Form**. If the property is a leasehold, then there will be a **Leasehold Information Form** as well.

2. *Read the reports*

Your solicitor will then read through everything and explain it all to you in a document called a **Report on Title**, which will include the results of **searches** such as **flood**, **planning**, **drainage** and **environmental** (and any others applicable to the area you're buying in). The searches will also highlight any public rights of way across your land, and who is responsible for maintaining roads and drains (normally your local council, but if you're posh and buying in a private road or estate, a management company will be responsible instead). Your solicitor will also tell you about any rights on adjoining properties, so if, for example, you're buying somewhere with a shared driveway or wall, he'll explain who has rights to what.

It's pretty important you pay particular attention to the environmental search as the property you are purchasing could have been built on previously contaminated land (this occasionally happens when a developer has bought a plot that was previously a rubbish dump or sewage works then reclaimed the land to build on). Or, the place may be in close proximity to a mobile phone mast or something else you may think is undesirable. At the end of the day, it's a personal choice whether you want to live next to something that resembles Goonhilly, but it's important you go into this with your eyes wide open. You also need to think about how many people it may put off when you come to sell the property. Remember what I said about the first thing you should think about when buying a place is how you're going to sell it? Yep, that's what I'm talking about, right here. So consider carefully what the search results show up, and contemplate how a future buyer may perceive them.

Once you've gone through your Report on Title, your solicitor will then raise any queries you have with the vendor's solicitor, particularly if you're buying a leasehold property, where there may be quirks in the lease that you want answered upfront.

At the same time that all of this is going on, your lender will have instructed a survey on the property. Yep, I know I mentioned this earlier, but now we're going to talk about it in a bit more detail. Because this is something that so many people just let fly over their heads, and it's actually pretty darn crucial. First off, you need to make sure that you get a surveyor who is a member of the **RICS** (Royal Institution of Chartered Surveyors) on the case. Surveyors are highly skilled and have completed years of training and exams and are the only folk qualified to undertake this sort of work. You can find one via the RICS website (**www.rics.org/uk**). I think it would be most likely, though, that your mortgage lender will organise it for you.

There are in fact three types of surveys available, which vary greatly in their detail and what the surveyor checks for. So, a quick lesson in surveying for you:

- **Mortgage Valuation Survey (sometimes called a Condition Report)**: This is your 'entry level' survey and gives a pretty basic level of detail. The surveyor will check the value of the property and highlight any really obvious problems, like a hole in the roof or the fact that it has subsidence. A Mortgage Valuation or Condition Report is perfectly OK if you're buying a brand-new property or one that's less than ten-years-old (because it will probably come with an NHBC guarantee, but do check). But fundamentally, this version is just going to tell you it's worth what you want to pay for it and that it won't fall down next week. It's really more for the benefit of the lender, so that they know that if you default on your mortgage, heaven forbid, they can sell it and get their money back. Helpful, but it's not going to safeguard you much. Expect to pay up to a couple of hundred quid, although some lenders chuck a Mortgage Valuation Survey in for free – always worth asking, I find.

- **Homebuyer's Survey**: This version goes into a bit more detail. In addition to reviewing the value of the property and the basic checks involved in a Mortgage Valuation Survey, the surveyor will give the place a bit more of a going over and look more closely at things like rainwater goods (that's guttering, downpipes and hoppers), signs of damp, problems with timber (such as woodworm or rot), and the condition of any insulation or damp-proofing. If you're buying a flat, they will also take a look at the communal areas of the building both internally and externally that may affect you. A Homebuyer's Survey will alert you if there are things that you need to fix in the near to mid-term, so that you're more informed about what you're getting yourself into and can raise any expensive to fix issues with your vendor – you may even be able to negotiate a discount on the purchase price if there is something serious that needs sorting. Expect to pay anywhere between £300 and £600, depending on the size and value of the place.

- **Full Structural Survey**: This is the daddy of all surveys and, in an ideal world everyone who buys a property would get one of these. The sad truth is, because of the level of detail involved, they are too expensive for a lot of people, and generally only those buying either a wreck that they are going to redevelop, a listed building or a higher value property will go down this route. Which is a shame, because a Full Structural Survey really is a full MOT for a building. It will flag anything wrong and highlight any potential issues that you may experience further down the line. You probably wouldn't bother with a Full Structural Survey for an apartment or new build property – that would be overkill – but if you're going to be doing a serious amount of work, spending a serious amount of money, or if the place has a listing, then this is the ideal way to go. Expect to pay upwards of £1,000 depending on the size and value of the place.

3. Leasehold lingo

Just to mention leasehold properties for a moment, because a lot of first-time buyers purchase flats, which are normally leasehold. There are two main types of **tenure** (ownership) of a property. The first is **freehold**, which in the simplest terms means you own the property and the land it's sat on outright. Then there are **leasehold** properties, whereby you own the property itself (so a flat for instance) but you don't own the building it's in or the ground that it's built on. In some instances, you can buy a property which is **leasehold with a share of freehold**. This means that you own the flat *and* have a share in the building and land it's built on as well. If the property you are buying is leasehold, then you will have a pay a charge, normally a few hundred pounds a year, to the Freeholder for what's called **ground rent**. If you are buying a property that is leasehold with a share of the freehold, then you won't have to pay ground rent because you're a Freeholder yourself.

If you're buying a leasehold or leasehold with a share of freehold property, there is extra paperwork to deal with in the form of a **lease**. This is a document that outlines your responsibilities, and also those of the **Freeholder** – sometimes referred to as the Landlord – if relevant.

You need to be aware of the length of the lease, which can vary greatly. Most modern leases start at 125 or 999 years, but depending on how old the property is depends on how long the lease has to run. Many mortgage lenders won't lend on properties that have less than 65 years left on the lease, so this is a question to ask before you even put your offer forward. Also, do bear in mind that a short lease on a property decreases its value. So if you've fallen in love with a place that does have a short lease, you may want to think about negotiating an extension to the term of the lease as part of your offer. But just be warned, this won't be a quick process.

Because a leasehold or leasehold with share of freehold property generally involves multiple units, you'll probably also find that there will be a **managing agent** involved that is responsible for maintaining the fabric of the building: for example, internal communal areas, gardens, rainwater goods, the roof, windows and external walls. So if, for example, there's an issue with the guttering, you would contact the managing agent, who would then review the problem and arrange the repairs. Ideally, the managing agent should be a member of the RICS, so it's a good idea to ask who the company is and what their credentials are.

The managing agent will also deal with the accounts for the building maintenance, so it's important that your solicitor asks if there is a **sinking fund** – the posh name for a separate bank account, where a portion of your service charges are saved and used for repairs. This can also be used for major works that aren't covered in your regular maintenance charges (for example, windows, external wall painting, rainwater goods repairs, etc.). Best to find out what the deal is in advance, or you could be hit with a massive one-off payment a week after you complete.

That all done, your solicitor will also negotiate any changes to the Sales Contract should anything have cropped up.

Don't forget, as well as working for you the solicitor will also be acting on behalf of your lender. So, if there is anything relevant to them (e.g. if there is a problem with the lease) he will let the lender know because this may affect whether or not they are willing to actually stump up the money to complete the purchase. Some lenders don't like lending on purchases for leasehold properties, so just be aware that if there are any slight niggles, your lender may want them investigated further to ensure that they are happy to lend you the money against the property.

Whilst you're at it, if you're buying a leasehold property you may want to speak to the **Chairman of the Residents' Committee** just to get a feel for what the 'unofficial' rules are around the place. Whilst there will be a long list of things you can't do in a leasehold contract – make sure you get your solicitor to run through this clearly with you so that you understand the limitations – you may also find that a Residents' Committee have in addition imposed their own set of guidelines that everyone lives by. It pays to take an hour out of your life and go and meet the Chairman because that way you are showing willingness in terms of being a nice neighbour as well as getting the lowdown.

It's likely that you will have to attend **Residents' Meetings**, either every quarter or twice a year. This is when everyone gets together to discuss various topics about the upkeep of the building and agree if any action needs to be taken, discuss the sink fund and anything else relevant. Anything major agreed at the Residents' Meeting will typically be actioned by the management company, which will liaise with one point of contact within the Residents' Committee, normally the Chairman, who speaks on behalf of everyone.

Last thing: if the leasehold property you are buying doesn't have an external, professional managing agent but is 'self-managed' by the Residents' Committee, I'd be very, very wary. Professional property management is a specialist skill and unless there happens to be a qualified RICS surveyor, a solicitor *and* an accountant living in the other flats who are helping the residents manage the place, it's possible to end up in all sorts of bother. Also, if you have an issue with a neighbour and there is no independent management company in place, you're then into all sorts of politics to get things sorted, rather than an external company simply reminding the individual of their responsibilities under the lease.

Many Residents' Committees self-manage under the impression that it saves money on fees they would otherwise spend with a professional managing agent, which of course is true. *Until* you run into major problems. And that *will* happen because, with all good intentions, unless you also manage property as a day job, you don't know what you don't know. I've seen (and experienced first-hand) some real horror stories where self-managed Residents' Committees have neglected basic property maintenance and caused thousands of pounds of damage to people's properties and devalued them in the process. In one case, an old chap looked after the buildings insurance for nine flats and didn't administer the policy correctly, leaving some of the properties uninsured. Which went un-noticed until there was significant storm damage.

So, word to the wise, if your solicitor finds out that the pad you're buying is self-managed by the residents, approach with caution. Don't say I didn't warn you.

4. Paperwork

The process of checking through the paperwork and it going backwards and forwards between your solicitor, the vendor's solicitor and your mortgage lender will take approximately six or seven weeks, although if you get a couple of hotshot lawyers on the case it can be done considerably quicker if it's a freehold property. Above all, remember that you can only proceed at the pace of the slowest in the chain.

If you're buying a brand-new property most developers ask for either a 21 or 28-day exchange, which is generally non-negotiable (and, to be honest, I find it a bit cheeky, but there you go). This means that *if you are buying a new build you need to let your solicitor know when you first instruct them, so they are aware of the timescales you need them to work to*. Be aware, they may charge extra to get the job done quicker.

If the survey has come back with questions on it (for example, they have found a problem with the roof or evidence of subsidence) then your solicitor will raise this with the vendor's solicitor. It may be that the problem is easily rectified and that the vendor will agree to have the work carried out as part of the Sales Contract, or it may be that the problem is so serious that you consider pulling out of the purchase and finding somewhere else. If the worst happens, yes, it's upsetting, but better you find out now rather than buying a money pit. *Listen to the advice of your solicitor – it's what you're paying them for.*

Whilst we're talking about paperwork, just a thought but do keep copies of all the guarantees for building works, planning consents, electrical and gas certificates, boiler service records and anything else that your solicitor sends you as part of the conveyancing process in a safe place. Why? Because it's likely that at some point you'll want to sell. I know, I know, you haven't even bought this place yet. But trust me. When the time comes, if you can easily lay your hands on all this paperwork then you've just saved yourself an awful lot of time and inconvenience. Time to start a filing system, methinks.

5. *Exchanging*

OK, so you've ploughed your way through a rainforest of highly confusing and scary legal paperwork, at which point your solicitor will then ask if you're happy with everything (it's a rhetorical question by the way: the thought of parting with hundreds of thousands of pounds rarely fills anyone with joy).

If so, he or she will then proceed to **exchange**. But what exactly does that mean? Well, in simple terms, it means that the contract is drawn up between you and the vendor where you put down your deposit, which is normally 10% of the agreed purchase price (you can put down 5%, but if you fail to complete you will have to find the other 5%) and agree to complete the transaction on a certain day. This contract is then exchanged between the two solicitors, yours and the other side's. It's your solicitor's responsibility to make sure that all is in place and that you are able to actually complete – that's to protect you so that you don't get sued if the wheels fall off between exchange and completion. So take this bit seriously, it's for your benefit.

Once exchange has taken place, you're now both committed; the vendor can't sell to anyone else, but you can't back out either. If you do welch on the deal you'll lose your contractual deposit of 10%, but you may also be sued by the vendor for damages and, worst case, forced to complete the sale. Suffice to say, it's not recommended that you proceed to exchange unless you are absolutely 100% happy for the whole thing to go ahead. It's not like you're going to get a receipt with a 30-day refund policy.

6. More paperwork

After exchange, your solicitor signs off the **Certificate of Title** to the lender. This means your solicitor certifies that the property is good security for the advance (in other words, it's a good bet to lend money against). The solicitor will have also checked for and sorted out any special conditions that were included in your mortgage offer. He will now draft the **transfer deed** (TR1), if this wasn't done before you exchanged, which is then sent to the vendor's solicitor together with a final set of **requisitions** (a last set of questions that the vendor's solicitor answers prior to completion, which confirm that none of the details which were provided before exchange have changed). Your solicitor will also raise any necessary pre-completion searches with the Land Registry, just as a final tick in the box.

If it's a leasehold property there will also be some questions about apportionment of **service charges** and **ground rent**. This effectively means that if the vendor has paid for a slug of charges upfront earlier in the year then he's entitled to some money back since he won't be living in the property. Between them, the solicitors will work out how much you need to pay, and an amount will go back to the vendor. The vendor's solicitor will also give an undertaking to discharge any charges/mortgages that are secured on the property, and provide details of the vendor's bank account, which is where the money is hopefully going on completion day. Bunking off with it in a suitcase instead is not recommended.

7. *The final countdown*

As soon as possible before completion your solicitor will send you a **Completion Statement**, which shows you the total amount of money you will need to complete the deal. Check this carefully, and more than once. This will include solicitor's fees, searches, any maintenance charges (if relevant), along with details of any extra money you've agreed to pay for fixtures and fittings you may be buying with the property, e.g. carpets, curtains, white goods, etc.

Now, a quick word in your shell-like about Completion Statements. I nearly got caught out about twelve years ago when I was selling a property and buying another one because my solicitor couldn't add up and basically calculated my statement incorrectly. He put the mortgage redemption penalty that I had to pay to my lender in twice. Which nearly cost me over three grand. When you're talking about a couple of hundred thousand to buy a place, plus all the fees for solicitors, mortgage fees for your new deal etc., you could argue that I had just been a bit out with my figures and calculations. But I knew I hadn't because, as I'd gone along, I'd been keeping a careful note of everything on a spreadsheet.

When my Completion Statement came through, and it was out by such a large amount, I was able to go back through my notes and quickly work out what the solicitor had done wrong. Cue very interesting conversation with the solicitor's secretary – who tried to tell me at first that I couldn't use a calculator – and then a very embarrassed solicitor on the phone making all sorts of excuses.

The moral of the story? Don't assume that, just because a solicitor sends you a Completion Statement, it's right. Check numbers and then check them again and don't agree to anything until you are 100% happy. If you don't think it's correct, stand your ground and ask the question. Don't forget, *you* are paying the solicitor and *you're* the customer. The most important thing is that you are happy and confident that your affairs are being dealt with professionally and correctly.

Ideally, ask your solicitor to send you your Completion Statement ten days or so before you complete so that you can make sure that you have the dosh ready to go. The reason I say get this as early as you can is because mistakes do happen – you've had a lot to think about in the last few weeks, I know – and even if your solicitor has calculated your statement correctly (fingers crossed) you may not have been totally on the ball and allowed for all the disbursements and fees. Knowing what you will have to pay as soon as possible means that you can figure out how to make up any shortfall. Do not get in the situation that many people do which is finding out that they are short the day before completion, and then end up trying to sell a kidney (or worse) to find the extra they need. Ask your solicitor as soon as you can after you've exchanged, and keep nagging – nicely – until you get it.

8. Completion

On the day of **completion** your mortgage lender will transfer the money to your solicitor (by CHAPS). Your solicitor then sends the agreed completion amount to the vendor's solicitor, again electronically, whilst you wait anxiously on the end of the phone, knowing that somewhere in the ether an awful lot of dosh with your name on it is winging its way into someone else's bank account.

Finally, the vendor's solicitor confirms receipt of the money and completion, at which point they'll phone the estate agent to confirm that he can release the keys to you. When that call finally comes, expect to feel any or all of the following: fear, elation, hysteria, the need to find the nearest pub.

But my friend, if only it were that straightforward. What we must remember is:

- The ineptitude of *some* estate agents.

- The fact that *some* of those employed within the legal profession only work six hours a day, don't answer the phone after five o'clock or during their lunch hour, and have an approach to technology that would leave a Luddite speechless.

The reality is that when the process stalls, as it inevitably will at *some* point, you can't ring the vendor's solicitor to chivvy things along. Oh no. You have to rely on the estate agent who's handling the sale to go back to the vendor's solicitor and put the pressure on.

In theory, seeing as the sooner the sale completes, the sooner the agent gets his commission, you'd think they'd keep on top of stuff like this, wouldn't you? Err, then you'd be wrong. The good estate agents have specific individuals called **sales progression executives**. Their role is ensure that solicitors on both sides are up-to-date with their paperwork, and to take appropriate steps when they aren't.

If you are unlucky enough to be buying through, shall we kindly say the more *traditional* type of agent, it's going to be down to you to nag and keep tabs on things. Don't worry about winning popularity contests here. Just be polite, businesslike and, where possible, back up conversations by email – so if push comes to shove, you've got a record of what you've requested and when.

There are a couple of other 'little' issues that may come up. Again, best I tell you about these things now, so you know what you might potentially have to deal with.

9. *Gazumping*

Gazumping is a despicable trend that started in the eighties, and reappears every once in a while when the property market is booming and there isn't enough stock to keep up with demand.

Typically, you will have put your offer in, the vendor (who at this point seems perfectly reasonable) has verbally accepted, all is moving merrily along and you're racking up legal fees left, right and centre. But ... just before exchange (in fact, the worst-case scenario is the morning you're due to exchange) the once perfectly nice vendor decides to pull out of the deal in order to accept another, higher offer.

Sadly, although very naughty, this is totally legal in England and Wales and there isn't much you can do about it, other than match or beat the higher bid or indulge in the use of a lot of profanities and write off the money you've already spent on solicitors, mortgage fees and surveys. I wish I could tell you different, but there it is.

As I write, some areas of the country are in the grip of a bit of a property bubble, so worryingly, gazumping is rearing its ugly head once more. If it makes you feel any better, the decent estate agents out there don't condone the practice. But they are, at the end of the day, powerless if their vendor directs them that he wants to accept a higher offer when a sale is already proceeding. You can, of course, counter offer (if you can afford to) and sometimes that can tip the balance back in your favour. It's up to you to do the maths and work out how much money you will lose by pulling out at that stage in terms of legal fees, mortgage application fees and surveyor's reports and see if you can find the extra money required.

This is why getting to exchange is such a crucial point – because once you've exchanged contracts, all bets are off and both you and the vendor are locked in. And you can relax (well, almost anyway).

10. Chains

When I talk about **chains**, I don't mean a nice piece of jewellery or part of your treasured mountain bike. This is just the technical term for the series of people buying from each other, with one purchase depending on the sale of another property and so on.

This situation is pretty much as bad as it sounds, and best avoided if at all possible. First-time buyers are generally considered golden applicants because they don't have anything to sell, so the whole transaction usually moves a lot quicker. And trust me, if you're selling, you *really* want to sell to someone who is 'non move-dependent'.

But, if you are stuck in a chain, be prepared for things to take a while and potentially get a bit sticky. If your vendor's purchase falls through – and that does and can happen – they may decide that they don't want to move at all. If it's prior to exchange, they can withdraw from your deal and there's nothing you can do. Sometimes, although rarely, you find a situation where the chain breaks because a sale falls out of bed, and then in extreme cases a buyer is quickly found who offers less money for the property, so everyone else in the chain then contributes to the difference in order to keep the whole thing moving. Not great for anyone and causes a lot of grief until it's all resolved.

It's worth being aware that *a third of all chains fall through at some point in the transaction, and in the majority of cases it's due to people not having their ducks in a row with regards to their mortgage.* Which is hugely, massively frustrating – but there's nothing you can do about someone else's financial ineptitude. So, now you can probably understand why, if you can, it's good to buy a property that's chain-free if at all possible.

Conclusion

As if getting a mortgage isn't hard enough, the laws surrounding how property in England and Wales is bought and sold make going to the dentist for root-canal surgery sound like a fun day out in comparison. Buying your first home isn't for the faint of heart, but the more you understand about the process, the more you can keep tabs on the key players as you go along. Always remember that no one else is as incentivised as you are to get the deal done, other than maybe the estate agent who'll be receiving his commission from the vendor.

However, the feeling of achievement and happiness that you get when you do, finally, get the keys and walk across the threshold of your new pad and realise that it's all yours is pretty hard to beat. If you ask me, it makes the whole process worthwhile. So savour that moment because you've worked hard for it.

Opening a bottle of something fizzy to celebrate is optional but highly recommended.

5.
Sale Agreed

S O, you've decided to sell, have you? Cast your mind back to the day you completed the purchase of your current home. Do you remember the relief that it was all over? The elation that all the hassle and stress could now be forgotten? Hmmm. Well, if you thought that was bad, you haven't even begun to consider the turmoil involved in *selling* a property...

Partly, this is because in the majority of cases, although you are selling something, you are also going to be buying something else. To put it bluntly, if your sale falls through, you won't be going anywhere at all.

The other reason that selling a property is sometimes riddled with problems is, quite simply, because of some estate agents.

Now, forgive me if I come across as being negative about them. I'm lucky enough to know and work with some of the best estate agents in the business (some of whom have even helped me to write this book, so I can't be too disparaging about them) and on the whole, the general standard of estate agency in this country is pretty high. But, there *are* sadly still a *few* agents out there who are a bit of a pain in the behind. It's these numpties that you need to be wary of. Unfortunately they unfairly give the rest of the industry a not-so-good reputation, despite the fact that most agents you'll come across are hard-working, professional and passionate about what they do.

The good ones (the majority) are switched on. They're clued up about demand in their area and will be able to educate you on

market trends (how prices have gone up/down/sideways in the last three months), the **demographic breakdown of current registrants** (basically, the income level and budgets of the people who've contacted them recently to see what property they're selling) as well as all sorts of facts and figures about **footfall** (the amount of people they show round a property before securing an offer). This is all valuable stuff and exactly why you get a professional on the case. However, the few rotten apples in the barrel tend to forget that customer service is king and that they are dealing with your most precious and expensive asset – your home.

So, as far as choosing an estate agent goes, you have to be a bit on your toes. Unlike any other party that you'll deal with in the process of selling (e.g. your solicitor, surveyor, financial advisor and mortgage lender), *there is no mandatory requirement for estate agents to be professionally qualified or regulated.* Think of it another way – you could be selling double glazing/mobile phones/cars on a Friday, then start up in business as an estate agent on the Monday, *with no training or qualifications.* And there is no law out there to stop you. Bit of a worry, isn't it?

However, there is a voluntary body called the **National Association of Estate Agents** (NAEA), of which roughly half of all agents in the country are members. Fundamentally, if they've signed up to this, your agent has taken basic competency exams, has committed to a code of conduct and customer care charter, has undergone a criminal record check and, essentially, is going to play by the rules. There is also a really good redress scheme, so if you do find yourself having problems, you can get some help. If you go to the NAEA website at **www.naea.co.uk** you can put in your postcode and get a list of members in your area. This is probably the best place to start your search.

Another professional body that you should look out for when selecting an agent is the **RICS** (Royal Institution of Chartered

Surveyors). They carry the royal warrant, so these guys are the best there is, and the examination and training process is pretty brutal. An estate agent bearing this logo really will be the cream of the crop. If your agent is a member of the RICS, you're in good hands indeed. You can find member estate agents by going on their website at **www.rics.org/uk**.

When you come to select your agent, you've got a few choices. There are the large national chains, such as Knight Frank, Your Move and Savills, which are a good bet if you don't know where to start and feel safe with a 'big brand'. Or you may prefer to go with a local independent agent; someone well-known and respected in your area who comes highly recommended. Neither would be the wrong thing to do – it's who you feel most comfortable with at the end of the day. Another option is the recent new entrant to the market, **www.purplebricks.com**, who are online based so able to offer a more cost-effective approach.

The key things to weigh up when considering which agent to appoint are how much you will pay in fees, their skill at marketing your property, and the quality of service you'll receive in terms of 'sales progression' – in other words, managing the process efficiently from offer to completion.

A real positive for consumers is that in the last few years legislation has changed and estate agents are now required by law to have signed up to a redress scheme, managed by The Property Ombudsman (TPO). Which is great, but unfortunately it's only useful when you have a problem. It's not a preventative measure but good to know it's there. You can check to make sure that the agent you are potentially going to use is registered with TPO by going to their website (**www.tpos.co.uk**).

So, you've checked your potential agents out and you've got a shortlist. Now you need to ramp up the selection process. Don't – whatever you do – ring them up and say, "I've got a house to sell, please would you come round and value it". You'll only get the nice side of the agent because they're trying to sell their services to you. *What we really want to find out is how well they treat prospective buyers.*

That's because, as long as your estate agent is marketing your property, he or she is the shop window for it. What you want is someone who is friendly and approachable, so that when a potential buyer spies your pad on the internet and excitedly rings the agent to arrange a viewing, they get a professional and courteous response.

So, you need to 'mystery shop' a bit. Ring the agents you're considering and pose as a buyer for the type of property you are looking to sell. You want to judge:

• How long it took to answer the phone – was it picked up within a few rings, or did you get an answer phone? Try calling a different times during the day and different days of the week to see how their response varies.

• Whether the person on the end of the phone was friendly, personable and courteous.

• How professional their response was to your initial enquiry, e.g. did they actually listen to what you asked for before talking to you about specific properties?

• How many properties they have got on their books which are in your budget and match your criteria, and if they were able/willing to promptly email you over particulars.

• If they offered to take your details, having had a helpful dialogue with you about what you're looking for, to register you on their database of applicants.

• Whether you have come off the phone from them feeling as though you've had a reasonable conversation with someone who is going to try to help you.

Bottom line: *if you think the agent is disinterested or rude, then what will your potential buyers think?* Precisely. Now's not the time to settle for second best. Apart from phoning the agents you've shortlisted, think about how effective their marketing strategy is. So check out the following:

- Their own website. Is it up-to-date? How good are the photographs of the properties they have on there? Are there floor plans? What about Energy Performance Certificates – are they clearly displayed?

- What property portals do they advertise on? The biggest are **www.rightmove.co.uk** and **www.zoopla.co.uk**. These are where the majority of buyers go to find property, so if the agent isn't on one (or both) of the above, then you won't be getting your property in front of a huge audience.

- How many 'for sale' and 'sold' boards do they have around the neighbourhood? This is a good way to tell how proactive they really are.

- Look at how much advertising they do in the local papers. Whilst the internet is now the place where 90% of buyers seriously look, a presence in local newspapers is essential to maintain brand awareness. Most good agents take either half a page or a full page in their local newspaper every week.

Once you've completed your reconnaissance, you can now decide on the three or four agents you would like to get round to value your home. Again, in theory this sounds simple, but you need to be aware of a couple of tricks of the agency trade. You see, depending on what the market is doing, and how well your estate agent is doing, he or she *may* undervalue or overvalue your property. Amongst other ploys.

1. Estate agents (sometimes) overvalue properties

This is one of the first tricks in the book for the less scrupulous estate agent. You invite them round to your home to value it – but essentially, the agent is bidding for your business. So, he or she looks round the property, tells you how nicely it's decorated or how lovely the garden is, then proceeds to value the property at significantly above what you thought it was worth. You're so pleasantly surprised by this valuation that you instruct them on the spot, presuming that's what it will sell for.

Wrong. What they've done is basically got you to sign on the dotted line, and in super-quick time.

From here on in, the game is to get you to reduce the price to what it can realistically be sold for, without you realising. How do they do that? Well, not sending anyone around to look at the property for a few weeks is a classic trick. Sooner or later, when there aren't any viewings, you'll ring up and ask why there's no interest. They'll say it's because there are loads of other comparable properties on the market, and you may get somewhere if you drop the price slightly to be more competitive. See? Easy as that.

A good agent, however, will give you a realistic price first time and talk you through how they arrived at their valuation, showing evidence of comparable properties and educating you about current local market conditions. *These* are the guys you need on the case.

You can really help yourself here by understanding property prices *before* you get an estate agent round to value your place. Check online with **www.zoopla.co.uk** to see what other homes in the same street sold for and what your property could be worth now.

Also look at your local newspapers to find comparable properties and how much they are on the market for. It's worth doing this research because, after all, we're talking about selling your biggest asset here, so you need to be on the ball.

2. Estate agents (sometimes) undervalue properties

You have to remember that estate agents are out there to make a living, and they get paid commission when a deal goes through. If it's a tough month or a tough market, and they don't have many deals on the table, the best way to get a property to sell quickly is to price it cheaply. A speedy sale equals fast commission payment. Again, this doesn't happen every day and the majority of agents would never dream of employing such methods. But this does occasionally occur, so I just want to put it on your radar.

Watch out for comments like:

> *"We have a few properties like this on our books at the moment already, so vendors are having to be realistic about pricing to be competitive."*

Or another classic line:

> *"The way the market is going, I really think that you need to be careful about pricing this, so it doesn't sit on the market for too long."*

If the agent says they have other properties similar to yours on their books, ask them to prove it. And ask him how many viewings those properties have had and what offers have been made (if any). If the agent is telling you to price a property realistically, do your research so that you know what 'realistic' *actually is*.

Now, it's entirely possible that the agent is telling the truth and that the market in your area is still in one of the cooler spots, there aren't as many buyers out there as you'd like, and prices are a little lower than you were hoping for. In that case, you do need to be able to trust what your agent is telling you. If they're saying you need to price realistically to sell, then to be fair, that is what you may need to do.

This is why I was banging on about getting three or four agents round to value your home. You need to get a clear idea in your head about which agent you feel will really act in your best interests and has also got their finger on the pulse of the market in your area. You'll then get three or four valuations which should, in theory, all be roughly the same. If there are any outliers, then you now know the potential reasons why.

3. Negotiate the fee

So, a clear winner (or winners) has emerged, and you feel comfortable enough to sign up. As you know, the majority of estate agents work on commission. That means they are – in theory – incentivised to get you the best price for your property.

Unless you decide to sell your home yourself, there's no way you can get out of paying the estate agency fees, but you *can* negotiate with them to make sure you're not paying over the odds.

Most agents charge between 1.5% and 3%, depending on the value of the property. Some will charge only 1% if you decide to instruct them as **sole agents** – meaning you won't instruct any other agents or try and sell the property any other way, such as on one of the **For Sale By Owner** websites.

If you've done as I've suggested and got three or four agents round to value your property, make sure you tell them that you are getting other agents round. This should ensure they give you their most competitive rates right away.

Once you've had the valuations back, you can begin to play one off against the other. If you can, get two agencies on the case – this is known as **joint sole agency** – and negotiate them both down to 1.5% or 2% tops. Don't go for **multiple agency** (that means as many agents as you can get to sell your property). It rarely works as all the agents involved feel that someone else will do the job and it also makes you look desperate to sell, which won't help you achieve the best price.

Once you've selected your two agents, tell them that they've both got six weeks to get you an offer, and if they don't perform, you'll be reviewing your choice of agent. Make sure you only sign up to a six-week period and read the small print in the terms and conditions to make sure that they can't stiff you for any commission after you've dis-instructed them. If they won't sign up to that, find another agent who will. Don't forget, the agent needs you and your property more than you need the agent. *You* are the customer, at the end of the day.

You need to get yourself sorted out with a **solicitor** early doors as well. Whilst your agent is working hard to secure your buyer, your solicitor can be pulling together your Contract Package (remember that from when you bought? If not, take a look at the previous chapter, 'Buying Your First Home') so that it's all ready to go when a buyer is found. The sooner you get a conveyancer to get on the case with that the better.

If you had a good experience with your solicitor when you bought the place, I'd suggest you go back to their firm again – you at least know what to expect and you may even get lucky and deal with the same person you did previously.

Remember, you don't have to use the solicitors or conveyancing service your estate agent will no doubt recommend to you. It's your choice. Use who you want to. All I'll say is, I highly recommend you use someone who is a member of the **Conveyancing Quality Scheme**.

If you're buying as well as selling (in which case, good luck) expect to pay a bit more for your conveyancing this time round: your solicitor will have twice as much work to do. Get a quote in writing first, and if you are in a position where the sale has to complete quickly, make sure you put this in writing clearly to the solicitor from the start. That way he or she can make sure you get the express service. You may pay a bit extra, but if you're trying to meet your buyer's deadline to exchange, it's money well spent.

4. Read the small print

One of the most important things I can encourage you to do is read the terms and conditions on the back of *any* paperwork an estate agent asks you to sign. Some unscrupulous agents will try to tie you in to them for as long as possible, and include clauses in their terms and conditions that aren't acceptable. A classic one is that if you dis-instruct them, you can't market the property with another agent for a certain period of time – say, six weeks – and if you do, and the other agent successfully sells your property, the agent you sacked is still due the commission payment you agreed.

Yes, it stinks and it's unfair, so make sure you read *everything* they ask you sign – carefully and without being rushed. It may mean you decide to take a day or so to check it through in your own time, and that's fine. You're the customer here. If there's something you don't like or don't understand, talk to the agent, explain the problem and ask them to change the terms for you. They can do so – normally with the branch manager's permission.

Make sure any changes to their documentation are initialled by both you and the estate agent and that you keep a copy. If you have any questions that the agent doesn't cover for you satisfactorily, then talk to someone either at your local Citizens Advice Bureau (**www.citizensadvice.org.uk**) or, if the agent is a member, contact the NAEA or RICS.

Right, so you've done the deed, and instructed your chosen agent. Well done. Now, you need to make sure they do their job effectively and get your place sold at the right price, to the right buyer. How on earth do you do that then?

5. Be particular about your particulars

You want to sell your property, right? That means you need to show it off to its best advantage. So make sure that when the agent comes round to take the pictures, your property looks like a show home. Tidy up and de-clutter the place, make the beds, plump up the cushions on the sofa, open the curtains, mow the lawn.

All sounds obvious, doesn't it? So why do you see so many dodgy photos of properties then? That would be because it's not the agent's job to pick your PJs up off the floor before they take the picture – and by and large, they won't. They'll just point the camera and click. So it's up to you to be there and make sure that your photos look professional and highlight the best bits of the property.

Don't be afraid to say if you don't think the pictures present your home in its best light. The great news is that these days agents use digital cameras, so if you make sure you're at home the day the pics are taken, you can review them as you go round the house.

Also, check the details of the property carefully after the agent sends them over for you to go through. Make any changes you feel are sensible. If you can get the agent to include a floor plan on your particulars, go for it. Buyers sometimes find it difficult to visualise room size and layout from a set of measurements. Also, if they are putting your property's particulars online (which they should be) make sure they've got details such as the Google Earth street view correct and that the map shows the correct location of your property. Go over everything with a fine-tooth comb and make sure it's absolutely spot on.

In an ideal world, if you've already got your solicitor on board at this point, smile sweetly and ask them to **check your particulars** for you as well to make sure that they are 100% accurate. I can't tell you how important it is that you make sure that you don't end up with inaccurate information on your particulars – you'll be in a whole world of pain in terms of property mis-descriptions, which *you* as the vendor could be liable for. So belt and braces, charm your conveyancer and get 'em checked.

6. Energy Performance Certificates

EPCs are the last relic of Home Information Packs. You may remember there was a bit of a kerfuffle when HIPs were introduced in 2007 – many, many column inches were spent on the heated debate about the impact they would have on the then-booming housing market. A lot of people (mainly estate agents) thought that they were the work of Lucifer and would cause a calamitous crash in property values. Anyway, they were abolished in 2010, much to the cheers of most of the property industry. Now, only EPCs remain from the original requirement.

They're possibly one of the most pointless bits of the whole exercise because no one ever reads these things, but you have to have one by law if you're selling or letting out a property, so it's best you at least know what your forty quid is being spent on.

You've probably seen an EPC before (it's that colourful bar chart thing on the bottom of sales and letting particulars) and I wouldn't blame you if you've never read one. Basically, it's a software-based calculation of the approximate energy costs for running the property, together with an indexed value of the property's current energy efficiency and its potential energy efficiency after the relevant energy efficiency measures have been put in place. Still with me? EPCs rate a property's energy efficiency on a scale of A to G (A being super-duper, G being akin to having holes in your roof). They also contain the following key bits of info:

• The address of the property

• Property type, for example semi-detached house

• Date of inspection

• Certificate date and serial number

• The total interior floor area (excluding garages, porches or any areas that aren't internal to the building).

Generally speaking, if you're having a floor plan in your marketing details, the same company that your agent will get to create that will generate your EPC for you. So it's all a very smooth process and you don't have to do anything. You just need to keep nagging your agent to get them to sort it out, because *the agent can't advertise your property on the market until there's an EPC in place.*

Last word on this one: EPCs are notoriously inaccurate if you have an older property or one that doesn't have double-glazing. Don't be perturbed. I've never yet heard of a sale fall out of bed because someone was concerned by what the EPC said. Fret not, my friend. There are far bigger things for you to concern yourself with.

7. *Know the rules about 'for sale' boards*

You don't *have* to have a 'for sale' board outside your home, so don't be talked into it by your estate agent if you're not keen on the idea. On the other hand, boards dramatically increase your chances of selling, particularly in a tougher market, and if you are happy to have one, then it's a good way of promoting your property.

There are actually laws around estate agent boards – the **Town and Country Planning Act** (TCP) states that you can only have *one* post with a maximum of *two* estate agency signs on it. That means if you instruct three agents, technically, only two can have a sign. This rule is regularly flouted – because, let's face it, a board is free advertising for the agent – so it's up to you to make sure they don't break the law.

If additional boards appear in your garden without permission then ring the agent concerned and ask him to remove his sign immediately (make sure you also put it in writing; email is fine). Remove it from your garden and put it in a safe place until they retrieve it. No, you can't burn it. Legally it's someone else's property, so resist the urge to chuck it in the recycling pile. Once you've completed, by law the agent has to remove the 'sold' board within 14 days. Again, as it's free advertising very few do, but persistent nagging will yield results.

Ultimately, if they won't remove a sign when you've requested it then you can complain to your local authority planning office, who will enforce the law and can also fine the estate agent for breaking it.

Alright, so you've signed up your agent, your board is in place (so the nosey neighbours are well aware that you're potentially on the move), you've got your trusty EPC all sorted and your solicitor is preparing your Contracts Pack. Now what? Well, with a bit of luck (and if your agent is doing all the right things) they'll be breaking down the door to get in for a look around. You can help influence the success of these viewings by doing your bit, of course.

8. Staging your home for sale

You only get one chance to make a first impression, so make sure your property does the talking, rather than leaving the agent to have to flannel on about how much potential the place has. Pet hair, scruffy carpets, smelly rubbish bins, dust and dirt everywhere are not great turn-ons for any buyer, so clean up your act. Make sure the place is spotless. Every day. Particularly if you've left the keys with the agent so that they can carry out viewings whilst you're at work. You need to have a blitz once a week, then keep on top of it – every day. Yep, I know it sounds like a pain in the backside, but you want to sell the place, right?

If you have, dare I say it, more 'creatively' decorated your home, you may want to consider the merits of some neutral paint to calm things down a bit. Remember, you are trying to create a canvas against which potential buyers can imagine their stuff. You need to sell the lifestyle they will be buying into. So whilst you might be very fond of purple emulsion in the bedroom or bright orange wallpaper in the lounge, it might not be everyone's cup of tea. It's nothing that a can of paint won't fix, so bite the bullet and make the place a bit less personal.

Whilst we're at it, you really need to keep trinkets and ornaments to a minimum. Again, the buyer wants to try to visualise what their life would be like in the place as their home, and anything of yours which is massively personal is a distraction to that. Pack it in a box and save it all for the new place.

9. *Keeping out of the way*

This is one of those scenarios where you need to treat as you would be treated. Think about it. You're out there yourself, looking for a property to buy, and you know how annoying it is to be met at the front door of a place you're viewing by a gurning vendor who is desperate to sell. They've even brewed some coffee and sliced a loaf of fresh bread in the kitchen because they read in a magazine that it was supposed to subconsciously make people feel at home (it doesn't work, by the way, and most people are wise to it, so I don't suggest you do this).

They then follow you around, telling you all about how they chose that particular wallpaper, or the fact that they've only just had the bathroom done. You end up feeling claustrophobic and hassled, and can't wait to get out of the place, muttering politely about how great it is as you beat a speedy retreat. Nuff said? Right, don't become one of them. And it's really easy. Just go out, and leave the agent to it. That's what you're paying them all that commission for, remember?

If you have pets, I'd strongly recommend you get them out of the way for viewings too, as you'd be surprised at the amount of people who are either allergic to animal hair or just don't like animals. And you can't exactly explain to the cat that they need to behave like they've just visited the taxidermist when buyers come round, can you?

For example, I had some friends who were having trouble selling their immaculate house; when I went round there to take a look in order to try and solve the problem, it turned out that they had an elderly dachshund called Frieda who, as soon as you opened the back door (which of course, the agent would do to show the buyers around the beautifully landscaped garden) would rush out and have a rather large dump.

Apparently the agent had told them about this, but it hadn't occurred to them that some buyers might find it a little off-putting. Following a little chat about the merits of a poop-free garden, Frieda embarked on a short sojourn with some dog-loving friends, and within a week they had an offer on the table. Problem solved.

But what if you have to do a viewing yourself? For example, if it's a second viewing and the buyer wants to come back one evening or at a weekend and the agent can't accompany them. What then? Well, as they said in *Pulp Fiction*: "Be cool." Answer the door politely, then say:

> *"Look, I've got some paperwork to do, so you guys just wander around, I'll leave you to it … I'll be in the kitchen/study/lounge so if you need anything, just let me know."*

Smile and let them get on with it. They will have been round before, so should know where everything is, and trust me, if they are interested enough, they will come and find you to ask questions. In which case, don't get excited, just be straight with your answers and try not to waffle. Difficult, I know, when you can see pound signs flashing in front of your eyes, but this is no time to get emotional. You can do that after you've exchanged.

So, you've done everything right. After what feels like countless viewings, it's finally happened. Your agent calls to tell you the good news: you've got an offer. Before you crack open the champagne, take a deep breath and listen to what they are actually saying.

10. Accepting an offer

By law, your estate agent has to inform you of *any* offer made on the property, even if they know you won't accept it. So, if the number that your agent comes back to you with is a bit insulting, *don't shoot the messenger, they're just doing their job.*

If the offer that has been put to you seems reasonable, then by all means accept it. If not, and you feel it's a little low, discuss with your agent why you should take the offer and see what they think.

In addition, and this is very important, you need to ask what the potential buyer's situation is. Remember how, when you were buying, you had an advantage because you weren't part of a chain? Now the boot is on the other foot, and you're ideally looking for someone who is **non move-dependent**. If your property has been well-marketed and you end up with two offers on the table (unlikely in a tough market but it does happen when things are more buoyant), the better scenario is the one where your buyer has nothing to sell themselves. Yes, they may negotiate harder on the price because they know they can move quickly, but if you've found somewhere you want to purchase, then consider taking the chain-free buyer. Chances are the sale will go through a lot more smoothly.

If you've taken my earlier advice and have two agents on the case, ring the other agent to tell them that you have an offer and how much it is, and see what they have to say about it. If nothing else, it will light a fire under them and kick them into action to get you a counter offer at a better price.

But you're not home and dry yet. Remember when you bought, you held your breath until the day you exchanged in case the vendor sold the place to someone else? Well, it works the other way too. Until your buyer has signed on the dotted line they can withdraw their offer. So, in an ideal world you need to keep the property on the market right up until the day it's exchanged. The agent will advertise it as **under offer**, so any prospective buyers are aware of the circumstances, but it's worth doing if you can, particularly if you've found somewhere yourself which you have made an offer on.

However, if your buyer is nervous or the market in your area is cooler, then you may make the call to withdraw the property from the market as a show of good faith to your buyer to secure the deal. Neither is the wrong thing to do, you just need to make a decision based on the current climate in your area.

In a busy market, where there isn't enough property to satisfy demand, you can sometimes find that you have two buyers who decide to go head-to-head and try to exchange before the other to secure the property. This is called a **contracts race** and is a great position to be in if it's you who's selling the property. I wouldn't advise it if you're a buyer though, because there is a 50:50 chance it'll end in tears (and a lot of wasted money).

At the other end of the scale, however, there's **gazundering**. I've already explained **gazumping** in the 'Buying Your First Home' chapter, and this is exactly the reverse. I've been on the receiving end of it from a cheeky buyer so I know for sure it goes on. Basically, what happens is that your purchaser proceeds as normal through the exchange process, going through all the paperwork and getting their survey done on the property, progressing with their mortgage application and so on. Then, just before they exchange, they drop their offer.

It's a highly effective way to get money off the property because they've got you over a barrel. You're so far down the road, probably at about the same point with another vendor in terms of negotiating a purchase on another property, likely to have racked up two lots of legal fees (both on the sale of the current property and the purchase of another), and also have the added danger of losing the place that you want to purchase should you not complete on your sale. It is, to put it bluntly, a nasty thing to inflict upon someone. However, it's also perfectly legal, and there isn't much you can do about it.

Gazundering always makes a come-back in a tighter market. There is, though, a way you can potentially avoid it, but it rather depends on whether you want to play hardball with your buyer early doors. Remember I said that in an ideal world you should keep your property on the market until exchange? Well, here's where you can play on the anxious side of your buyer's nature if the market in your area is busy and there are few properties around to buy. They will be concerned about losing out on your property, so get your agent to negotiate a **lock out** contract with them.

Here, your conveyancing solicitor draws up a document confirming the selling price you've agreed, and that you will withdraw the property from the market in exchange for an upfront deposit (£2,000 to £5,000 is a realistic figure, depending on the value of the property that you're selling) which the buyer will forfeit if they fail to exchange, other than if the property doesn't pass the survey, etc. It works both ways, though, so if you withdraw you'll be liable to your buyers for the same amount.

If they sign it, it's a win-win situation for both parties as you both know where you stand and it does take a lot of the pressure off. Not everyone will go for it, but as with everything in life, if you don't ask, you don't get. Be warned: lock outs *can* take a couple of weeks to get in place, and that's time lost that you could have spent working towards exchange. Also, in a cooler market, the buyer really has a bit more power in the transaction than you do, so they are unlikely to agree. However, everything depends on the scenario you're in, so it's worth knowing you *can* do this in case it comes in handy at some stage.

By the way, a lot of estate agents don't like lock out clauses much because it slows the process down – ergo, they have to wait for their commission a bit longer – but the good guys will be able to advise if your situation merits considering one.

Conclusion

I'm not going to sugarcoat it, selling a property – particularly if you're buying another one at the same time – can be a very stressful experience. All you can do is appoint the best estate agent and solicitor you can find from the outset. They really are the key to making sure everything runs as smoothly as possible. So take your time, do your beauty parade and work on recommendations where you can.

No matter how good they are, you need to keep talking to your agent to make sure that they are progressing the sale as efficiently as possible, and keep tabs on your solicitor to make sure that they are turning paperwork and any enquiries around as quickly as possible. Nothing winds up a buyer more than the vendor's solicitor taking longer than they should to provide key documents, so keep a close watch on proceedings to make sure this doesn't happen.

Remember, it's perfectly normal to feel a range of emotions (and have a few sleepless nights) when you're selling a property. I know I do, and I've been doing it for over twenty years. I find the best way to deal with it is to remain pragmatic. I'm a big believer in 'what will be, will be' when it comes to property. Sometimes when a deal falls through it feels like your world is crashing down around your head. But generally I've found that the eventual outcome is better than the original plan. Everything happens for a reason, as they say.

If not, I find gin very useful in such situations.

6.
Virgin
Landlords

Sometimes life throws a curveball when you least expect it. You're all settled in your pad, and then an amazing job offer comes up that you can't turn down … but it's a hundred miles away. Or maybe, you meet 'The One', and after a whirlwind romance come to the conclusion that you want to live together. Just not in your gaff. At the opposite end of the scale, after breaking up with someone you thought was the love of your life, perhaps you've woken up one morning and decided that you have to go and spend a year backpacking around Asia to 'find yourself'. There's just one small flaw in your plan … you're a responsible homeowner now. Eeek.

Before the cold, hard light of reality ruins your dreams, don't panic. There is an easy way to deal with this that will enable you to fulfil your heart's desires *and* keep your property. Welcome to the Accidental Landlords Club.

You see, landlords fall into two distinct categories. The first are what I'd call professional investors. They own a portfolio of properties which they acquire after careful consideration about how much rent they can charge each month and how much capital value each place will accumulate over a certain period of time. They employ clever accounting to offset gains on one property against losses on another to exploit any tax loopholes. In short, they're just in it for the money, and it's a business.

Then, there's the second type, AKA the Accidental Landlord. You didn't set out to be a property magnate or to build an empire, it just happens that you've bought a place and, for whatever reason, don't want to or can't live it in for a while but don't want to sell it either. So you've come to the logical conclusion that you'll rent it out.

And you wouldn't be alone. Due to the credit crunch of the last few years and the financial difficulties faced by thousands of homeowners, there are many people who through absolutely no fault of their own just aren't able to afford their mortgage payments at the moment. The short-term solution is to let their property out for a while. It's a smart move, and can actually make the difference between keeping your home and preserving any equity you have in your property, or losing it all to your lender.

This chapter, then, is aimed at people who never thought they'd be a landlord, *not* the Buy To Let Brigade. So, for the purposes of this book, I'm going to assume you know nothing whatsoever at all about letting out a property and all of this is news to you.

But before I get into the detail, I can hear you asking why is letting your property out to a tenant a wise move? Well, if you decide to sell the place, it's going to cost you a fortune in estate agent's fees, legal costs and possibly even hefty redemption penalties from your mortgage lender. Sure, if you're lucky – and it's a big *if* – you may end up with a bit of money in the bank after all that, but then if it's only a short-term move, why put yourself through the hassle?

If you are able to let the place out and cover your mortgage you've got the convenience of being able to move back and when it suits you (within reason), together with the immediate advantage of someone else paying the mortgage and the long-term benefit of the property increasing in value over time. What's not to like, as they say.

Have I convinced you? Good. In that case, there are a few things you need to know about being a landlord, which I'll explain here.

Also take a look at the earlier chapter 'The Realities of Renting'. There's quite a bit of detail there which is relevant to you too, so take five minutes and have a read through. No, it's not that I'm being lazy and can't be bothered to write it here again, it's just that it makes for a bit of a boring book if I keep repeating myself, OK?

1. Keeping everyone important in the loop

Even though when you own a property it's pretty much yours to do what you want with, there are a couple of parties who will want to keep tabs on what you're up to. No, it's not your parents, it's your mortgage lender and the tax man.

If you were just living in the place yourself, minding your own business – annoying the neighbours now and then, but hey – and doing your own thing, provided you pay the mortgage on time each month you'd be left to your own devices. But, if you want to let the place out, you'll need to inform the bank or building society, and make arrangements with them before you do anything else.

Why?

Well, properties that are let to tenants are sometimes seen as a greater risk than those which are **owner occupied** in terms of the owner defaulting on the mortgage. Oh, and your lender does have a vested interest in your property because, well, they lent you a huge chunk of money to buy it, so until such time as you've paid that off, they want to know what you're doing with it.

If you bought the property as your main residence and have lived in it for a sufficient amount of time, your lender may take the pragmatic view that since you never set out to be a Buy To Let investor, and after considering your change in circumstances, they'll just confirm your request in writing that you've informed them you want to rent the property out and they're OK with it. This is called a **Letter of Consent**. Be warned, they may charge you a small administration fee for the pleasure of doing so. Lenders that are more risk-averse may decide to raise the rate of interest that you pay, or even switch you to a specific **Buy To Let** mortgage.

The key thing here is to approach the situation not as a fait accompli, but to ask your lender's advice *before* you get involved with anything. A quick conversation that starts along the lines of, "I'm considering letting out my property, how do I go about that in terms of my mortgage?" should provide you with all the information you need. Get them to put their response in writing, though, so you can reference it later should you need to.

And the likelihood is that you will, because if you are going to let your property via a letting agent (and if they are on the ball), they will ask to see the Letter of Consent or proof that you have a Buy To Let mortgage. For more information on why, see the 'Be fussy about letting agents and landlords' section in the 'The Realities of Renting' chapter. Suffice to say, getting your ducks in a row early is the best way to go.

If you own a flat which is a leasehold, do check that you are allowed to rent the property out. Most modern leases are fine, but with older leases you sometimes find that there are specific clauses forbidding the letting of properties. Also, out of politeness, it's a good idea to tell someone from your Residents' Association or management company know what's going on. If you are going to have a letting agent manage the property whilst it's rented out, let them know who this is and provide their contact details. This is a good move for two reasons: firstly, the curtain twitchers in your block can keep an eye on your tenants for you, and secondly, if there are any issues they know who to get hold of in an emergency (either you or the letting agent).

Then you need to deal with that other slightly terrifying prospect, HM Revenue & Customs. It sounds scary on the face of it, but really, it's not that bad. The way it works is simple: you need to declare any **net profit** that you make on renting out a property.

For example, if your monthly mortgage payment is £1,000, and you're going to charge £1,100 a month in rent, you'll 'make' £100 per month after paying the mortgage. But allowing for letting agent's fees and taking into account any other expenses such as insurance or repairs that you have to pay for, then your net profit may well be less.

In this example, you might end up declaring an annual income from your property of £400 (or thereabouts), which you would then pay **income tax** on.

If you're **employed** and the net income that you'll get from the property is **less than £2,500 a year**, it's really simple to deal with. Your Pay As You Earn (PAYE) tax code can be adjusted to collect what you owe, which then adjusts the amount of tax you pay each month. You need to ask your local tax office to send you a P810 form to report your income each year – it's one form to fill in, and you'll just need to keep records of what rent has been paid to you, what it's cost you in mortgage fees, letting agent fees, expenses, etc. and the rest will be done for you.

However, if you're employed and the net profit that you receive from the property is **more than £2,500 per year**, then you'll need to declare it on a tax return form. There is a specific section on property, which has help notes to make it a bit easier (these days, you can also complete your tax form online, which calculates everything as you put the figures in and makes life somewhat simpler).

If you're **self-employed** and have an accountant who looks after your books, make sure you mention to them that you are letting out your property so that they can take it into account in all of their calculations when doing your tax return for you.

For those in doubt, you can find further advice about how to pay tax on any net profit from a rental property on **www.hmrc.gov.uk**. If you would feel better talking to a human being, there are numbers on the website to call. Or, if you prefer, speak to an accountant (make sure they are a member of the Institute of Chartered Accountants, **www.icaew.com**) who can help you out with submitting a tax return form and working out what your net profit is on your rental property.

Just make sure that you keep receipts for everything (any repairs that you have to carry out, or furniture that you buy specifically for the purpose of renting, any accountancy fees you incur etc.) because you'll be able to offset an amount of tax against the costs of renting the place out.

If it sounds off-putting, don't worry, this is all about being organised, and there are people around who can help you with this. Once someone has sat you down and explained it all, it's a lot less terrifying, I promise.

One last thing to bear in mind. You may have to pay **capital gains tax** on the proceeds when you sell the place. This will depend on how long you lived in the property before you let it out, and how long you end up letting it out for. Something to consider, and definitely one to ask your solicitor or accountant about before you put the property on the market.

2. Getting the place ready to rent

So, you've done the legal stuff and got the green light to go ahead. What next? Well, a bit like preparing a property to sell, you need to smarten your place up to make it as attractive to potential tenants as possible before you instruct an agent to market the place.

First off, you need to think about whether you're going to be letting it furnished or unfurnished. If it's the former, then take a good look around. Are there any family heirlooms or expensive items that you'd be really upset about if anything happened to them? If the answer is yes, then you're going to need to arrange for them to be put into storage, and replaced with something that's cheaper and 'tenant proof'. I use that term not to disparage anyone, but if you've ever rented a place yourself, you'll know what I mean when I say that you don't *quite* treat it with the same care that you would if it were your own.

That doesn't, however, mean you can put any old junk in there and expect to charge top whack. Good tenants – the sort that will look after the place and pay the rent on time – are selective, and will want a property that is in good condition and well coordinated throughout. Try and go for neutral tones (avoiding cream sofas and light carpets, though; that's just a recipe for disaster), which will form a great canvas both for the furniture you're supplying and any personal items the tenant will bring with them.

If you're letting it unfurnished, the same sort of rules apply. Allow for the fact that your tenants will want to make the place feel as much like home as possible, and that's difficult to do if you've inherited someone else's 'personalised' colour scheme. Ideally, if you're going to let the place unfurnished, remove all the furniture before you instruct a letting agent, so they can photograph it and show it to prospective tenants in its empty state. This makes it much easier for people to envisage how they might utilise the space.

Conversely, if you're letting it furnished, then get everything up to scratch and together so that what tenants see when they visit the property is what they are actually going to end up with when they move in. Needless to say, whether letting furnished or unfurnished, you'll also need to get the place professionally cleaned, and dejunk any outside storage space, such as the shed or garage (if you're allowing the tenants to use those areas).

Also, do have a read of Section 7 in this chapter, 'Your responsibilities as a landlord'. It's good for you to know upfront what you're getting yourself into so you know what's coming later on.

3. Letting agent

As I've ranted about previously in an earlier chapter, the best advice I can give you is to use a letting agent who is a member of **ARLA**, **UKALA**, **NALS**, **RICS**, **NAEA** or, if you're in London, the **London Rental Standard**. This can be either on a **tenant find only** arrangement – just to get a tenant in place and sort out all the paperwork and deposit – or on a **full management** basis, where they not only get you up and running, but then manage it for you on an ongoing basis. The latter is ideal if you're going to be moving out of the area or just don't know what you're doing and would rather leave it in the hands of people who do.

A letting agent will also be able to administer the deposit paid by the tenant, and secure it with one of the Tenancy Deposit Protection schemes. For more detail on deposits, it's worth referring to the 'Deposits' section in the 'The Realities of Renting' chapter.

Expect to pay a fee equivalent to the first month's rent for finding the tenant and sorting out the paperwork. If your agent will also be managing the place, you're probably looking at anywhere between 8% and 12% of the rent each month. This will include collecting the rent, and the agent being the first point of contact for the tenant if there are any issues. You can of course negotiate, but the best agents are normally pretty realistic with their fees because they know that they offer a good service and will get the job done quickly.

Any charges you do agree, always confirm in an email so you've got a paper trail should you need to refer to it in future.

Other than dealing with the paperwork, the most important thing any agent will do is market your home to get it let out for as much money as possible, as quickly as possible, to the best quality tenant available. So, as with anything else, do your research.

I'd highly recommend you consider doing a bit of mystery shopping. It's imperative that the first contact your prospective tenant has is with a friendly, approachable individual who is professional, puts them at ease, and offers good customer service – this is even more relevant if the agent is also going to manage the property. So *ring around and see who you like the sound of.* Pretend that you are looking for somewhere to rent, and see how the letting agent deals with your enquiry. Are they polite? Do they listen to your requirements and proactively suggest properties for you to view? They are going to be representing your property, so make sure you like what you hear. Also, if you are going to be employing a letting agent to manage your property on an ongoing basis, check to make sure they have a 24-hour emergency number for tenants to call if they have a problem.

Whilst we're talking about first impressions, the majority of tenants go online to start their search, so ideally you want to use an agent who advertises on one of the larger property portals, like **www.rightmove.co.uk** or **www.zoopla.co.uk**. Take a look and see how their properties are presented online – are the pictures clear and professional, rather than fuzzy and a bit wonky? Are there any spelling mistakes in the descriptions? Can you see their website on a mobile device, like a mobile phone or a tablet, as well as on a PC? Remember, this is the shop window for your property, and over 90% of tenants start their search online, so it pays to go with a letting agent who is savvy in terms of their digital presence.

Whether you go for an agent on a tenant find only or full management basis, the way that an agent will go about finding you suitable tenants is, broadly speaking, the same. First off, they'll arrange to visit the property to appraise the place and then calculate out how much rent you'll be able to charge, similar to the way that a normal residential sales agent would work. You'll also be asked to sign their terms and conditions, which, as with selling your home, will tie you in to marketing the property with them for a certain period.

You know what I'm going to say here, don't you? Yep, that's right – read it through carefully. Ideally, all you want to sign up to is *six weeks maximum*. If they've not found you a tenant after that, you want to be able to dis-instruct them and get another agent on the case.

Also watch out for any clauses that mean you'd potentially owe them a fee, even if you've fired them, should another agent manage to find you a tenant. If you're not sure of anything, do ask the question. Don't feel stupid for asking the agent to explain exactly what something means in the contract. Whatever you do, if you've subsequently agreed something different to what's on the original contract with the agent, mark the changes up clearly, send the letting agent a copy and make sure you keep a copy with the amendments that you've made.

Once you've formally instructed them, your agent will then start to pull together the marketing particulars for the property. This will involve them paying you another visit to prepare the EPC (Energy Performance Certificate), write the description of the property and take photos. At which point it's advisable to get the place looking show-home-tastic. Those pictures are going to be used to get tenants through your front door, so you want them to look as good as possible. You may also want to consider having a 'to let' board outside your property. If you don't want a board (and don't forget it *is* your choice) then tell your agent in writing so that they don't put one up by mistake.

When the particulars are finished, get them sent to you so you can check them for accuracy before the letting agent starts sending them out. If you haven't already, ask the agent whether they have a mailing list of prospective tenants who have registered to receive updates on new properties that meet their criteria via email. This is the quickest way to stimulate viewings, as the agent is simply matching tenants' requirements with suitable properties.

When enquiries start to come in, your letting agent should conduct all the viewings, even if they are working for you on a tenant find only basis. If you do have someone who's keen and up for a second viewing at an evening or weekend when the agent isn't available, it's worth considering agreeing to show them round yourself.

Top tip for ladies: If you're a single gal and live on your own, maybe have a pal or parent around so you're not on your tod with a complete stranger if you are conducting a viewing and the agent isn't with you. (Yes, I know, call me a worry guts, but I'm just trying to look out for you, OK?) For more tips on personal safety with regards to property go to **www.suzylamplugh.org**.

Inevitably, you're going to have to furnish your agent with a set of keys, and much in the same way you would keep the place spotless if you were trying to sell, it's important that you don't forget your home needs to be pristine for viewings, so a quick whizz round every morning before you go off to work is essential. No dirty pants strewn about the place, please.

4. Credit check and references

Once a tenant has been found for you, they'll normally be asked by the letting agent to put down a **holding deposit** so the place can be taken off the market whilst the agent runs a credit check and validates their references. As with everything else, they'll do all the work and just ring you once the results are in to let you know whether the prospective tenant is a good bet, or a complete nutter with a criminal record as long as your arm and no bank account. We're aiming for the former not the latter, obviously. This is one of the most important jobs the agent will undertake for you, because if your tenant fails to pay their rent, you still have to pay the mortgage and that leaves you out of pocket.

Tenant screening, as it's referred to in the trade, normally looks into the individual's status and basically determines if they are good for the rent each month. The main areas tenant screening reports cover are:

- A credit check – whether the applicant has any history of county court judgements (CCJs) against them, or a bankruptcy or insolvency within the last five years.

- Affordability check and income verification – how much they earn, where they work and whether they're employed or self-employed.

- Bank account validation – who they bank with and how long have they held an account there.

- Checks with previous landlords – if your applicant has rented a property before, the agent will request a reference from their previous landlord to make sure they didn't trash the place, keep a gorilla in the kitchen or default on the rent.

- Immigration checks – in certain circumstances, it may be relevant for your letting agent to check your prospective tenant's immigration status to make sure they have the correct paperwork in place.

Depending on the tenant and their income, they may need a **Guarantor** – someone like a parent who guarantees that the rent will be paid and will, if necessary, pay the rent if the tenant can't pay it themselves. This is quite common if you're letting to students, for example. In that case, as part of the tenant screening process, it's essential that the Guarantor is credit checked as well.

The other option is that a company will be paying the rent each month – this is quite common in big cities where companies pay for accommodation for employees. It's called a **Company Let** and generally speaking, this is a great situation for a landlord. If a company is large enough to be paying the rent for its staff, it means your rent is pretty much guaranteed – I've let my properties out on company lets before and it worked out really well. Don't take it for granted, though – make sure your letting agent runs a full screen on the company to ensure that they have the money to pay and that they are who they say they are.

For tenant screening, letting agents generally use a specific professional service (such as HomeLet). If anything comes back and you're not sure, ask your letting agent to clarify with the tenant so that you feel happy they can, ultimately, afford their rent. If that means you would like an additional employer's reference or a letter from their bank manager, then speak up and ask for it.

5. Insurance

Whilst your tenant is being vetted, it's a good idea for you to sort out some insurance for the various eventualities that may occur once they've actually moved in. There are a few things you need to think about, which I'll run through now.

Buildings cover

You should have this if you've got a mortgage anyway, so just ring your insurer and let them know you're letting the property out. This is important because companies look for any excuse they can to not pay out on claims. If the tenant sets fire to the kitchen and you've not told the insurance company you've let the property, you may find your policy is invalidated. Not good. Once you've spoken to your insurer, put it in writing too (and keep a copy) to prove you've informed them.

Landlord's contents insurance

You'll need this regardless of whether you're letting the place furnished or unfurnished. Why? Because the term 'contents' actually covers anything that you could theoretically take with you when you move house, for example, carpets, light fittings and curtains.

Be aware that taking out contents insurance will only cover you and *not* the tenant in the event of something occurring. Pretty obvious really, but I thought best to mention it. Also, it's always worth paying that bit extra and getting accidental damage cover. It doesn't cost that much more, and it means that if you do end up in a 'red wine on light coloured carpet' situation, you can sort it without it costing you a fortune.

Either your letting agent will be able to arrange landlord's contents insurance for you as part of their service, or you can ring around a few local insurance brokers. Failing that, go online to one of the numerous price comparison sites. There are plenty of options, it just takes a bit of research.

Rent guarantee and landlord's legal cover

This is genius. Basically you pay a one-off premium (from about £100 to £250, depending on how much the monthly rent charge is) at the start of each tenancy, which then pays out if your tenant doesn't pay their rent: meaning that you can still pay the mortgage, and aren't out of pocket.

Legal cover is normally also thrown in, so that if you have to take the tenant to court to get a possession order, those costs are covered too. Ask your letting agent about it. If they don't offer it, you can buy this kind of policy from **www.moneysupermarket.com** (look for 'Rental Protection').

I can't recommend landlord's rent guarantee and legal cover enough. Having found myself with a tenant who lost her job and then couldn't pay the rent, this kind of insurance made a massive difference. Ultimately it meant I didn't lose thousands of pounds and get myself in mortgage arrears. I know it's a bit more money to find, but it really is worth it so you can sleep at night, especially if missing just one or two months' rent from your tenant would throw your own finances into turmoil.

Landlord liability insurance

As a landlord you are responsible for the safety of the property that your tenants are living in. Fair enough, you may think. But this also means that if your tenant harms themselves due to something dangerous in the property (which could be as simple as them falling down the stairs after a particularly wild night out, breaking their leg and then claiming that the carpet wasn't properly fitted and caused them to trip) they can make a claim against you for damages.

Landlord liability cover will pay for any damages you may be ordered to cough up for, as well as covering you for any legal costs. Again, your letting agent will probably be able to arrange this, or you may find you can upgrade your rent guarantee and landlord's legal cover to include it as well.

6. Dealing with deposits

I've covered this in some detail in the 'The Realities of Renting' chapter, so I'm not going to bore you with it again. Have a read through and you'll get the gist. Suffice to say, from the landlord's perspective your agent can handle it on your behalf if you wish. To be honest, this is what I'd recommend, as that way at least you know it's done properly. Also, you're paying them handsomely to get things sorted, so let them earn their crust. They will secure the tenant's dosh in the appropriate manner with one of the three alternatives available under the Tenancy Deposit Protection Scheme.

Whilst your agent can manage this process for you, it's crucial that you make sure they *do* get everything sorted and in place. Because ultimately, as the landlord *you* are responsible, not the letting agent.

The letting agent must let the tenant know which scheme their deposit is being protected with (this is normally noted in the tenancy agreement). The letting agent should also issue the tenant with an important document called **Prescribed Information**, which contains information about their tenancy. The scheme used by the letting agent to secure the deposit will send the protection certificate direct to the tenant. All you need to be sure of is that your agent gets that deposit protected and issues the correct documentation within 30 days of the tenant handing over his or her money. If they don't, you as the landlord could be liable for a hefty fine, not to mention the fact that it could affect your ability to remove the tenants later on. Not cool. So make sure you keep tabs on this bit of the process and also that the updated deposit registration regulations are followed to the letter.

Something else to note here is to ensure that the inventory, which will be prepared for you by the agent, is as accurate as possible. Check it thoroughly before the tenant moves in. If there is any damage to the property at the end of the tenancy, you are going to have to prove to a third party that the tenant hasn't looked after the place, and will need evidence as to why you need to withhold some of their deposit.

This process is easier if you have laid the foundations upfront and made sure the inventory is accurate. I know it's not the most exciting thing you'll ever do, but trust me on this, it's vital that you protect yourself. For more on inventories and how they work, take a look at Section 5, 'Safeguard yourself' in the 'The Realities of Renting' chapter.

7. Your responsibilities as a landlord

Okay, this is dull, but it *is* important. As a landlord you have responsibilities – other than counting the rent that comes in every month. Assuming that you're letting your property on an Assured Shorthold Tenancy basis (see the 'Understanding your lease' section in the 'The Realities of Renting' chapter) the three main points are as follows.

1. Maintenance and repairs

You are obliged to maintain the structure and exterior of your property, maintain all water supplies and sanitary/drainage installations and ensure that all sinks, baths, showers, toilets, etc. are fit to use. You also have to provide and maintain adequate lighting, heating and ventilation, and treat any damp that may occur as a result of structural problems with the property.

2. Safety of any gas and electrical appliances

The Gas Safety (Installation and Use) Regulations 1998 – a riveting read, if ever I saw one – specifies that you have to maintain all gas appliances you provide in the property (boilers, gas hobs, gas ovens, gas fires, etc.) and arrange and pay for an annual service and safety check by a CORGI (Council for Registered Gas Installers) approved engineer. This is commonly referred to as the **Landlord's Gas Safety Certificate**.

The engineer visits your property, checks the various appliances to make sure that they aren't emitting anything hazardous like carbon monoxide, then issues a certificate. You need to keep this to prove you've had the inspection carried out, and your tenant will also need a copy.

You also need to make sure that any electrical appliances you supply are safe to use. This falls under the Electrical Equipment (Safety) Regulations 1994. It applies to all electrical appliances you supply with the property, and is why a lot of landlords, even if they are letting a place furnished, stop short of including items like kettles and toasters as it's just more hassle to get them inspected each year to make sure they are all safe for use. To do this, you need to arrange what's called a **PAT (portable appliance test)** for all electrical equipment annually, and also give your tenant all the instruction booklets for things so they know how they work. Also, make sure that any appliances you are supplying carry the British Standard Safety sign.

In addition, you'll have to make sure that you get a certificate for any electrical work you have done, such as any re-wiring, because the Landlord and Tenant Act 1985, Housing Act 2004 and the Plugs and Socket etc. (Safety) Regulations 1994 state that the landlord has an obligation to ensure that all electrical equipment is safe. This should be issued by a registered electrician, and you can find one of those by searching the Competent Persons Register at **www.competentperson.co.uk**.

Now, I read all of that legislation so you don't have to. And yes, I *am* great fun at dinner parties, before you ask.

3. Fire safety of the furnishings and building

You also need to ensure that any furniture or furnishings that you are leaving in the place meet with the fire resistance regulations specified in the Furniture and Furnishings Fire (Safety) Regulations 1988 (see, I told you this was thrilling stuff, didn't I?). In practical terms, it means you have to check that anything you are leaving in the property carries the appropriate label on it somewhere to show that it has passed the various safety tests in order to comply. This doesn't apply to carpets, curtains and duvets, oddly enough. Just everything else.

Don't forget about **smoke alarms** either – it's *your* responsibility to install them (although normally it's the tenant's responsibility to make sure they work). Not only that, you should install a small, multi-purpose fire extinguisher and a fire blanket – make sure you put it somewhere easy to find and logical, such as in a kitchen cupboard. At the risk of sounding like a stuck record, this is exactly why you've got a letting agent on the case, so if you're not sure about anything, ask questions and get it sorted.

The full extent of your responsibilities will be laid out in the tenancy agreement and government legislation. Your agent should talk you through this before you sign it to make sure you understand everything, as well as answering any questions you have. There are a couple of other things to be aware of. Firstly, as a landlord you can't be barging in on the tenant every five minutes. You have to give them reasonable notice if you want to inspect or visit the property – this comes under the tenant's right to 'quiet enjoyment of the property'.

The other issue is that you have a responsibility to get any necessary repairs to the property sorted within a reasonable amount of time. In other words, if the boiler decides not to work in the depths of mid-winter, you can't leave your poor tenant shivering for too long before you do something about it.

There are also a couple of bits of important paperwork you need to provide to your tenant. The first is an EPC (Energy Performance Certificate), which the agent should have produced before they marketed the property (they need one to advertise the place). Even though the tenant will have seen this in the marketing particulars, the EPC has to be issued to them again, along with their tenancy agreement. This is law and there are penalties to both the landlord and letting agent if you don't comply. I've covered EPCs in more detail in 'The Realities of Renting' chapter (Section 4, 'Important questions to ask'). Now, whilst your letting agent will sort your EPC out for you, it is *your* responsibility to make sure they get it sorted and issued, otherwise it will be you who ends up in trouble.

The second bit of information you should give your letting agent is either the Letter of Consent from your lender (proof you have permission from them to let the property out) or confirmation of a Buy To Let mortgage. In truth, you don't have to do this by law, but I would say it's best practice. It proves to your tenant that you are a responsible landlord, which at the end of the day is of course what you are. You can find out why a tenant will need to know you've jumped through this particular hoop by reading 'The Realities of Renting' chapter (Section 1, 'Be fussy about letting agents and landlords').

8. Handling emergencies

With the best will in the world, even a perfect tenant is going to have a problem at some stage. Don't get uptight about it, just take a deep breath and deal with the problem. If your place is managed by an agent then they are the tenant's first port of call. The agent should then inform you of the problem, and get your authority to make any necessary repairs before they arrange for the relevant tradesperson to attend. Unless it's a dire emergency and you can't be contacted – in which case they will need to do whatever it takes to make the place safe and habitable, and deal with the consequences afterwards.

The majority of professional letting agents have a specific mobile phone number for emergencies, which is answered 24 hours a day. If this is the case, check that both you and your tenant have got this number. If you're managing the property yourself, give your tenant any and every contact number you can. If you're out of the area (or country, for that matter) give them the details of someone you've nominated to look after the place in your absence.

Whichever way you do it, it's important to ensure the tenancy agreement states that they need to make reasonable efforts (and prove that they have done so) to contact either you or, if appropriate, the letting agent, before authorising any repairs –

emergency or otherwise. What you don't want is them running up a horrendous out-of-hours plumbing bill just because there's a leaky tap in the kitchen keeping them awake on a Saturday night.

Another top tip if you're managing the place yourself is to have a list of tradesmen to hand that you've dealt with before who you trust and are reliable, so that you don't waste time ringing around to find a plumber/heating engineer/locksmith when you really need one. Which, I guarantee, will be at around 2am on a Saturday night, when you're tucked up asleep and your tenant has managed to lose their front door keys/blow up the boiler/flood their bathroom and the downstairs flat into the bargain.

And when that call comes, resist the urge to call them a moron. Ask them if they are alright, and then get them to explain what's happened so that you can make a judgement call on whether or not it can wait until the morning.

Don't forget, if the damage is due to the tenant – for example, if they've let the bath overflow or locked themselves out because they are inebriated and have lost their keys – *they* will have to pay for any necessary work. You're not liable. You only have to cough up if something has broken due to normal wear and tear, or if it was faulty in the first place.

Make sure you get a receipt for any work that's carried out, including labour and materials, as you'll need it at the end of the year when you're working out how much income tax you need to pay. That's because any expenditure you make on property maintenance can be offset against your income, thus reducing your net profit – and the tax you owe.

9. *Dealing with naughty tenants*

If you let your property for any length of time, chances are that at some stage you'll have a tenant who is a bit of a problem. Yes, it's a pain in the backside, but it happens, and like most other things in life, you just need to keep a cool head, take the best advice you can and deal with the issue.

But before we go any further, if you're smart, you should be able to prevent quite a few problems before they get serious. How? Well, if you arrange regular inspections of the property you'll soon know if your tenant has trashed the place or sub-let it to a few 'friends'. I'd recommend a quarterly inspection to keep on top of things. You can either do these yourself, or get an agent to do it for you. If you've got a letting agent who is fully managing the property, ask if inspection visits are covered by their monthly commission. If not, ask how much extra they are going to charge.

If you're going to carry out the inspections yourself, you need to give the tenant reasonable notice – a week is ideal, with 48 hours the minimum, but either way do confirm it in writing (email is fine). This isn't a military parade, so no matter how tempting, do not run your fingers over surfaces checking the level of dust that's accumulated. You are there simply to ensure that everything is in reasonable order. If the place is excessively dirty, or you spot any issues, then send a short letter to your tenants outlining the issue and requesting that it be resolved within a reasonable amount of time. Keep a copy for your records, as ever.

Remember, every individual is entitled to his or her 'unique' lifestyle. *It's only when that lifestyle causes damage to your property that there is a potential breach to the letting agreement.* So try not to be too judgemental. Just look to make sure that everything is where it's supposed to be and there aren't any causes for concern. Provided you keep up inspections, a lot of things that could cause issues further down the line can be dealt with pretty easily.

However, sometimes tenants can appear perfectly reasonable when you arrive for your regular check, then exhibit all sorts of outrageous behaviour the following day. If you find yourself on the receiving end of such tactics dear reader, well, this section is just for you.

If problems do arise, issues need to be dealt with in a business-like, calm and efficient manner, and definitely documented in writing (email and/or letter) at every stage of the process. Should you end up going to court to get a repossession order (which you'll have to do if you want to evict someone), you will have to provide evidence for why you believe their behaviour to be unreasonable, and show that you've done all you can to resolve the dispute before taking the ultimate sanction of chucking them out.

When you boil it all down, there are three main types of issue you might encounter with a tenant:

1. Not paying the rent.

2. Damaging your property.

3. Breaching the terms of the lease.

Assuming that you've got an Assured Shorthold Tenancy agreement which clearly states when the rent is due, as well as the tenant's obligations and responsibilities, then as soon as you become aware of a problem you – or the letting agent acting on your behalf – need to write to the tenant outlining the issue, and giving them a reasonable amount of time to rectify the problem or their behaviour. Depending on the severity of the situation, that could be 24 hours or a month, but your agent will be able to advise you. If you're managing the place yourself, your local Citizens Advice Bureau would be a good port of call.

Generally speaking, non-payment of rent is the easiest one to deal with. That automatically entitles you to serve notice on the tenant should you wish. Usually, the threat of eviction is enough to get most people to cough up, but in extreme cases you'll need to take legal action to get a court order for an eviction notice. Needless to say, you'll have no rent coming in, mortgage payments going out and the legal fees to pay, so the whole exercise is going to sting a little. However, you *will* be able to take legal action after you've had the tenant removed to reclaim the rent you're owed (how long it will take to get it back is anyone's guess). All this is why I mentioned rent guarantee and legal cover earlier – at least you wouldn't end up out of pocket should something like this happen.

If, on the other hand, your tenant has decided to breach their lease, perhaps by 'entertaining' the neighbours late at night with a choice selection of club anthems at a high rate of decibels, or by smuggling a dog in with blatant disregard for the 'no pets' clause in the lease, then the process is a bit more challenging. You will need to write to them, explaining why their behaviour is a problem, and requesting that they rectify the issue within a reasonable amount of time. Set a deadline for the issue to be remedied, and remind the tenant that they may forfeit some – or all – of their deposit and/or get themselves evicted if they fail to comply.

That should sort out the problem. If it doesn't, write to them again with another warning, again setting out why they've breached their lease, what they need to do to sort the problem out, and when they need to do it by. If *that* goes unheeded, it's time to go legal and apply for that court order.

If you have a letting agent, they will be able to manage this process for you – though discuss with them any additional fees they may charge for the pleasure of doing so. If you're managing the property yourself, I'd suggest you find yourself a good solicitor who specialises in landlord and tenant law and employ them from the get-go. If you were smart and have legal cover on your insurance, then check to see if it will pay out to cover your solicitor's fees (chances are it will, but best check before you run up a big bill).

Should your troublesome tenant suddenly stop paying rent as well (just to be *really* difficult), then your life just got a bit easier. You've now automatically got grounds to get them out pretty much straightaway. If not, however, be prepared for things to take a while. Just accept that, according to the law of averages, everyone is likely to get one tenant who's a handful sometimes, and you just got yours. The upside is that the odds are now in your favour that it won't happen again. Fingers crossed, anyway.

10. At the end of the tenancy

At some stage, either you'll decide you want to move back in, sell the property, or the tenant will want to move on. Whichever way round, either party will have to wait until the relevant break clause in the contract. This then allows your tenant to give you one month's notice, or you as the landlord to give them two months' notice. (I'm basing this on an Assured Shorthold Tenancy agreement, although other types of lease will vary.)

Once notice has been served, a moving out date will be agreed. This is when the check out will take place. If you appoint a letting agent on a tenant find only basis to get another taker for the place, the good news is that they will probably (for a fee) be able to deal with the check out of your old tenant for you too. If, on the other hand, you have an agent who is fully managing the place, then it'll all be dealt with automatically, along with getting the next tenant lined up for you – if indeed that's what you want to do.

The check out procedure is basically the check in reversed. An inventory clerk will go around the property with the tenant after they've moved all their stuff out, checking the state of the property against the notes of its condition when they moved in. Any damages will be reported, along with details about general cleanliness and any wear and tear, together with the appropriate meter readings.

In my experience, the best thing you can do is attend the check out personally. If that's impossible, make sure you visit the property the same day to run through the completed inventory, comparing it to your copy of the original check in notes. That way, you can make sure that you agree with the check out. If there are things that the inventory clerk hasn't spotted (this does happen) you can call the agent and get it documented within 24 hours of the tenant handing in their keys. This is important because if there is a dispute about the deposit, your check out inventory will need to prove how bad a state the property was left in. Oversights now mean no leg to stand on later.

If the place is furnished, check the inventory to make sure nothing has mysteriously gone missing (I've heard of beds, sofas and even boilers vanishing). Take photographs of any problem areas. Once the inventory has gone back to the tenant, and any damages which need to be deducted have been agreed between you, the agent will arrange for the deposit (or what's left of it) to be returned to the tenant by the scheme it's protected with. Any monies you are owed are then sent to your bank account.

If there is damage and you want to claim money from the tenant's deposit, you need to prove why and present estimates for repair work or replacement items to the tenant. Again, if you're using a letting agent they may be able to help you with this. However you do it, don't forget that in the majority of cases *you need to make sure their deposit is back with them within 10 days of them moving out*, so you can't drag your heels on this. If you do, expect to end up with a fine or a court order against you. Also don't forget that both you *and* the tenant have to agree on deductions in order to release the deposit from the protection scheme you're using. If you can't agree between you, the various schemes have processes in place you *must* follow in order to get both parties' agreement.

Conclusion

I know it sounds like being a landlord is terribly complicated and daunting, but the reality is this: sometimes, needs must, and if you get a good letting agent on your case, and your tenant is a reasonable human being – both of which are eminently doable – the whole thing should pass off without too much difficulty.

The hardest thing I've found as a landlord is trying to remain emotionally detached if you're letting out a property that you once lived in. It's very difficult to be rational when you feel that someone is violating your home, even if that's just them putting a nail in the wall to hang a picture. But remember: to your tenant this is just a place they are renting. You have memories and a strong sense of attachment; they don't.

So keep things in perspective. One day, if you want to, you'll be able to move back in. For now, though, your life is elsewhere, and you need to concentrate on that.

Getting a letting agent to manage the place for you will cost a percentage of the rent, but will also largely allow you to put the whole thing to the back of your mind. It should also give you the comfort that if things do get a bit tricky, you've got professionals to help you deal with it.

One last thing. If you do decide to move back in, don't expect the place to look the way you left it. Even the best tenant will have scratched something or spilt stuff on the carpet. Accept that before you start the process, and it'll be a lot easier. It also feels weird to know that someone else has been living there. That's only natural, and it'll take time for you to settle back in, but redecorating the place might help you to make it feel like your home again, even if it's just sloshing a bit of fresh paint on the wall.

Changing the toilet seat might help too. If it's still there, of course.

7.
Breaking Up is Hard to Do

If you're reading this chapter you are either:

(a) Exceptionally financially astute and trying to avoid a problem before it even happens – in which case, hats off, I salute you, have a gold star.

Or (as is more likely the case),

(b) In that most awful of situations: the person you thought was the love of your life has turned out not to be. And it's far more complicated than that, because you've bought a property together.

I feel your pain, I really do. Having been married and divorced (which is actually a little easier to deal with in terms of practicalities, because once you're married the law regarding property is a lot more straightforward) and having gone down the 'living in sin' route, I can tell you the emotional fallout in both cases is relatively similar.

There's that awful sinking feeling that everything in your world is about to change, and not for the better. No wonder emotions can reach boiling point and things can degenerate very quickly, even if you both wanted to remain on amicable terms and be reasonable about it.

What can make matters worse for partners who never got married is the common misconception that, after a certain period of living together, you both have some rights regarding the property. You don't. There is no such thing as a **common law spouse**. At the time of writing there are moves to put some measures in place, but they haven't been finalised. So unless you are married or in a civil partnership, you need to take steps early on to protect yourselves when you buy somewhere together.

It doesn't matter what you've paid in terms of housekeeping, or how much money you've sunk into a property, *if you haven't clearly specified who gets what in the event of a break-up then be prepared for it to get very messy and expensive.* There's every chance you'll come out worse off than when you started the whole caper.

Have I got your attention yet? Good, because this is serious stuff.

But let's take a couple of steps back and look on the positive side. If you are about to embark on the romantic adventure of buying a home together, as well as going through the usual rigmarole of deciding where you want to live, what sort of property you're looking for, applying for a joint mortgage, etc., you also need to think seriously about what you would do should it not work out. Not easy, I know, when you're looking at your beloved with rose-tinted spectacles and picturing long Sunday lie-ins and sex on tap, but there you go.

Think about how much money each of you are going to be contributing to the whole deal. Are you both putting down an equal amount of money to cover the Stamp Duty, legal fees and deposit? Will you be going exactly halves on all household expenditure and the mortgage? What's more likely is that one of you might have more savings (or generous parents who are going to gift you the dosh) and the other may earn slightly more, so is going to take the hit for more of the bills each month.

You'll reason, in your loved-up state of bliss, that it all works out fair in the end. Well, you may think that now, but trust me, when the other party has decided that a one-night stand with Debbie/ Wayne in accounts was acceptable behaviour at the Christmas party, even them breathing will seem unreasonable to you.

I don't want to sound like a pessimist; I'm not, honestly, I ended up getting re-married, which just goes to prove it all works out OK in the end. I appreciate that it doesn't sound like the most loving gesture you'll ever make, but *if you want to do the best for each other, it's really important that you have the 'what if' conversation before you sign on the dotted line.*

So, if you're not quite ready to tie the knot, but want to live together, then you've got a few options, depending on your situation. In this chapter, we're going to take a little look at the various scenarios just to make sure that you're fully up to speed.

One last thing before you read on, folks: for the purposes of this chapter, I'm assuming that you don't have little people in your world yet. If you do have kids and aren't married, things are slightly different in terms of your rights around property. My advice to you is see a solicitor before you do anything else.

1. *Splitting everything 50/50*

If you are one of those rare couples where everything you do financially is going to be based on equal contributions when you buy your property together, you need to make sure that you are on the deeds as **Joint Tenants**. This means that, should you sell the property, you are both entitled to half the proceeds (after you've paid off any mortgage).

This is the simplest arrangement. All you'll need to do is inform your conveyancing solicitor at the beginning of the process that this is how you want the deeds held, and they will make the necessary arrangements.

As for fighting it out over the Emma Bridgewater mugs and who gets custody of the cat, well, you can figure that out for yourselves.

2. *If one is contributing more than the other*

In this scenario you need to be a bit more on the ball. What we're basically saying here is that, should it all go Pete Tong, one of you will have put more in than the other – either as a deposit, in terms of paying the mortgage, or by contributing to works and improvements on the property. That person will then naturally want a greater proportion of the proceeds should you decide to go your separate ways.

This means that you need to discuss calmly and rationally who's going to put what in (easier said than done, I know) and who will want what out in the worst-case scenario. Then you need to speak to your solicitor and draw up the deeds as **Tenants in Common**. You'll end up with a document attached to your deeds that clearly states who gets what in terms of how the proceeds of the sale are split.

So if one of you has put in the whole of the deposit, coughed up for the Stamp Duty and paid most of the mortgage each month, the amount left over after you've sold the place and paid off the mortgage, legal fees and estate agent's bill will be split accordingly.

Still sounds complicated? OK, here's an example of how proceeds are calculated in the event of property being held as Tenants in Common:

Daisy and Will are splitting up, having lived together for ten years (without getting married). They bought their property in 2004 for £249,950, and although they haven't done any work on the place, they've seen it rise in value – it's now worth £320,000. When they bought it, Will had saved up enough to cover the initial deposit; he also earns more than Daisy and therefore has paid more of the mortgage. They held the property as Tenants in Common, and agreed that, should they split up, Daisy would receive less than Will because she'd contributed less financially towards the property. This is how the figures work out:

- Initial purchase price of property = £249,950

- Deposit, Stamp Duty, legal fees and moving costs associated with purchase = £50,000 (paid for by Will).

- Monthly mortgage payment = £1,100 (of which Will paid £770 and Daisy paid £330).

- Current value of property = £320,000

- Outstanding mortgage = £184,000

- Legal fees and agent's fees to sell property = £6,500

- Net proceeds of property (if sold for £320,000) = £129,500

(N.B: I've kept the figures really simple here, and haven't included horrible stuff like mortgage redemption penalties, etc. This is really just an illustration of the basic mechanics of the situation, but you need to remember that the proceeds will be split as per your agreement, after you've paid off all costs associated with the sale of the property.)

The agreement was that Will would get back the money he'd initially put in, plus 70% of the proceeds of the sale, as he'd paid 70% of the mortgage each month. Daisy, on the other hand, would be entitled to 30% of the proceeds of the sale *after* Will had taken out his initial investment, as she'd not put anything into the purchase of the property and had contributed less to the mortgage each month.

So the final figures look like this:

- Net proceeds of property = £129,500

- Less Will's initial investment of £50,000 = £79,500

- Will's share (at 70%) of £79,500 = £55,650

- Daisy's share (at 30%) of £79,500 = £23,850

As you can see, this is going to require an honest discussion between the pair of you *before* you buy a property. It's a sensitive topic, and it can be tricky to broach the subject without having a row about it before you've even started. But I hope you can see the benefits of having the conversation.

3. Living together when one of you already owns their place

This is potentially the trickiest situation of all to deal with, for a couple of reasons.

Firstly, you're not starting with a blank sheet of paper here, so the emotional implications of moving into another person's property are that it may never, really, feel like it's *your* home.

I've been in this situation personally, and even though we replaced the kitchen and bathrooms, plus I gave it a makeover that would put Kelly Hoppen to shame, it still never felt like the place was mine. You may feel differently, in which case, great. But it is something to consider.

Once you've got over that little hurdle, you need to think about the financial side of things. If you are the party who owns the property, and you've invited your beloved to move in with you, think about how the finances are going to work. Is your partner going to put a cash lump sum into the property to pay off a chunk of the mortgage, or are they perhaps going to pay for improvements or building work? Maybe they're going to be making a generous contribution towards the bills and housekeeping budget. If so, and you want to give them some security, you can put them on the deeds of your property as either Joint Tenants or Tenants in Common (depending on what is relevant to your situation).

It's a lovely gesture, but it *will* cost you. You see, the government – which will have already gleefully grabbed your contribution to the coffers when you bought the place in the form of Stamp Duty – will now charge your sweetheart Stamp Duty on the proportion of the property you are transferring into their name.

Charming, isn't it?

It's also a little-known fact, and catches a lot of people out. So get advice upfront from your conveyancing solicitor about how much you'll need to pay. Remember, the amount of Stamp Duty will be charged on the current value of the property, *not* what you paid when you bought it. You'll also get clobbered for Stamp Duty if you decide to wait until your current mortgage deal comes up, and then apply for a re-mortgage in joint names. Nice. Don't blame me, I'm just the messenger.

Here's how it works in practice:

Caroline and Mark are moving in together, and aren't married. As Mark already owns his own home, Caroline will move into his house. To give Caroline more security, Mark has suggested adding Caroline to the deeds of the property and the mortgage. Caroline has some savings she is going to use to pay off a chunk of the mortgage, as well as contributing 40% of the mortgage payment each month, so they've agreed Caroline will be noted on the deeds with Mark as Tenants in Common, and Caroline will have a 40% interest in the property.

In this scenario, the figures work out like this:

- Current value of Mark's house: £525,000

- Outstanding mortgage: £425,000

- Deposit from Caroline: £40,000

- Mortgage outstanding once Caroline's deposit is paid: £385,000

- Value of portion of property transferred into Caroline's name: £154,000

So in this example, Caroline will pay Stamp Duty (at 1%) on the following elements:

- £40,000 contribution to the outstanding mortgage.

- £385,000 of outstanding mortgage at 40% = £154,000

- Total = £194,000 at 1% Stamp Duty = payment to HMRC of £1,940

You can't get away with not paying the Stamp Duty in this situation *even if you do get married*. If you're transferring assets between you and noting your new spouse's details on the deeds, you will *still* have to pay Stamp Duty, unless you receive a court order to transfer the asset over to an ex-partner in the event of divorce or legal separation. The only way you won't have to do this is if you work on the basis that, as a married couple, you have a claim over each other's assets and just agree that you're both contributing to the costs of the mortgage and running the property without adding your new husband or wife to the mortgage or deeds. Or buy somewhere together from the outset, in which case you'll both be on the mortgage and the deeds from the get-go.

4. Deed of Trust

No ladies, this doesn't mean letting your man go off to that stag do in Riga without reading him the riot act about strippers. If you are moving in with your other half and you have both agreed that you don't want to start mucking about with the deeds and writing out a fat cheque to the Treasury, you can safeguard yourselves another way. This involves getting your solicitor to draw up a separate document called a Deed of Trust, which details exactly what your other half has put in (either as a lump sum or percentage of the monthly bills) and what you've both agreed they would get back out again should things break down and they move out.

It's a much simpler approach, though for some it doesn't give the same sense of joint ownership as having both names on the deeds.

It's a personal choice at the end of the day – neither way is wrong, and you're equally safeguarded whichever route you choose.

5. Mortgage meltdown

One of the most common problems that people ask me about is what to do concerning the mortgage if one of you moves out and the other continues to live in the property. A lot of people think that, if they're not living in a property, they don't have to pay their share of the mortgage. They're wrong.

Simply put, when you take out a joint mortgage, regardless of whether you're on the deeds as Tenants in Common or Joint Tenants, you are both what's called **jointly and severally liable** for the payments. Doesn't exactly trip off the tongue, but what it means is that once you've signed on the dotted line, if the other party doesn't pay their share of the mortgage then you have to cover it yourself, regardless of whether either of you are living in the property or not. If you don't pay *all* the mortgage payment, you will be in arrears and liable to being repossessed, and with a black mark on your credit rating to boot.

Many people end up in the sticky stuff because their partner moves out but isn't paying their bit towards the mortgage, and the one staying in the property thinks that by keeping up *their* contribution towards the payments they will be okay – the lender will go after their ex for his or her share. But it doesn't work like that, so don't make the same mistake.

If you can't live in the same place whilst you're working through the mechanics of splitting up, then at least agree that you will both continue to make the mortgage payments.

If your ex isn't coughing up, the best thing you can do is talk to your lender as soon as possible and let them know the situation. Ideally, get an appointment with your local branch and explain that you will be covering the payments until the property is sold or let. At least they'll be are aware of what's going on.

If you simply can't afford to pay both your contribution *and* your ex's share because you don't earn enough, then you will need to prove this to the lender by showing wage slips and bank account statements. If it's clear that there is no way that you'll be able to make the payments on your own, you may be able to come to an arrangement with the lender, where they will transfer you onto an interest-only mortgage until the property is sold, or perhaps allow a period where you don't have to pay the mortgage to give you the chance to take legal action against your errant ex and/or sell the property.

Either way, talk to your lender sooner rather than later.

6. Making a will

Now, this isn't the most romantic thing in the world, and I know you probably don't want to think about it, but have you considered making a **will**? If you're not married and one of you dies, the fact that you lived together does not guarantee that your beloved will inherit your estate – and that includes your home.

Technically, if you're not married and you do snuff it before you've made a will, all your worldly wealth would be left to your **immediate family** (for example, your parents). That would leave your grief-stricken other half at worst, homeless, or at best, having to juggle a lot of finances in order to pay off your family to stay in the home you owned together.

That's not a situation anyone wants to leave their nearest and dearest in, so get it sorted. There's no excuse – a solicitor can write a will for you very cheaply (about a hundred quid for a basic one) at the same time they're sorting out your other paperwork when you're buying a property. It's a bit of a no-brainer, to be honest.

If you're sat there reading this and thinking, "We didn't do that", it's not too late. A solicitor can put something in place for you retrospectively and advise you of the best way to get yourselves organised.

7. Buying the other party out

It's a disaster. The worst has happened. You've had the "I think we need to talk" conversation, and you've agreed that you're going to go your separate ways. After the dust has settled and you've stopped playing 'All By Myself' and 'Love On The Rocks' on repeat, you've realised that, heartbroken as you are, you're going to have to live *somewhere*. Moving house is a pain in the ass and expensive. So, the logical conclusion for some is to buy your ex out of the property. You can either live there on your own or, perhaps to help bolster the finances, rent out a room (in which case, see 'Fantastic Flatmates' for some pointers).

That being the case, firstly you need to agree between the pair of you how much it's going to cost to do this. Remember when I said that no matter how reasonable you promised each other you'd be, things tend to get acrimonious when money enters into the equation? This would be one of those situations.

The fairest way to go about this is to get the place professionally valued by three estate agents, then take the average valuation, and agree from that what you will pay in order to buy the other party out. Remember, if you've taken my advice, you will be on the deeds as either Joint Tenants or Tenants in Common, so you need to make sure that you've taken into account the fact you're either going to have to split the proceeds equally, or pro-rata, depending on what you'd agreed.

This is definitely one for a solicitor, because as well as having to go back to your lender and prove that you can afford to take over the mortgage on your own, you're also going to have to make the necessary arrangements to get your ex's name *off* the deeds (once you've got everything sorted). This means they will no longer have any claim over the property and everything is documented, so no one can argue later in the day that actually you said one thing but agreed something different.

Don't forget Stamp Duty, either. This will apply (again) if one of you is taking over ownership of the whole property. Whoever is doing the 'buying out' will be charged Stamp Duty on the value of the portion of the property that is being transferred into their name.

So it's really clear, here's an example:

Emma and Damien are splitting up. They bought their house in 2009 for £425,000. As property values haven't risen in their area since they purchased, Damien has decided to take on the mortgage for the whole property so Emma can move out.

Because Emma and Damien bought the property as Joint Tenants, they both contributed the same to the deposit and half each to the mortgage each month, and as they have also made significant overpayments to their mortgage there is quite a chunk of equity in the property. So, the figures work out like this:

- Original purchase price of property: £425,000

- Outstanding mortgage on property: £200,000

- Current value of property: £425,000

- Equity in property: £225,000

In this example, Damien will pay Stamp Duty (at 1%) on the following elements:

- £112,500 to Emma for her half of the equity to buy her out.

- £100,000 for the other half of the mortgage value that will be transferred into Damien's name.

- Total = £212,500 at 1% Stamp Duty = payment to HMRC of £2,125

It sounds complicated, but the reality is it's pretty straightforward. You just need to make sure you've got a good solicitor on the case who'll ensure you've ticked all the boxes to avoid any serious repercussions in the future.

Also, don't forget to take your ex's name off all the utility bills, especially the Council Tax. If you are going to be living in splendid solitude for a while, you can claim a 25% single person's discount, which is worth having. Just ring or email your local council to let them know of your change in status (nope, they won't figure it out from your Facebook update) and they will send you a form which you simply fill in. Just remember if you then subsequently have a friend or lodger move in with you the single person's discount no longer applies and you have to let the council know, OK?

Last thing to mention whilst we're on this subject: if you were sensible and made a will, you'll need to change that too in order to avoid being the most generous (dead) ex-boyfriend or girlfriend in the world.

8. Practical co-habiting tips for soon-to-be exes

Some of what I'm about to say may seem like I'm stating the obvious (so apologies in advance if I offend anyone) but for those in the depths of despair/heartache/rage, it's probably worth mentioning a few ideas to help you try to keep the status quo and your sanity when you're trying to live in the same property whilst going through a break-up.

MANNERS

It doesn't matter that you think it was all his/her fault, while you are still living under the same roof, extend your ex the courtesy that you'd like them to offer you. Which means now isn't the time to start bringing randoms home from the pub, emptying the joint bank account or deciding to run a regular poker night with all your mates until 3am during the week.

PRIVACY

Designate bedrooms so that you've each got some privacy (easy if you have a two bed property, tough if it's a studio, in which case, best start ringing around to find an available couch). If you are the dumper, then you get the spare bedroom – no question, it's the least you can do. Keep clothes and personal possessions in your own room, so you don't have to go raking around and disturbing the other person in order to get dressed in the morning.

Communication

Keep the other party informed of your movements, so if you're going to be late home let them know (particularly if they are in the habit of double-locking the door from the inside, as you'll end up locked out 'by accident' if you're not careful).

Three's a crowd

Under no circumstances bring a third party back to the property whilst your other half is still under the same roof, even if you don't think they will be there. Should they come home unannounced, you will have started World War III and it's pretty difficult to retrace your steps from there.

Paperwork

Meticulously document what you pay in terms of contributions to the housekeeping (keep bank statements and copies of bills to prove what you've paid should things disintegrate) and keep the standing order for the mortgage payments going until everything is sorted and you've either sold the place *or* been bought out and all the paperwork is finalised.

Keep it covered

An ex parading around in their underwear or low-slung bath towel in the kitchen is both confusing and disconcerting for the other party. Don't do it.

Tidy up

Try to keep the place tidy, respecting the other person's right to a clean bathroom and kitchen.

TV PRIVILEGES

Be generous about shared television rights – if you can't agree, then for the short term either go down the pub to watch the football, or get a TV for your own room so you can retreat to the privacy of your boudoir to get your 'Enders fix in peace.

OVERNIGHTERS

If you are staying out for the night, gently broach the subject without going into too much detail. Your ex doesn't need to know where you are or with whom, just that you're going to be away that evening and will be back at a certain time the following day. Interestingly, from both personal experience and also that of friends, this appears to be one of the major flashpoints that can lead to heated disagreements in the 'living together but not' environment; even if you're innocently going to be away with work, the assumption by the other party is normally that you are 'staying out with him/her' – even if there isn't anyone else involved. Remember, it's a tough situation and there are a lot of raw feelings involved here. Tread as carefully as you can.

TIME LIMITS

Finally, jointly agree a timeframe by which either you will have got the situation sorted and paperwork finalised, or one of you will move out (but continue to pay the appropriate contribution to the bills until such time as it's no longer necessary). By putting a time limit on it, there will be light at the end of the tunnel for both of you.

9. Getting the right advice if you've not protected yourself

I'm not going to say I told you so. If you're currently going through a break-up and you haven't made the appropriate provisions, you're going to need some good advice to ensure that you come out of the experience as solvent as possible.

In these situations, *a specialist property solicitor will be worth their weight in gold*. Many will give you an hour's free consultation. My advice is that you thoroughly do your homework first: pull together bank statements (particularly if you have a joint account), copies of bills and your mortgage paperwork, and write yourself a list of questions that you want to ask, so you don't waste time in the appointment or forget to ask something important. Make copious notes as there will be a lot of information and detail that you need to remember, and in your emotional state you may not want to rely on your memory. Make sure the solicitor you use is a member of the Law Society (you can check by going to **www.lawsociety.org.uk**).

You can also go to your local Citizens Advice Bureau, who will be able to give you basic advice on your situation – although this isn't a substitute for engaging with a qualified solicitor. Find your nearest office by going to **www.citizensadvice.org.uk**.

10. What changes if you get married?

You mean other than the contractual obligation to bring each other breakfast in bed at weekends, and annoying your single friends by referring to your state of loved-up conjugal bliss at every opportunity?

Seriously, once that ring is on your finger life does change in all manner of ways (mostly for the better). But when it comes to property, there is a definite difference in the eyes of the law between a co-habiting couple and those who are married or in a civil partnership.

When you get spliced the status of your individual assets changes. Each of you has the right to claim against the assets of the other in the event that you separate. What you end up actually getting is down to either agreeing sensibly between yourselves, or in the case of total communication breakdown a court will decide for you. At this point of course, you need a good solicitor.

As a married couple you can hold your property as Tenants in Common, which (as we've covered) means you can document who put what in and who gets what out. Or you can draw up a pre-nuptial agreement. All I would say, though, is at the time of writing, a pre-nup isn't legally binding in the UK, though more and more judges are referring to them when cases go to court, and upholding what was originally agreed.

Good legal advice isn't cheap, but there are cost-effective ways to get a fair result without giving all your life savings to lawyers. Increasing numbers of divorcing couples are using **mediation services** as an alternative to full-on 'my solicitor writes longer letters than yours' tactics. In these situations, the mediator is an impartial qualified expert who makes suggestions, based on the couple's circumstances, as to how the matter could be resolved positively. A mediator also ensures that both parties remain as calm as possible during the process. It's a cheaper and more constructive way to find a resolution, but it does depend on the relationship you have with your soon-to-be ex.

Top Tip: If you're living together but not married, the law treats you *as two separate individuals with no financial responsibility to each other.* This is why you're not automatically entitled to anything and why it's important to agree upfront the 'what if' scenario should the worst happen. You can get a solicitor to write you a **Co-habitation Agreement**, which is like a pre-nup but for people who aren't getting married, outlining who gets what if you decide to go your separate ways. Just make sure that it's drawn up correctly and includes details of your financial situation and assets. Also make sure you've both received independent legal advice about what the contract you're entering into means.

Conclusion

Please don't be put off. Living together is great (most of the time) and *could* be a sensible option for those who just want to 'make sure' before they go down the marriage or civil partnership route.

I think what trips a lot of people up is that, these days, it's sometimes actually harder to disentangle yourself from a jointly owned property than it is to get a divorce. So, make no mistake; if you've got a joint mortgage and bought a property with someone then be aware of what's involved.

Get the paperwork in place to safeguard each other. That way, should it all go pear-shaped, at least money will be one less thing for you to argue about.

8.
Nightmare Neighbours

One of my good friends Nick, who is a lawyer, gave me probably the best bit of advice ever with regards to neighbour disputes. Bearing in mind he's one of the most highly qualified in his field in the country, whatever he says, I pay attention to. It probably best sums up everything you need to know on the subject:

> *"Don't fall out with your neighbours unless you absolutely, really have to. The only people who come out of it well are solicitors."*

He followed up this statement by explaining that, in the majority of cases, by the time a dispute has reached court, the costs are such that no one is going to come out of the situation financially better off. One of you might feel vindicated that your principles have been upheld. But if it has cost you thousands to get to that point, then that's scant comfort.

However, we are all pre-programmed to defend our properties if we perceive there is a threat. I suppose it all goes back to that old adage, "An Englishman's home is his castle." And of course, in some instances, where there is anti-social behaviour or damage to property, then there is absolutely no choice but to take action.

I write from bitter experience: I can tell you, it ain't fun. The anxiety when you bump into the individuals in question. The sleepless nights caused by toxic notes shoved through the door and heated arguments. The inevitable taking of sides by other neighbours.

Really, it's not cool. In my case, I was lucky as the law was pretty clear-cut and on my side, and once this had been clearly explained to the offending individuals by another neighbour who kindly agreed to mediate, the situation settled down and was resolved, although it took a long time before things were anywhere near amicable again.

There is another reason for not getting into a protracted and legal dispute with next door. When you come to sell your property, *by law you have to declare if you have taken any legal action against your neighbours or lodged any complaints against them with any local authority.* Any way you look at it, that's going to put a lot of buyers off. If you fib or withhold this information and it gets found out after the sale has completed, you can be sued by the new owners. Yes, really.

How you deal with neighbour disputes also depends on the sort of property you live in. It may seem counter-intuitive, but it's actually slightly easier to deal with problems if you live in a leasehold rather than a freehold property.

Why? Well, there will be a lease that sets out a list of stuff that you can and can't do. And most modern leases cover pretty much every eventuality. Which makes it slightly easier, because if the lease says that you can't cause noise or disturbance after 11pm at night, and yet at 3am there is a party upstairs that would rival the Notting Hill Carnival, then it's a pretty clear-cut case. You can go to the lessor (or freeholder) with your complaint and, providing you can evidence your claims, they will have to take action.

Now, same situation, but you live in a freehold semi-detached house. It's slightly trickier because there is no rulebook you can point to that says, "You can't play loud music in your garden at 1am on a Wednesday morning." So no matter how wild the party, you've got quite a battle on your hands.

Then you get into the reasons why people fall out in the first place. Usually, it's because someone is thoughtless, and their actions, unknowingly, impact others around them but they just blunder on regardless until such time as they are brought up short and made aware of their responsibilities. Then you have those who realise they are causing a nuisance, but frankly don't give a damn. These folk are harder to deal with, because their belligerence, even when the law is presented to them, means that there is just no reasoning with them.

So in this chapter we're going to take a look at the most common reasons for falling out with 'them next door', what your rights are, how best to manage a dispute yourself and when to call in the cavalry: the local council, a specialist solicitor or, if all else fails, the police.

1. Trees

A bit of greenery always improves a property's outlook. However, it's probably not a surprise that **trees** can create a lot of tension between neighbours – whether it's overhanging branches, encroaching roots or boughs blocking out light.

As with any issue, your ideal starting point is to try to approach the situation amicably. Before you speak with your neighbours, it's best to understand your legal rights as fully as possible. Not that you want to be quoting statute over the fence, but it helps to be aware of what you can reasonably request before you start.

So, looking at the common causes of arboricultural aggravation, let's start with **overhanging branches**. You are allowed to cut back any part of a tree (or any other bush or plant, for that matter) including roots, that encroaches on your boundary. Clearly it's much friendlier to politely mention first that you're doing this, rather than next door seeing you taking a pair of shears to their prized Magnolia.

The law states that the bits you chop off are actually still the property of your neighbour (because the tree, bush or plant is on their land) so you do have to return the lopped branches to them. Again, if you've told them that you plan to prune the shrub or tree in advance, it won't be a shock when you do this, which is why it's always best to have an open and friendly dialogue before you start. You may agree between you that they are happy for you to trim whatever is overhanging and remove the garden waste, or they may even offer to cut it back for you.

If it's a tree that's overhanging, always check first to make sure there isn't a **Tree Preservation Order** (TPO) in place. A TPO is put in place by a local council to protect a significant or rare type of tree. If a TPO is in place, then you can't carry out any work on the tree without the council's permission. Yep, that's right, even if the tree is a nuisance or causing damage, you can't do anything without consulting them first. You can find out if a tree is protected under a TPO by contacting your local council. Likewise, if you're in a conservation area other rules will apply, and before you do anything to a tree you'll need to check what you can and can't do.

If the overhanging branch belongs to an apple tree, for example, the fruit which grows on it is technically the property of your neighbour, even if the branch is growing over your fence or boundary. So, to the letter of the law, if you pick the fruit from the tree, that's scrumping. However, if the fruit *falls* onto your land, it's classed as abandoned, so feel free to use that in your jam or pie with a clean conscience.

Now, on to slightly more serious matters: **tree roots**. In certain circumstances, these can be a major cause of subsidence and create structural challenges for property if they grow under the foundations, so this is something that you can't afford to ignore. If you suspect your property is being damaged by tree roots, speak to your buildings insurer as soon as possible. They'll be able to guide you on the correct course of action.

If a tree grows on your neighbour's land but its roots encroach onto your property and undermine your foundations, you are legally entitled to have the roots removed up to their boundary line. However, you need to remember that, in doing so, you may actually damage the tree. In this situation, your best starting point is to find a qualified arboriculturist (tree surgeon) and ask them to investigate and provide a written report.

You can find a tree surgeon in your area by going to the Arboricultural Association website (**www.trees.org.uk**). Once they've submitted their findings, you can discuss the situation with next door. Strictly speaking your neighbour should pay to rectify the situation, but be prepared to compromise. You may, to keep relations peaceful, offer to pay half so that they agree to getting the work completed promptly before it causes more damage, or indeed you may just decide to pick up all the costs, so that there is no argument whether it can be done or not.

Whatever you decide to do, it's best that you document it in writing (email is fine), so that you and your neighbour both have a written record of what's been agreed. Keep your buildings insurers informed of your actions and be guided by them. They will be able to advise what costs are covered under your policy.

Alternatively, you may be concerned that a tree on a neighbour's land could fall on your house (not a great way to wake up in the middle of the night). Again, a tree is the responsibility of the owner of the land it's growing on. If a tree causes damage to your property, the owner of the tree is liable.

If there is clear evidence that your neighbour has been negligent – for example, if it's obvious that a tree is rotten or damaged in some way, and they've not taken any action but you think there is a risk to your property – it's best to raise this as soon as possible verbally but back it up in writing (or an email). Ask them to get an arborist to 'health check' the tree and provide you both with a report. Should this fall on deaf ears, speak to your local council. If there is a real risk and your neighbour doesn't want to do anything about it, the last resort is to get a court injunction if the tree is classed as dangerous, or you may find that your council will step in and take action, especially if there is a danger not just to your property but also to the public (e.g. if the tree is near a pavement).

A less hazardous issue, but still one that has the potential to cause confrontation, are **leaves**. For example, if your neighbour is complaining that the leaves that fall from your tree are blocking their guttering, what do you have to do? Well, the answer technically is not a lot – leaves aren't controllable so it's highly unlikely that you could be legally held responsible.

However, it all comes down to maintaining good relations, so whilst you don't *have* to do anything about it, if you are able to easily lop off an offending branch you may choose to do so as a gesture of goodwill.

Likewise, if trees in your garden have grown so high that they are interfering with electricity or phone cables, the utilities companies do have the right to cut them back. Other examples are where a tree overhangs a public footpath or blocks a right of access. In these instances, it's better that you manage the situation proactively before this becomes a problem, otherwise the council can deal with it for you then send you a bill. Prevention is better than cure, as they say.

A really good source of information about the do's and don'ts regarding trees is the Tree Advice Trust (**www.treecouncil.org.uk**). They even have a helpline, allowing you to talk through any issues with an expert. Failing that, you can find out more about tree disputes and who to talk to at your local council on the Communities and Local Government website (**www.communities.gov.uk**).

2. Fences and hedges

Now, before we get into the nitty-gritty, let's try to tackle the daddy of all gardening gripes: **leylandii**. So much has been written about this alleged horticultural thug over the years, and I've lost count of the amount of people that have asked my advice on it.

Bottom line: contrary to popular belief it is **not** illegal to plant leylandii in your garden and to grow it as a hedge. Properly trimmed and managed it's an effective way to create privacy, and it grows in most types of soil and conditions. Personally, I think it gets a worse rep than it deserves, but then again it's not something I've ever had to argue about with a neighbour.

Why does it cause problems then? Well, it grows very tall, very fast, would be the answer. And some people find that once it gets past a certain height, even though it's on a neighbour's land, it can create an issue in terms of blocking out light. Which is where the arguments tend to start.

Leylandii or otherwise, **hedge disputes** are up there with trees as a common cause of neighbour fallouts, often causing a very straightforward issue to escalate. But before your blood boils, take a step back and understand the basics, which hopefully will not only make you feel slightly better about the situation, but once informed, will also help you to avoid starting a conflict with next door.

It's worth bearing in mind that, at the time of writing, whilst there is legislation in place (it's actually part of the Anti-Social Behaviour Act, 2003) your neighbours can grow their hedge to any height they like, quite legally, *just because they can*. Yes, really. So pick your battles and approach with caution.

To have any grounds for complaint, the hedge in question must be as follows.

- evergreen (in other words, have green leaves on it all year around)
- more than 2m high
- and blocking out light or access to your property or causing you to suffer "lack of reasonable enjoyment".

If you can't tick any of those boxes, then frankly, it's not even worth talking about.

Lack of reasonable enjoyment is, as you can imagine, pretty tough to quantify, and you need to look at it from your neighbour's perspective as well here – did they grow the hedge to create some privacy from you, maybe?

Yes, I know, tough question, but you need to see it from all angles. To make sure that you have a case to discuss, consider contacting your local council and asking for further information so you understand if your predicament qualifies.

Once you've assessed the situation, approach your neighbour amicably. If things do escalate, you need to be able to prove that you have tried to do everything you can to sort it out yourself reasonably. So to start with, be as friendly as possible and, with a smile fixed on your face explain why the offending shrub is a problem, and ask if they would be able to cut it back. As a sweetener, you could offer to contribute towards that cost, or even pick up the bill yourself. They may not have even realised it was causing a problem, so be nice.

If the softly-softly approach doesn't work, write to them (email is fine or write a letter and keep a copy). Again, you need to be as polite as possible as you may need to prove later on that you've tried to resolve things amicably. As I often say, treat as you would be treated yourself.

If diplomacy fails, then you can make a formal complaint to the council. Clearly that's not going to be a quick process, as you are going to have to fill out a form setting out your side of the story in detail, and provide evidence of the steps you've already taken to get it sorted. That's why it's so important to keep copies of correspondence and, if you need to, keep a diary and take pictures to back up what you are saying.

You should send a copy of the form and evidence to your neighbours – if you don't, your council will, so you may as well just do it anyway. Be aware that you will have to pay a charge to your council for getting involved, and you will have to pay this regardless of whether or not your complaint is upheld.

Once the council has received your form and evidence, they will review it to make sure that it passes the legal tests to qualify as a case. If it does, they will contact your neighbour to ask for their side of the story, then send out a council officer to view the hedge and surrounding areas for themselves. They will check whose land the hedge is on, how far away it is from your windows and measure the hedge itself.

Once the officer has been round (and it may take three months to get this far), the council will weigh up all the evidence and decide if it needs to issue a remedial notice, setting out what your neighbours need to do about the hedge and when they need to do it by.

If all this seems overly complicated, well, I'm sorry, but them's the breaks. Which is why I said before, think long and hard before you start this off. Also, you'll have to declare the whole caper when you come to sell the property.

Fences have the potential to provoke just as much trouble as hedges, but for slightly different reasons.

You are allowed to install a 'barrier' up to 1m high if the wall or fence faces a road, or up to 2m high anywhere else (e.g. between you and your neighbour's garden) without planning permission, providing you erect it on your own boundary and don't encroach on your neighbour's property. If you want to build higher than your rights within permitted development, you need to seek the necessary consents. You can find out more about what you do and don't need permission for in Chapter 9, 'Adding Value' under 'Permitted Development and Planning Permission'.

Generally speaking, by law as a property owner you don't have to erect and maintain any type of 'barrier' if you don't want to (unless of course it's noted in your Title Deeds; have a read of them to check). Obviously, the majority of homeowners *do* decide to erect some kind of fence, hedge or trellis. And there are certain situations where you are required by law to create a barrier between your property and others – for example, if the house is on a street and it would be dangerous if you didn't, or to keep any animals you own on your land and stop them straying onto neighbouring property.

If you do decide to erect a fence or wall, then the most important thing to figure out is where your boundary line is. If you put it an *inch* over the boundary and on your neighbour's property, you're going to land yourself in all sorts of steaming doo-doo. Look on your Title Deeds before you start – you can download them from the Land Registry (**www.landregistry.gov.uk**). If it's not clear where your boundary is, then get professional advice from a solicitor or RICS surveyor. It may cost you, but better a few hundred pounds now than thousands and thousands on legal bills, court costs and therapy down the line. Check out the next section, 'Boundary Bother', for a bit more on this.

Another common flashpoint is the maintenance of *existing* walls and fences. There is a very widespread misconception that the ownership of a fence is determined by which way the fence posts face, in other words, if the posts face 'your side', your neighbour owns the fence. This isn't strictly true. The letter of the law states that the owner of the fence is the person on whose boundary the fence posts are. It doesn't matter which way they face.

Again, it's worth checking on your Title Deeds in case ownership of a fence or hedge is noted and you are responsible. This is exactly why it pays to understand more about boundaries and other legal responsibilities before you start picking a fight about it.

Legally, you are not obligated to repair or maintain a fence or wall even if it's on your land, but if it does cause injury to your neighbour or damage their property you would be liable. So, as with most things in life, prevention is better than cure. If, on the other hand, your neighbour's wooden fence is rotting and could cause injury to you or your family, in the first instance it's probably best to discuss it calmly and rationally to see what they may be prepared to do to repair it.

If you think that they haven't repaired it due to the costs involved, and it's bugging you that much, you might like to offer to contribute financially towards the work. After all, you can either spend a couple of hundred quid towards the costs of fence panels or spend thousands on getting a solicitor involved if it gets nasty. Which would you rather do? Exactly.

Sure, it may not be your fence but if it's causing you a problem, then it may be a quicker solution to write off a small amount of money to get it fixed and then move on with your life and keep next door on side. Of course, it's all going to depend on what you can agree with your neighbours, but if you present it tactfully and in a way that makes it a no-brainer for them, then all but the most antagonistic of individuals won't really be able to justify saying no.

However, the bottom line in all of this is that if your neighbour really doesn't want to repair or replace their own fence, *they don't have to and you can't make them.* The only thing you can do is erect your own fence on your own boundaries. Providing it's on your land and within permitted development rules or you have planning consent, then you can do what you like.

Within reason, of course.

3. Boundary Bother

Boundary disputes can cause untold anxiety and stress, in some cases over just a few inches' encroachment, and are one of the main causes of legal action between neighbours.

Your most useful ally is still pragmatism, because it's really, honestly, not worth spending thousands of pounds and months (if not years) of arguments and anxiety for something that, with a bit of common sense and compromise, can be resolved pretty amicably.

I spoke to another one of my legal eagle friends, who is a specialist in boundary disputes, and her advice was clear. Before taking on any boundary case, Kate always asks her prospective client:

> "*What have you done?*"

In other words, even though there may be a legal case for encroachment, depending on the actions of the 'aggrieved' before it got to the stage of instructing a solicitor, their behaviour or approach to the dispute may have prejudiced the case before it's even started.

The other thing Kate tells her clients is, "You have to come to court with clean hands." In other words, anything and everything you have done, said and written to your neighbour will be scrutinised. You need to be beyond reproach to even stand a chance. So think long and hard before you make rash decisions.

Quarrels over boundaries generally start either when there is an issue with whose fence, hedge or wall belongs to who because it needs maintenance or replacing, or when someone is trying to build up to a boundary line but the other party perceives that there has been encroachment (or breach) onto their boundary.

Every property does have precise, legal boundaries. These are invisible lines that separate your land from next door. However, what tends to confuse people is the fact that these aren't documented precisely in your Title Deeds. Your Title Deeds instead represent what's called the **general boundaries**. In the majority of cases, the most common example of general boundaries is a hedge – it delineates your garden from next door but is only a general indicator of where the line between the two is, because it's not precise to the millimetre.

Take a step back from all this for a moment, and consider what you are going to have to go through to establish your exact legal boundary, which is called **determining the boundary** (if you don't already have it documented).

You are going to need to get a chartered surveyor to review the land and complete a survey, check the deeds and plans for both properties and also refer to historical documents and aerial photographs. That's not going to be cheap.

Then, if you and your neighbour can't agree between yourselves, you'll have to go to court, where a judge will decide where the legal boundary is. This will then be documented via new plans, which need to be lodged with the Land Registry.

It may come down to a surveyor having to physically mark out the line on the ground between the two of you, and oversee a fence or wall being erected to ensure there are no further arguments.

Given that it's going to cost you the price of a very nice holiday to the Caribbean to sort out – plus all the time and hassle involved – I'd say your best bet is trying to resolve the issue between yourselves, if at all possible.

The best way to avoid all of this altogether is, of course, when you are in the stages of buying the property. *During the buying process, it's your solicitor's job to identify any potential boundary issues*, but it's up to you to be on the ball and make sure this happens.

Before you exchange, get your solicitor to send you an official copy of the Land Registry **Title Plan**. This will show the general boundaries (unless the current owner has established the legal boundaries previously). When you visit the property, take the Title Plan with you and compare it to what you can actually see. If you're concerned that, say, the wall between the properties looks like it may be in the wrong place, take photographs and ask your solicitor to speak with the vendor's solicitor before you go any further.

Remember, your solicitor is not going to see the physical property, so he's going to assume that the general boundaries as shown in the Title Deeds are where they should be. Make sure you get any discrepancies sorted *before* you exchange, or you are storing up problems for later.

If you didn't do this when you bought your property and are now finding yourself in a bit of a pickle, the RICS (**www.rics.org/uk**) do have a neighbour dispute service that provides access to a specialist panel of expert surveyors who can help you to mediate with your neighbour and (hopefully) avoid costly legal action. They also have a helpline where you can get 30 minutes' free advice from a specialist surveyor. Well worth the call.

A last word on this subject. If legal action is unavoidable, and you have an unblemished case which your solicitor believes may stand a chance, it's worth checking your **contents insurance** to see if you have **legal cover** on your policy. If it's included, ring your insurer, give them the heads up and see if you will be able to make a claim in respect of your legal fees. Whilst it won't save you the stress and sleepless nights, it may save you thousands of pounds, so it's worth a few minutes of your time to find out.

4. Noise Nuisance

Problems with **noise** take many forms – music and televisions turned up too loud, dogs barking, children screaming and burglar alarms. All can be responsible for interrupting your peace and quiet. Ongoing issues with noise are a common source of stress and can cause untold upset between neighbours, as well as having a negative effect on your health and general enjoyment of your home.

However, there is an element of needing to go into situations with one's eyes open. If you buy a property near a pub, and then decide subsequently that you don't particularly care for the decibel count at kicking-out time when the inebriated are singing their way home, it would be very difficult to make a claim against the establishment in question on the grounds that, frankly, the pub was there when you purchased the property. So, caveat emptor; this is why it's so crucial to do your research into an area *before* you buy.

Also, unless you ask the vendor specifically if they have ever had a noise problem before you exchange, it's going to be mighty difficult to prove that the seller knew when they sold the property that there was an issue but withheld the information. So make sure your solicitor is explicit in his enquiries to the other side during the conveyancing process.

It really is important to retain a sense of perspective though. If it's a one-off, and your neighbours have given you advance notice that they are having a birthday party that might 'go on a bit late', to be fair, you have been warned. Of course, if they are still spinning the decks at 4am, you're absolutely within your rights to knock on the door and politely ask them to turn it down a bit. No one is going to think that's unreasonable. It's all about give and take; one soiree that goes on until the early hours doesn't constitute an ongoing noise pollution issue. So, grit your teeth, pop in the earplugs and wave nicely when you see them the next time.

Repeat offenders, on the other hand, need to be dealt with differently. And in that respect the law is on your side. But even then, before you start on that particular path, it goes without saying that it's still best to try and deal with things amicably first. Something that I've found very effective is to ask the noisy neighbour into your property so that they can hear what *you* hear. Often, they're not aware of what's audible through the walls, and have no idea how much they're disturbing you. It's worth giving them the benefit of the doubt first time round. If that approach doesn't work – and sometimes it doesn't – then it's time to start looking into the more official channels.

If your neighbours are **tenants**, then your first point of recourse is to the landlord or letting agency. You will need to provide evidence of your complaints, so keep a diary of all disturbances, and if you can, record the noise so that you can prove exactly how much of a nuisance they are being. In other words, make your problem someone else's problem. Give the landlord or letting agency a reasonable amount of time, say a week, to contact the tenants and deal with the problem. If they don't, contact your local council.

If your neighbours **own their property**, then it's a slightly different process, but not much. Keep a diary note of all disturbances with the date and time and how long the noise occurred for. Record it, if you are able, in case you later need to prove the level of noise that you could hear. Write to your neighbours (email or letter is fine, just make sure you keep a copy) and outline the problem. Give them a week to rectify their behaviour, and let them know that you are recording and logging any disturbances to use as evidence should you have to start proceedings against them. That way, you've invited them for a drink at the last chance saloon. If they don't take up the offer, you can at least prove that you tried to settle the matter amicably. Make sure your letter is polite and cannot be construed as threatening or aggressive – you need to retain the moral high ground on this one.

If the behaviour continues, then your next port of call is your local **Environmental Health Office**. Give them a ring and explain the problems that you are facing, that you have an issue log and recordings of the noise and that although you have tried to settle the situation amicably, your neighbours are ignoring you. The Environmental Health Office has to investigate your complaint, and if the disturbance is ongoing then chances are they will send an officer out to listen and assess the noise at different times of the day on multiple visits. The Environmental Health Office can also lend you noise-monitoring equipment to help you gather evidence, as well as imposing an on-the-spot fine, issuing a noise abatement notice and instigating a prosecution.

A few other things to remember:

- Noisy children aren't in themselves considered a 'nuisance' unless the situation involves anti-social behaviour, e.g. aggression towards you and your property. If this occurs, then see section 9 in this chapter, 'When to call the police'.

- If the Environmental Health Office does decide someone is causing a statutory noise nuisance and issues a noise abatement order, and this is breached, the offenders can be fined up to £5,000. So even if an order is issued, it's important to still keep your issues log up-to-date and record any incidents.

- Noise isn't just loud music. If your neighbour has a penchant for completing deafening DIY tasks (that aren't emergency repairs) at unreasonable hours, that would constitute a nuisance.

- Noise disturbance is noise disturbance, whether it's at midday or midnight. If you can hear it, that's all that counts. There are no noise level restrictions set in law in terms of when loud music can and can't be played.

- It is very difficult to bring a complaint about being able to hear washing machines or hoovers, footsteps, shouting, slamming doors, babies crying, children playing or any other type of 'general living noise'. You will need to prove that the noise is unreasonable and could be contained, which in most cases you won't be able to.

• Under no circumstances would I recommend you start a 'war of noise'. You can leave yourself wide open to all of the above action if your neighbours decide to turn the tables and accuse you of anti-social behaviour. All you are going to do is just make an already bad (and loud) situation worse.

5. Parking

Another source of disagreements is car parking. It tends to bring out the territorial streak in even the most peace-loving citizen, especially in areas where there aren't enough roads without double yellow lines to go around.

If you have your own private driveway, the only thing you need to worry about is if someone parks across your drive and effectively blocks your entrance or exit. If they do, it's pretty easy really: just call the police (on 101 *not* 999) and give them the car registration number and they will deal with the problem on your behalf. Take a picture and keep it for your records should the offender move their vehicle before the police arrive as it may be required for evidence. A snotty note on the windscreen telling the driver they are inconsiderate, have breached the Highway Code and that you've informed the police is optional (but quite satisfying).

If you have a shared drive, but next door are continually parking in such a way as to block you in or make it difficult for you to park your car, then you need to refer to your deeds to see where the boundaries are on the driveway (see the section earlier called

'Boundary Bother' for more information). This should be pretty clear, and a quick (but friendly) chat to remind them that you need to be able to park there as well, together with a copy of the Title Plan to show them where they should be parking, ought to solve the problem.

If you don't have your own driveway or allocated parking space and have to park on the street, things are slightly different. Contrary to popular belief, you don't have the right to park directly outside your property. That's purely a courtesy observed in many a nice neighbourhood, but you can't get upset if you can't park outside your front gate. Providing that no part of the Highway Code is being contravened – i.e. the car is roadworthy, taxed and isn't parked on double yellows, a red route or in a permit holder's space – people can park wherever they want.

Bearing that in mind, don't start an argument that would make the Battle of Hastings look like a vicar's tea party. If you happen to see your neighbour at some point, you could (having softened them up with a bit of small talk) explain that if it's OK with them you'd really like to park outside your own house. But be careful how you go about it. You can't demand the right to do it, so you're only going to get your own way by being charming.

As my mother always says, "You get much further in this world by being nice."

6. Dogs

Now, before we get started on this particular topic, I must say that I am an ardent animal lover, and desperate for a dog of my own. I have to say this, because otherwise what I'm about to write next could be misconstrued as the rantings of an anti-canine activist, and that's not the case.

Dogs aren't everyone's cup of tea, and an out-of-control pooch can cause mayhem, even if it is cute and just being a bit mischievous by crawling under the fence and digging up your neighbour's flower beds. And if we're talking about a dangerous dog next door, we're into a whole different league of problems.

The most common issue with a dog in a neighbouring property is noise. Even the most adorable mutt will bark if left alone for a long period of time. Now the owner won't necessarily be aware of their furry best friend's separation anxiety, because they aren't there to witness it. However, you will clearly be very conscious of the howling, whining and woofing that's going on, so it's up to you to put it very firmly on their radar. As with other types of noise disturbance, keep a diary of all the occurrences and record the noise so that you have evidence should you need to take the matter further. But in the first instance, it's probably a good idea to try to calmly speak to the owner and explain that you are worried about the dog's welfare because it barks all the time. If you say it with enough concern you might be able to convince them that you too are an animal lover (even if you're not) and that will get them on your side, before you then say, "And of course, the barking is quite noisy and we do hear it a lot, so it is a bit of a nuisance."

The likelihood is that they will get the hint.

If they don't, and Fido keeps on bellowing, follow it up with a polite letter; email is fine, just make sure you keep copies for further evidence if required. If that fails, then you'll need to take more official action. Have a read of Section 4, 'Noise Nuisance' for more information about getting the local Environmental Health Office involved.

However, if the hound next door is aggressive – in other words if you are afraid that the dog may bite you or your family – then under the Dangerous Dogs Act you can legally take action to prevent being attacked.

The Dangerous Dogs Act now applies to *all* dogs, not just the previously 'banned breeds' such as pit bull terriers and the like. So if you think you might get a nasty nip from Tinkerbell the Jack Russell next door, you have just the same rights as if she were a naffing great Rottweiler.

The new rules make it illegal for any dog to be 'out of control', bite or attack someone. If you are concerned about the behaviour of a dog, particularly if you have small children who are playing in your garden with a snarling beast next door, the law is on your side.

It's also worth knowing that the law now covers dog attacks on private property. So if you get chomped (or worse) by next door's hound in your own garden, for example if your neighbour's dog escaped, you would have grounds for action. In the event of an attack the owner is highly likely to be prosecuted, as it constitutes negligence on their part to keep their animal under control.

If you are concerned about your own or your family's safety because of a dog next door, then call the police (on 101 rather than 999) or the RSPCA and report your neighbours. Not only is it the safest thing to do for yourself, but the poor animal may be suffering or being abused, which is probably what is making it aggressive. If the RSPCA find that the dog is dangerous, anti-social or mistreated, they will remove it. But the sooner you get the wheels in motion, the better for everyone involved.

Remember, you are protecting yourself, your family *and* doing what's right for the canine in question, so don't feel guilty about it. It's not your fault and it probably isn't the dog's fault either; the only person who can be blamed is the irresponsible owner.

Shame you can't put *them* in a cage with a muzzle on, eh?

7. Disputes when you live in a leasehold property

As mentioned earlier, if you live in a leasehold property and your neighbours misbehave (or if indeed you do) then things are a whole heap more clear-cut than if you reside in a freehold property. Why? Because your lease is pretty much the rulebook for do's and don'ts and, by virtue of the nature that you and everyone else bought a leasehold property, you're all bound by the same rules. Which means it's a lot easier if someone doesn't play ball.

Basically, as a leaseholder (whether or not you have a share of the freehold) you all have a responsibility to abide by your responsibilities as a **Lessee**. And that gives you a fair degree of protection because if your neighbours do something they shouldn't, rather than relying on the Environmental Health Office or other legislation to get things sorted out, you have an immediate course of action: refer to the lease. So, if someone is playing their music very loudly late at night and the lease forbids such activities, it's easy; your neighbour is breaching their lease. End of. Or, if for example you are not allowed to hang your washing out on your balcony or patio but your neighbour does it anyway – boom, they are contravening the lease and there is nothing they can do to defend themselves.

The remedy for these issues depends on your individual set up. If you have a Residents' Association, for example, you can complain to them and ask that the Chairperson approaches the culprit to point out they are in breach of their agreement and therefore need to modify their behaviour. This normally works because the type of person who tends to take on the responsibility of being Chair of a Residents' Association is rarely someone to be messed with.

If you don't have a Residents' Association, it would be sensible to approach the managing agent for the property, and explain the issue to them so that they can take appropriate action.

If this kind of intervention doesn't work (and sometimes it doesn't), the next step is to up the ante and write to the **Freeholder** (sometimes referred to as the **Landlord**) with evidence of your concerns and an outline of the problem. The Freeholder will then have to investigate the problem under their obligations in the lease. If there is a clear breach, they must enforce the lease on the leaseholder. This can be achieved by the threat of legal action, which if undertaken could result in a Leasehold Tribunal hearing, or worse still, a court order which may see fines applied and damages awarded against the guilty party. The ultimate sanction is that the Lease can be forfeited and the ownership of the property of the offender be returned to the Freeholder. However, such an outcome is rare. Normally the threat of legal action or Tribunal is enough to get even the most difficult of individuals back in line.

As with every other issue that could possibly arise when you have neighbours, the best course of action is always to take the most diplomatic route first. Talk to the Chair of your Residents' Association and see if they can mediate on your behalf or suggest a way to approach the situation that will mean the next encounter with the guilty party won't be quite so awkward. When neighbours fall out in leasehold communities it can affect everyone as there is always an inevitable taking of sides, so it's likely that other people in your apartment block or complex will want the situation resolved as quickly and amicably as you do.

8. Mediation services and when to call a solicitor

When you're dealing with a problem that's right on your doorstep that interferes with your daily life, matters can, and usually do, escalate very quickly. Whilst no one is going to be able to wave a magic wand, it is certainly worth taking a step back from the brink and talking to an expert who can give you a pragmatic view before the situation descends to the point of no return.

Many solicitors are happy to provide a free half an hour consultation or informal chat over the phone to discuss your problem. Contrary to popular belief, they aren't just in it for the fees, and the good ones will probably advise you that it's not worth getting them involved, then explain to you how to sort it out yourself without the need for formal legal intervention. To find yourself a specialist litigation solicitor in your area, go to the Law Society website (**www.lawsociety.org.uk**) and contact one of their members. Remember, *the sooner you get legal advice, the sooner you can make sure that you don't do anything to damage your case in the long run.*

Of course, if the situation is complex, you might want to consider instructing a solicitor, but in an **advisory capacity** only. That means that they don't start writing letters on your behalf to your neighbour (something you would need to disclose when you sold the property), but instead work with you in the background, acting as a sounding board and providing their expertise. You can quite legitimately use a solicitor for guidance on your rights and how best to approach your neighbour and resolve a dispute yourself, which can help you to manage the situation in a way which keeps things as amicable as possible.

The other thing that all solicitors are advocates for is **Alternative Dispute Resolution** services, or **mediation**. This isn't just due to a change in the law, but because they genuinely do see the value in a structured and facilitated meeting between the two parties where disputes can be discussed calmly and rationally, in a neutral environment where practical solutions can be found. This is a much cheaper approach and probably the best route you can go down because it helps to preserve relationships between neighbours as it avoids further legal action (if you can come to an agreement).

For mediation to work, though, both parties have to sign up to it and understand the process. You'll need to use a qualified mediator who you jointly appoint; again, to find one in your area, check out the Law Society website.

It won't work for everyone, but before you spend all that money on legal fees it may just be worth a go.

9. When to call the police

This is pretty self-explanatory, but I wanted to include a couple of lines on this because it's important.

If at any time during a confrontation with a neighbour you feel physically or verbally threatened, or suffer from verbal or physical harassment due to your sexuality, religion or ethnic background, then report it to the police.

That sort of behaviour is not acceptable – you shouldn't have to put up with it and *you don't have to*. Disputes can get out of hand, especially if you are both seeing red with no one to mediate, but the last thing you want is to put yourself or your loved ones in danger. Get yourself out of the way inside your property and lock the doors and windows until the police arrive.

Likewise, if your neighbour is in breach of the peace – being disorderly in the street, making a lot of noise in their garden or outside your property, or if they start to damage your home, for example by throwing a brick through your window, or try to force entry – then that's one for the boys and girls in blue as well.

In these instances, dial 999, report the incident and, once you are safe in your property with all doors and windows locked, try filming the incident if you can (on your phone is fine) as you may need this (together with your witness statement) as evidence should the police decide to prosecute.

10. What you have to declare by law when you move

Inevitably, regardless of whether a situation with your neighbours is resolved or not, you *will* eventually want to move house. Now, I know you won't thank me for telling you this, but if you have had a dispute with your neighbours that involved legal action or the involvement of the local authorities – e.g. the Environmental Health Office – or if the police have been called at any time due to your neighbour's behaviour, you will have to declare it to your prospective buyer as part of the conveyancing process.

Yes, I know you're thinking, "Why? Because if I do as she's saying, I will never sell my house!" Well, the answer is pretty simple. You have a legal responsibility to correctly and fully complete your

Property Information Form (or TA6 to give it its proper name) which, amongst other things, asks you if you have had any disputes with your neighbours. So unless you decide to tell a little (not-so-white) lie, or in fact, a bit of a whopper, you're going to have to come clean.

What if you do decide to fib? How is your buyer going to find out? And what happens then? Well, if your buyer did happen to speak to one of the other residents in the street once the sale had completed and found out that the next door neighbours have long been a complete nightmare with a full matching set of ASBOs and you didn't declare it, they can sue you for damages due to loss of value of the property. The law states that if you provide false information or purposefully omit information on your Property Information Form, you are liable to face court action if, later on down the line, it's proven that the information you supplied was incorrect or inaccurate. So that's why it's better to come clean in the first place. If you don't, it could well come back to bite you on the arse.

There are some situations where it's *not* necessary to mention an issue that's come up with a neighbour. So if, perhaps, next door went through a phase of having noisy, late-night gatherings but (following a corrective chat) this is now in the past, or if you had a problem with next door's dog barking but you've settled it amicably and everything is now under control, it's likely that you wouldn't need to declare it as an issue. And clearly, if the offenders have moved on, the problem has effectively gone away, so you probably don't need to worry about disclosing that either. But do check with your solicitor first. You're paying them to protect your best interests, so *tell the truth and let the experts advise you on what and how you should disclose relevant information.*

Conclusion

There are few winners in disputes with neighbours. The time, energy, anxiety and financial implications are rarely worth it, and whilst you may score a moral victory by confirming that a fence is an inch over your boundary, in the grand scheme of things, if you then have to declare that you've had an issue when you come to sell and have to slash the price of your property to move on, you have to ask yourself, *was it worth it?*

In some cases it can be unavoidable: with genuinely anti-social behaviour, you need to stick to your guns and take whatever action is necessary to protect your home and your family. There is no question at all that this kind of behaviour is not acceptable, and you shouldn't have to put up with it.

But if the situation is less serious, such as the odd burst of loud music or late-night party, it's important to step back and think about the bigger picture. Because let's face it, for the grief and aggro it's going to cause in terms of seeing that person in the street or on the stairs every day, do you really want to start creating a difficult situation on your own doorstep? Precisely.

Besides, you know what they say about 'love thy neighbour', don't you…

9.
Adding Value

If I had a pound for every time someone asked me, "What's the best way to add value to my property?" I would be a rich woman indeed. The answer, sadly, isn't straightforward. It depends on so many factors: where you live, what type of property you have, the size of your budget, how long you intend to stay there and what it's worth before you undertake any refurbishments.

So I guess what I'm saying is: there isn't a 'one size fits all' answer.

Before you do anything it's good to question your own motivation for starting any major works. Apart from the cost of undertaking a big project, make no mistake, living in a place whilst you're doing it up is no fun. It's a bit like camping but slightly less glamorous. Plus you can't go home and have a hot shower if you don't like it, because chances are you ripped that out, along with the tiling in the bathroom and that's the next job on your list. Ask me how I know this.

Your first consideration should be your **long-term plans** for your property. Have you just bought what you consider to be your 'forever home' and are going to be there for ten, fifteen or twenty years? Or is this a pad that you will probably outgrow in three to five years, at which point you'll want to move up the ladder?

If you are going to be in your current abode for the long haul, say ten years or more, then it's best to give priority to improvements that will enhance your lifestyle *first*, then what will add value as a very close second. Because if you're going to be living with whatever changes you make for a long time and spending your hard-earned money on the place, you need to enjoy the benefits from that investment every day.

For example, swimming pools and hot tubs can be quite divisive – some buyers baulk at the cleaning and upkeep costs, for others the idea of a dip in your own private pool is irresistible. But if you and your family will regularly use a hot tub and are going to be there for many years, then you'll get your money's worth long before you come to sell.

Of course, it's absolutely the right thing to have an eye on the future and incorporate things that will add value and desirability, but that's not the number one priority if you're going to be living there for a long time. At the end of the day, unless you move every year your house is a home first, an investment second. You have to live in and love the place, which is hard to do if you've ripped all the heart, soul and character out.

However, if you *are* only going to be living somewhere for just a few years, I would recommend a slightly different approach. Whilst you've still got to live in the property, you may want to be a little more commercially-minded when it comes to making improvements: using neutral colours for décor and flooring, for instance, and speccing out your kitchen and bathroom with future buyers very much in mind.

Any alterations also need to be sympathetic to the type of property. For example, if you live in a period cottage, a sleek, contemporary kitchen may look out of place unless you mix in clever elements such as exposed brick or beams to allow for continuity with the rest of the house. Conversely a modern, city-centre apartment might not suit a Victorian-style slipper bath, unless you then work the rest of your interior design scheme to include other vintage pieces alongside the more *avant-garde* to create an eclectic look. Rather the way that those clever folk at Hotel du Vin do (I will admit to being an HdV fiend and love the way their designers juggle contemporary with antique to create their beautiful interiors).

Then there are things that add desirability but not necessarily additional value.

A beautiful garden that you've toiled hard over will never fail to impress, and certainly will enhance a property's 'kerb appeal', but it won't add thousands to the value of your house. However, the *extent* of a garden does have a bearing on what a property is worth. Those with a bigger plot would be able to ask for a bit more when they put their property on the market. It's one of those cases where size *does* indeed matter.

Another highly desirable element is storage. Built-in wardrobes need to be tastefully done – and one woman's heaven of a closet with sliding mirrored doors is another's hell, so be careful – but storage space throughout a property, with plenty of concealed cupboards under the stairs, in hallways, kitchens and utility rooms is extremely useful and desirable. It means that when you do come to sell, people looking at your property won't be walking around thinking, "Where on earth do I hide the hoover/kids' toys/ironing board?", especially in smaller properties and apartments where space is at a premium. And it doesn't have to cost a fortune either.

If you've bought a property with the intention of redeveloping and then selling it on for a profit, I highly recommend you invite the agent you bought it through round for a cuppa. Ask them what improvements they feel would add value to the place and increase the 'desirability factor'. You'd be amazed at the amount of good agents that will do this for you, so just ask. They're keen because chances are, you're likely to go back to them to sell the place when the time comes. For half an hour of their time they can help you to consider changes that will create a positive impact and make your home appealing to buyers rather than being lumbered with a property that will be hard to shift. It's a a win-win for everybody so take advantage of their knowledge (and the fact it comes for free).

Whatever you do, don't assume you know what other buyers in your area will want without doing a *lot* of research (unless of course you redevelop properties for a living). Let me give you an example. I was speaking to a friend of mine the other day who is an estate agent; we were discussing a property he had recently taken onto his books. It was in a very 'good' road, on a big plot, and was a nice 1930s 'Arts and Crafts'-style four-bedroom family home that had been redeveloped by the current owners not so long ago.

I looked at the photos. High-quality kitchen – check. Period details refurbished – check. South-facing garden and lots of internal light – check. Tasteful décor – check. I couldn't work out what the problem was. Until I looked at the floor plan.

The property had four bedrooms, and each one had an en-suite shower room. Not a huge problem, in itself, but the owner had then added another family bathroom upstairs because there wasn't a bath in any of the en-suites, and he thought it was important to make sure any potential owners could have a good wallow. He'd also shoehorned in *another* shower room and WC on the ground floor, just in case future occupiers had elderly guests who couldn't navigate stairs. This had compromised the layout and size of all the other rooms throughout the property.

The agent said the owner had thought that by adding extra bathrooms he was adding thousands to the value of his property. The 'refinements' had been made with the best of intentions and much consideration *but* were scaring buyers away.

This beautiful home had been on the market for nearly three years. Not the quick refurb-and-return they had in mind, that's for sure. And it was a real shame, because the finish of the works were of a very good standard. But buyers just couldn't get past the sheer number of toilets they'd have to clean and the rather quirky layout that having six bathrooms had created. Not to mention the potential bleach bill.

Here endeth the lesson. What *you* think will add value may not be everyone's cup of tea.

Financially, you need to be absolutely sure that any money you invest in order to add value will do exactly that. Many people think that by spending £30,000 on their kitchen – with cupboard doors painted in Farrow & Ball, special worktops made from granite mined from the foothills of the Andes, and appliances from the Starship Enterprise – will add, say, £40,000 to the value of their property.

In all but a few cases, they're wrong.

Sure, they will have added *something* to the value, but it's highly unlikely they'll recover their total investment unless they've actually extended a room to create a lot more space, or improved the layout.

So, in this chapter I'm going to take you through the do's and don'ts of what improvements you can make to a property without planning permission, along with what does add value and what really doesn't. And I recommend you read this pretty thoroughly before you even think about knocking that wall through in your lounge.

1. *Permitted development and planning permission*

Before you do anything, you need to know if you have to apply for planning permission. For those who breach the rules, hefty fines and the threat of having to pull down your grand design await. It's not worth breaking ground (or plaster) until you know exactly where you stand on this one.

The good news is that, in many areas, the majority of improvements can be made under what's called **permitted development**. That means providing you follow the regulations to the letter, you don't need planning permission – though you are likely to still need **building regulations**, depending on what you're doing.

Permitted development rights were first introduced in 1948, believe it or not, as part of a raft of legislation introduced by the Labour government who, at the time, were looking to get the country back on its feet after the Second World War and wanted to help those who were trying to renovate properties.

Unsurprisingly, legislation has moved on a lot since then and permitted development rights are constantly being reviewed and updated, with the latest amendments in 2014. The more recent changes have allowed homeowners to make large alterations to their property without planning permission. Given the complexity of planning law, this has made a lot of people's lives a lot easier. It's also cut down the burden on the poor folk in the local planning offices. Instead of having to wade through countless applications for loft conversions, they can now focus on the more complex cases where their skills are really required.

That's the good news. The potentially not-so-great news is that permitted development rights vary depending on where you live.

If your property is in an area called **designated land**, which includes National Parks and the Broads, Areas of Outstanding Natural Beauty, Conservation Areas and World Heritage Sites, your permitted development rights are likely to be reduced, or even removed completely. In which case you need to carefully check what you can and can't do. Likewise, if you own a listed building, whilst you will still have permitted development rights, you will also need **Listed Building Consent**, so there will still be paperwork to complete.

It's also worth bearing in mind that permitted development rights are available for houses but *not* apartments. So if you own a flat and the loft space above it, for example, you may want to convert the loft into another bedroom. Now, if you lived in a house, you'd probably be able to do that under permitted development. But as it's an apartment you won't be able to and you'll have to apply for planning consent. If you live in a leasehold property or your home is held as a freehold with **covenants**, you need to check your deeds or lease to see what you can or can't do. Again, research thoroughly before you proceed.

All right, so now we've got that bit out the way, I'll give you the heads up on what you can do under permitted development regulations.

The main elements covered under permitted development (providing you live in a property which qualifies) are here, but this list isn't exhaustive and I don't have the space to go into a lot of detail on each. So, I'd strongly advise that you take a look at the Planning Portal (**www.planningportal.gov.uk**) to find out more. As a rule of thumb, you can usually extend your home by about the space of a double garage, but of course this depends on the original size of your house to start with. If an extension has already been made to the property, you can't extend again under permitted development and will need planning consent for any further additional works.

Don't forget, if you live in a designated area, listed building, leasehold property or your house is held as freehold with covenants, you will need to check as your permitted development rights will *be restricted.*

- **Internal re-modelling**: In other words the moving of walls to change the internal layout of the property. Don't forget to check if it's a load-bearing wall, in which case you'll need expert guidance and building regulations on things like structural and electrical works.

- **Doors and windows**: Pretty straightforward, you can change/upgrade your doors and windows in most cases without applying for planning permission. However, installing bay windows (rather than replacing existing ones) does count as extending, for which you need to check if you qualify for permitted development or have to apply for consent.

- **Loft conversions**: Not only can you convert loft space into living space, you can install a staircase and dormer windows all without planning consent, providing you follow the rules. Remember, dormer windows don't require permission, provided they are no higher than the roof itself or extend further forward on the roof plane than the principal elevation.

- **Using attached buildings e.g. integral garages**, **to convert into living space**: Pretty straightforward, but one important thing to consider. You must consult the original planning permission for the garage to check for any restrictive conditions. If the original planning says it must be used as a garage, then you will need to get planning permission before converting it into living space.

- **Single storey extensions and conservatories**: These are subject to size restrictions, based on the type and overall area of the original house. Also, the extension must not sit forward of the principal elevation of the property and should be built of similar materials to the original building. But if you tick all the boxes correctly, you can extend under permitted development without the need for consent.

• **Roof windows** (also called roof lights): All good, providing they don't protrude more than 150mm beyond the plane of the roof slope. If you're installing them into the side of your roof, then you have to use obscured glass and they must either be non-opening or more than 1.7m above floor level.

• **Double height extensions**: You can build a two-storey extension under permitted development providing it's at the rear of the building and not exceeding 3m in depth or within 7m of the rear boundary. There are also regulations around the type of glass and glazing you're allowed to use.

• **Working from home**: You can work from home without planning permission, so if you have a study and tap away on your laptop all day, that's fine. However, if you work from home and your occupation changes the nature of the building – for example, if you have converted your spare bedroom into a hair salon and have a constant stream of customers and van deliveries, as well as employees that are based there, you will need planning permission.

• **Sheds and outbuildings**: It's OK to build them, but you need to be mindful that when you combine all of your buildings and enclosures (so your house, garage, sheds and outbuildings) they must all add up to no more than 50% of the coverage of the plot. Once they go over that, you need planning permission.

• **Knocking two properties into one**: A house that has been converted into two flats can be returned to its original state as one property under permitted development. But...it doesn't work the other way around. If you want to convert a house into two apartments, you'll need to get consent. Likewise, you can knock two semi-detached houses together to create one house under permitted development, which is a great way of extending if next door comes up for sale and you don't want to move.

- **Porches**: You can add a small porch to your property without seeking planning permission, providing it's no bigger than 3m^2 and no higher than 3m. But that should be big enough for your coats and wellies.

- **Decking and patios**: Go right ahead, no planning permission is needed for these, providing that the height of your decking is no more than 300mm and together with any other extensions or outbuildings (such as your shed or garage) it doesn't cover more than 50% of your garden.

- **Swimming pools**: It's OK to install a swimming pool or hot tub under permitted development rules, but only up to a certain size. You need to apply the same calculation as you would for sheds and garages. Add up the total area of the main property, any outbuildings, sheds and garages as well as the swimming pool/hot tub, and providing everything is under 50% or less of the size of the plot, you're all good to go.

- **Vehicular access**: You can create a new entrance to your driveway or property under permitted development providing it's on an unclassified road. So not straight onto the M1 or M25 then. If you do live on a classified road, you'll need consent.

- **Cladding**: Should you choose to, you can clad your property unless you're in a designated area or listed building, in which case you need to seek the relevant permissions. Anywhere else, you just need to bear in mind that you need to use materials similar to those which were used in the property's original construction. As a side note, think very, very carefully before applying the pebbledash. Once it's on, it's a bugger to get off.

- **Solar panels**: Not everyone's cup of tea from an aesthetic perspective, but you're OK to install solar panels provided they don't overhang beyond 200mm of the edge of the roof and that the highest part of the panel doesn't protrude over the highest part of the roof.

- **Basements**: If you already have a basement, or even if you don't and want to create one, that's fine, you can convert or excavate under your property within permitted development, but you do need planning permission and building regulations approval for the engineering work involved. Be aware that basement conversions are a very expensive and complex operation, therefore not for the faint-hearted.

- **Agricultural land**: If you live in the country and are lucky enough to acquire a bit of your neighbouring farmer's plot, you are allowed to incorporate agricultural land into your own garden. However, there still needs to be a barrier between your 'domesticated' garden and the agronomic acreage, and you must use it to grow vegetables, flowers or trees. Or keep pigs. You can't use it for BBQs, as a kiddie's play area or build a tennis court on it. The local Planning Department won't take too kindly those sort of frolics.

- **Gates, walls and fences**: You're allowed to go up to 2m high where a wall or fence doesn't face a public highway (so down the side of your house between you and next door, for example) and up to 1m high where a wall or fence borders onto a road.

- **Parking**: It's always a good thing to add off-road parking if you can to your property, and under permitted development you're allowed to create a parking area between the front of your house and the road. If it's more than 5m² – two normal-sized parking spaces – the area *must* be covered in a porous material so that the surface water doesn't run off into the street. Gravel is a good and cheap option but if you decide to go for a tarmac or paved driveway, you need to make sure that the water has sufficient run off *within* your front garden, and not onto the road, which will cause surface water flooding.

Above all, if you're not sure, speak to your local **Planning Department**. Don't be scared, they're human too and generally will only be too pleased to help. They'd rather give you the right steer now to avoid issues with retrospective planning permission in the future. Also, there is a fantastic interactive tool on **www.planningportal.gov.uk** which gives you loads of detail about what you can and can't do (for property geeks like me that means hours of fun, I can tell you).

If you are going to sell your house once your works are complete, I'd advise you to get yourself a **Lawful Development Certificate** to prove that your project complies with permitted development regulations. These usually cost around £75, and will give your prospective buyer (and their solicitor) peace of mind that you've ticked all the right boxes. You can apply for one from your local council and it's a pretty straightforward process.

Should your dream involve works that aren't covered under permitted development, you'll have to call in the experts and apply for planning permission. For something more ambitious, you're going to need a **planning specialist** and an **architect** to help you prepare the necessary documentation for submission to the local Planning Department.

Your planning specialist should be a member of the Royal Town Planning Institute and your architect will need to be a member of the Royal Institute of British Architects. You can find members in your area by going to their websites at **www.architecture.com** and **www.rtpi.org.uk**.

I always recommend to people that if you are going to be undertaking significant works, do talk to your neighbours first. By law you actually have to serve them notice if the works you want to undertake are close to the boundary of their property – but I would strongly suggest that you warm them up to the idea first so they know what's coming. You'll be all excited at the prospect of a swish new kitchen and living area or a playroom downstairs where you can shut the door on your children and their toys, but the noise and disruption for anyone else in close proximity whilst your project is in progress shouldn't be underestimated.

Treat as you would be treated; let them know when the works will be starting, how long they will last for and don't use heavy machinery or undertake noisy jobs at weekends. Remember, generally speaking you should restrict works that could cause disturbance to neighbours to between 9am to 7pm Monday to Friday, 9am to 5pm on a Saturday and 10am to 2pm on a Sunday, although policies for each council vary in terms of what they will enforce, so do check.

If it were me, I wouldn't undertake any works that could cause noise pollution on a weekend unless it's an emergency.

Also, to avoid heated arguments (and worse) check to see if any of the works you are proposing will fall under the Party Wall Act as well. You'd be amazed at the amount of people who don't do this, just to get into real doo-doo later when their neighbours, rightly so, raise objections. You can find out more about party walls on **www.planningportal.gov.uk**.

If you approach your neighbours first and let them know what's going on and give them plenty of notice, you should be fine. It gives them a chance to get their head around it all and perhaps to book their holiday to coincide with some of the time you'll be working. Do give them regular updates, particularly if the project is running late. The more you talk and keep your neighbours informed, the less likely you are to have harsh words over the garden fence. A bottle of wine or a bunch of flowers every now and again helps to grease the wheels too, as does a 'thank you for being so understanding' card when it's all finished.

Yes, it's extra effort at a time when you're busy and stressed, but you will thank me for this later, I promise.

OK, so now you know what you can and can't do, let's take a look at the best ways to add value to your property...

2. Creating open plan living space

In many cases, additional space adds additional value. Factoid. But over the last few years, the thing that most buyers are looking for is flexible living space that is light, airy and above all, multi-functional.

You know the deal: a beautiful open plan kitchen, dining and living area that allows families to eat, play and relax together, as well as providing the backdrop for entertaining in style. If you throw in bi-fold doors, decking and some nice outdoor lighting, you're talking most people's nirvana. As another of my estate agent contacts, Phil says:

"Open plan kitchen-diners always sell houses. It's one of the main things my buyers ask for."

When you consider the way that a lot of the housing stock in the UK has been built, you're likely to be starting with a separate kitchen, living room and in some cases dining room. I haven't undertaken a formal research project on this one, but just from personal experience, how many people actually regularly use their separate dining room as a dining room these days? Honestly? Other than for Christmas lunch and the odd dinner party, it's probably the least-used room in the house.

Also, people just like hanging out in kitchens. It's true; I've lost count of the amount of times we've been to see friends or family for dinner or had them over to ours and all spent most of the evening sat at the breakfast bar or kitchen table, rather than gather in the lounge.

So, when we come to think about what turns buyers on, a ground floor layout that offers the most options in terms of how you can use the space and layout of a property is a hands-down winner for the majority. The good news is, these sorts of projects can normally be undertaken within permitted development.

If you're lucky enough to have the space in the property and wherewithal in your budget, it's also a good idea to either retain or create a separate 'formal' drawing room – some people might call it a snug, TV room or 'grown up lounge' where no little people are allowed. It's not a necessity but it's a very nice to have and will only add further appeal as well as value, providing you're not compromising on the layout of the rest of the house.

Remember, you're looking for a layout that *flows*, allows for maximum flexibility and, ideally, incorporates an outside entertaining zone (hence the decking and fancy outdoor pyrotechnics). Incorporate as much storage as you can, but also think about how others may use the space – so allow for lots of power sockets and keep at least two walls clear of any built-in storage or a fireplace to give potential buyers as many options as possible as to where to place their furniture.

3. Additional bedrooms

Another excellent way to increase the asking price of a property is by increasing the amount of bedrooms. Now, this advice does come with caveats, so before you start bashing walls around, digest this for a second.

For most people, a bedroom is defined as a room *upstairs*. That may sound patently obvious to some of you, but think this one through. If you sling another room on your layout downstairs that you can only access via your kitchen or lounge, a bedroom that does not make. You've just created a study or playroom that you can put a sofa bed in, and that's an entirely different proposition. It doesn't add as much value as a bedroom.

Also, the definition for the majority (including myself) of a bedroom is that you can actually get a bed (single or double), a wardrobe and a chest of drawers in it and still swing a cat. Anything less than that and what you've got yourself is a box-room. Which isn't exactly the same thing, and doesn't really add value either.

So what I'm saying here is, when you come to think about additional bedrooms, look carefully at what you want to achieve and consider the additional amount of space you'll create. There is no point, whatsoever at all, in spending all that money and going through all that grief to create another 'bedroom' that at best will take a cot, worst-case golf clubs and the stuff you can't be arsed to put in the loft, and then finding out that you've only increased the value of your abode by a couple of thousand pounds, if that.

I've seen people who have proudly trumpeted that they've added twenty grand to their home by adding another bedroom, but when I've taken a look at the place all they've done is take one good-sized boudoir, added a wall down the middle and juggled the access to create two miserly bedrooms that you would struggle to fit furniture into. That sort of thing doesn't add anything to the asking price at all. Actually, it can hamper your chances of selling.

The best gains in terms of adding bedrooms are, realistically, going up to four bedrooms. If you can take a two bed to a four bed, all with good-sized rooms and with a layout that flows well and feels light and airy, you're really in the money. Go over four bedrooms, though, and you're into quite a niche market. I'd suggest you save your money and spend it elsewhere. A well-planned four-bedroom house with generous sized rooms is a much better bet than a five-bedroom house that has a compromised layout, and will be a lot easier to sell when the time comes.

4. Loft conversions

Many families are in desperate need of more room but the cost and logistical nightmare of moving is just too great. What a lot of people don't realise is that, if you do the maths, you may be able to convert your loft to create that extra space you need – and for much less than the price of a bigger property (as well as Stamp Duty and all those other moving costs).

Some people see loft conversions as a major renovation that will be expensive and complicated, but if you get the right advice and builder on the job, it's normally pretty straightforward (compared to other major projects you could undertake). And it has the potential to add a lot of value – if done well. Better still, depending on where you live and your property, it's something you can do under permitted development without the faff of planning consent (see Section 1, 'Permitted development and planning permission' for more information).

However, you will still need building regulations for the structural elements, such as reinforcing the strength of the new floor, electrical works (plus plumbing works if you're adding an en-suite) and ensuring that the new stairs have been correctly designed and conform to fire and safety standards.

Now, the main thing to consider in terms of adding value is what you are actually going to do with the additional space you create. If you are able to build a spacious master bedroom with an en-suite, together with a permanent set of stairs, the value and desirability you'll add to the property will likely exceed the cost of the works. If you're just talking about boarding it out, adding a Velux window and using it as space to have your Scalextric or sewing kit out permanently – and still have to use a pull-down loft ladder to get to it – that's an entirely different proposition. Don't expect that sort of an exercise to have any positive impact on what the place is worth.

Before you get excited, the first thing you need to do is get yourself into your existing loft space armed with a torch and tape measure and see what space you've got to work with. You'll need headroom of at least 2.3m, so you need to check this one out sooner rather than later. Also, if you live in a terrace or semi-detached house, check to see if you have a **party wall agreement** with next door. If you do, you'll need to get their permission before you do anything else.

If you're planning on adding a bathroom upstairs, think about your current hot water and heating system and how it's going to cope. It's definitely worth speaking to your plumber or heating engineer to find out what your options are. Then you need to consider your windows. Can you get away with a couple of Velux units, or do you need dormers to make the room useable in terms of adding headroom?

There's a lot to think about, which is why I'd recommend speaking with specialist loft conversion companies who do this every day and can provide you with a detailed project plan and price. At the very least this will help you understand the costs and timescales involved before you start to rack up expensive bills. Get the professionals involved early on; do your research and find reputable companies in your area then ask three to quote for the works involved.

Sounds like a lot of work? Well, it will be a bit disruptive whilst the works are going on (let's not kid ourselves here), but for sheer bang for buck, in terms of creating useable living space you'd be hard pressed to beat it as a way to add value.

5. *Additional bathrooms*

Top of pretty much any buyer's requirement list these days is multiple bathrooms. If you've got two bedrooms, be it in an apartment or terrace, then one family bathroom and an en-suite is pretty much the standard in terms of top turn-ons. If you're looking at a family house, then an en-suite to the master bedroom together with a family bathroom and a downstairs cloakroom will help you add value *and* desirability.

It's mainly down to changes in the way we live over the last twenty years or so. Kids are staying at home for longer (because it's so expensive to get on the property ladder) so everyone needs a bit more shower/bath/mirror space to avoid heated arguments. For others who've spread their wings and bought their own place, the additional income that can be generated by letting out a spare room is great, but to really make it work you need a second bathroom to give everyone some privacy.

The good news as far as bathrooms are concerned is that you can add value and appeal without spending a fortune or, in most cases, needing planning permission (although you know what I'm going to say: depending on what you're thinking of doing, check first).

Bathrooms are one of my favourite things to work on because you can create something that looks pretty expensive on a very reasonable budget if you're clever about which elements you spend your money on. Good quality bathroom suites can be picked up from places like Wickes or B&Q for two or three hundred quid –

if you go for plain white, you can't go wrong – and you don't have to spend a fortune on tiles to get the 'luxe' look.

My top tip is to have a wander around a couple of high-end bathroom showrooms to get a feel for the sort of thing you like the look of. You'd be surprised at what you can achieve if you really put some thought and effort into sourcing your materials. For example, try your local tile warehouse to get the designer look without the designer price tag.

I always spend any spare money in the budget on great taps, because they really are the focal point and can lift bargain sanitary ware to something that looks a lot more expensive. I find a good quality heated towel rail is also important, as is the best shower head I can afford.

In terms of where you're going to put your additional bathroom, just be aware of the existing available space and layout. Avoid cramming an en-suite into the corner of an already snug bedroom just for the sake of it. That's not going to help you sell the place later on. However, if you do have a generously sized bedroom and have factored in your water supply plus waste and soil pipes, then go for it.

Make sure you have some means of ventilation – I know it's another obvious point but it's overlooked by so many people, who then end up with serious mould and damp issues. Best of all is a bathroom with a window *and* an extractor fan. If you can't create a window though, just make sure you install an extractor fan man enough for the job.

Whilst we're on this subject, there's no need to go mad and add in various accoutrements just because you think they will add additional value. Unless you plan on getting your money's worth by using them yourself, forget things like whirlpool baths, HD water-resistant built-in TVs or one of those body jet and steam showers. You aren't going to add significantly to the asking price by having a waterproof X-Box in your bathroom. Buyers generally want new, freshly tiled, nice quality and spacious bathrooms. By all means, install a vanity unit and nice big mirror, because those sorts of things are always useful and appealing, but I wouldn't go too much further.

Do spend money on getting a reputable company in to do the job for you (unless you're super handy yourself) as the quality of your grouting, the fact that the tiles are straight and your shower doesn't leak will count for a lot more than a self-flushing toilet.

Last word on this one: downstairs bathrooms in a conventional house can be quite divisive. It doesn't bother some people, but for others it's a complete no-no. If your only option to add another proper bathroom is downstairs, think carefully about what you're going to spend and be aware that you may not get all of your money back. Adding a downstairs cloakroom is a more cost-effective way to add real value and appeal.

6. Creating off-road parking

If you live in an area where outside space is at a premium and you have to park on a road, you'll know how frustrating it can be to have to lug your shopping/children/luggage from wherever you've been able to park to your front door. I've had to do it in the past when I lived in London, and it drove me mad.

I hated the fact that I couldn't park right outside my house. Because I was working long hours, plus resided in a part of town where most households had more than one car, I often had to park a long way away from where I lived and walk on dark and not very well lit roads late at night. Then there was the fact that I couldn't (and still can't) parallel park so scuffed my alloy wheels to oblivion, together with the extortionate cost of a resident's parking permit and the fines I managed to incur when I did, out of desperation, on many occasions just dump my car in whatever space I could find which happened to be encumbered with double yellow lines.

Therefore, it won't come as much of a surprise when I tell you that being able to create an off-road parking space for your property has the potential to add *a lot* of value as well as real desirability when you come to sell. Depending on how much you spend on the job – you can do it for two or three thousand pounds in the majority of cases – and where you live, adding one or even two parking spaces is probably the biggest return on investment you can make.

You also get the untold joy of knowing you can park right outside your front door. Forever.

In most of London and other big cities, an off-road parking space can add tens of thousands to the value of your property, and for very good reason. Now that really is bang for buck.

It's also not hugely complicated to sort out. So what do you need to bear in mind? Well, first off, take a look at how you're actually going to get your vehicle into the space you're going to create. You are probably going to require a **crossover** (or **dropped kerb** as they are also referred to), in which case you'll need to contact your local council to get not only permission to change the pavement, but also costs for doing so. (It's highly likely that they will only let you install one if it's undertaken by one of their own contractors.)

This isn't normally too costly (expect to pay around £1,500, although prices vary), but you'll need both permission and the dropped kerb in place before you can say that you've created a bona fide off-road parking space. Also, check to see if you live on an unclassified road (in which case it's likely you can do the works under permitted development). If you live on a classified road, you will need planning permission; in which case, as well as the local Highways Office, you'll also need to speak to your local Planning Department. Same applies if you live in a designated area or listed building – check to see what consents you need before you start any works.

There are also rules about what materials you should use to construct your new driveway; these have to allow for adequate water drainage. You can find out more about this by looking on the planning portal website (**www.planningportal.gov.uk**). Common sense would also suggest that you need to make sure that the area of your front garden you want to convert into a parking space is actually big enough to take a car and that your vehicle won't overhang onto the pavement or road. Yes, yes, I know it's obvious but you'd be surprised how many people don't consider that one.

Another thing to think about is access to your new parking spot. Is there a bus stop, road sign, telegraph pole, speed bump, pedestrian crossing, grass verge or tree in the way? If you've got one (or more) of these obstacles between the road and your proposed driveway, should the council give you the go ahead you will have to pay extra for these elements to be moved. It's not insurmountable, but you do need to talk it through with the Highways Office and consider the financial implications.

So there are a few things to mull over but providing you do your homework, adding off-road parking is one of the least expensive yet potentially most profitable improvements that you can make to your property.

7. *The Don'ts*

Just because you can make some changes under permitted development rights, doesn't mean to say you *should*.

Over the next few pages, I'm going to tell you about common mistakes that some people make that, contrary to popular belief, generally don't add value and can, in many cases, actually make it harder to sell.

It's tough love folks, because I don't want you to spend your hard-earned cash on making what you think are improvements, only to find out later on that you've at best made things more difficult for yourself or, at worst, wasted money and devalued your property. I'm looking out for your best interests here, not trying to offend anyone, I promise.

Alright, now I've got that bit off my chest, let's look at the one of the most common gaffes people make when updating their gaff.

Converting a garage into living space

Sounds like a good idea in principle, right? Yep, it probably does until you consider this very obvious but often overlooked fact: a garage is a major selling point that adds considerable value.

Take that away to create a playroom and you've invariably devalued your property more than you would have done had you just left the place as it was and not added a few extra square metres of living space. Unless you have the spare land to erect a separate garage to make up for the one you've just used to enlarge your kitchen, it's not worth doing.

Why is this such a bugbear? Well, think about the amount of stuff you have and what most people usually keep in their garage. It's not their car, I can tell you. If you take that away, where else do you store your bikes, garden furniture, tools, extra freezer and deck chairs? Precisely.

The other common mistake on this one is to turn your garage into an additional bedroom, thinking that this is going to add thousands to the value of the property. Err, nope, in most cases it won't. As I said earlier in this chapter, most people only perceive a bedroom to be a bedroom if it's upstairs. So that's probably not going to work either.

If you're absolutely hell-bent on converting an integral garage then for goodness' sake think long and hard about your plans. Make sure that the new living area is *seamlessly* incorporated into your existing layout so that it looks considered and not 'tacked on'. Also, think about what I said in terms of adding additional outbuildings or a replacement garage to balance out what you've taken away. Just remember the principles around how much space on your plot these take up and at what point you will need planning consent.

If you're in any doubt about what I'm saying, let me quote one of my estate agent friends Nigel, who gave me the following advice to pass on to you:

> *"People think converting their garage will add value. In the majority of cases it won't. We see so many people who've spent thousands thinking they are doing the right thing end up with a property that sits on the market for months. Eventually they have to drop their asking price to sell. So in effect, they've not only devalued the property, they've also wasted the money they spent on the work in the first place. If someone is thinking about converting their garage, I tell them to spend the money on a new bathroom or kitchen instead. That's a far better use for the same budget and whilst it won't increase the size of the property, it will make it more desirable and easier to sell."*

Believe me now?

Swimming pools and hot tubs

Here's another thorny subject guaranteed to split opinion. Pools are considered by some to be the last word in luxury whereas others would say that they are expensive to run, a nightmare to maintain and a serious safety hazard for those with children or pets. Similar reactions also occur when it comes to hot tubs and garden ponds.

So choosing whether or not to install one really goes back to how long you are going to be in the property. It also depends on whereabouts you live in the country. If you reside in one of the balmier regions, such as the south coast, and are going to be in the property for a very long time, an outside pool may be something you'll get a lot of use out of. So it could be worth taking the plunge, so to speak.

But if you plough thousands into installing a pool and then fail to use it more than a few times a year because you live in a less temperate area, not only is it money you could have better spent on other improvements, it's also unlikely that a buyer is going to find it a turn-on when you come to sell.

The other thing that doesn't exactly help the case of any water feature is that if a buyer really doesn't like it, they perceive that it's going to cost thousands to remove. Now, you *can* fill in a swimming pool to create a massive ornamental flowerbed pretty easily and affordably, but a lot of prospective purchasers won't see it that way. It's an obstacle; another thing about the property they may have to change which will create extra expense and aggro.

A lot of agents are used to seeing negative reactions to 'water features' so advise clients selling properties with pools or ponds to have the costs of getting rid of them handy. That way they can address this objection with a potential buyer during a viewing should the need arise.

So, in short, if it's going to enhance your life and you're going to live in the property for a long time, go for it. But don't expect it to add thousands and thousands to your bank balance when you come to sell.

CONSERVATORIES

Oh no, here's another one I know some of you won't thank me for. Conservatories. One man's dream is another man's UPVC nightmare. They really are more contentious than most people realise and right up there in terms of the top ten things that turn some buyers off.

The question is, how much value do they *really* add?

Well, it all depends on what you actually consider a conservatory. If it's a high-quality build of a sympathetic design, using materials in keeping with the rest of the property (say, a period-style orangery on a Victorian house) you're reasonably safe. You should be able to recoup your costs when you come to sell. Adding additional value? Hmmm, tricky. You'd be lucky. However, a cookie-cutter UPVC jobbie tacked on the rear of any residence isn't going to appeal to everyone and has been known to put a lot of people off.

Another oft-overlooked fact is that a conservatory only adds real appeal if you can use it all year around. Yes, I know, it's one of those 'obvious' things again, but you'd be surprised how many people make this fundamental howler. They buy a lovely house with a south-facing garden. Then stick a double-glazed monstrosity on the back without any air conditioning. Thus creating an environment that would rival Dante's *Inferno* in the summer months, and which is chilly in the winter without a fan heater, thermals and a blanket. That's not going to work for a lot of people as a room you can use 365 days a year now, is it? But you'd be amazed at how often it does happen.

Then you've got the more serious structural issues that go a lot deeper than the aesthetics. Movement between the main building and conservatory is a common issue, normally caused because the addition has been built on minimal foundations. Then you've got problems with leaks, due to lack of flashing or cavity trays (that's lead work which seals the join between the house and conservatory) or overspill from insufficient valley gutters, along with complications that stem from blown sealed units. Make no mistake, unless you do the job properly and use a reputable company that will give you guarantees for the work, you could be storing up serious trouble for later. Have I put you off yet?

Most worryingly, even if you do spend a lot of money to get it right, you've got the unknown factor which is that if a potential buyer doesn't agree with your idea of good taste, they could perceive that the conservatory will be expensive and difficult to have rectified or removed. So they just won't bother and will end up buying somewhere else instead.

As with the swimming pool debate, if you're going to be in the property for ten, fifteen or twenty years and this is something that you will use all the time and are willing to spend the money to do it properly, well, proceed if you must – but with caution. Likewise, if you're shelling out tens of thousands on a pucker redevelopment project and you can integrate a space more along the lines of a garden room into your plans, with brick walls and a pitched roof as well as perhaps underfloor heating, air conditioning and classy sash-style windows (together with those ubiquitous bi-fold doors), then great, go ahead.

But don't expect to add *huge* amounts of value. It just makes for a more appealing prospect than the usual plastic-and-glass box.

A lot of people think that by adding on a conservatory they've gained about 20% on the value of their house. I'm sorry to tell you that's just not the case. Please don't hate me for saying it, but really think long and hard about this one. If you're smart and make it feel like it's part of the original fabric of the building, well, you may just get away without devaluing your property and if you're really, really lucky you might get some of your money back. But other than that, I beg you, please don't go there.

8. Other things to consider

There are so many things to ponder when weighing up the pros and cons of making improvements to a property, and to be honest there are far too many for me to cover in this chapter. Many other books have been written on and dedicated to this very topic. Suffice to say, all I'm aiming for here is to draw your attention to the more frequently experienced aspects so that you can consider carefully what your next steps are and ensure you do the correct research.

But I did want to mention a few other things that I think everyone should reflect upon before starting any sort of property enhancement. As with a lot of things I've written in this book, some of you may read these and think, "She's stating the bleedin' obvious." But I don't believe I'd be doing my job properly if I didn't point these things out. If nothing else, they will give you a giggle at other people's naivety (for that also read 'stupidity'). So sit back, enjoy and prepare to potentially feel very smug.

KEEPING ON TOP OF YOUR BUDGET

Before you start, get quotes – not estimates, there is a difference in law – for everything down to the last door knob and really be sure that you've got a handle (no pun intended) on how much the whole exercise will cost you. Add a 10% contingency budget in case the wheels come off. Then stick to it. Rigidly.

266

I see so many projects where people have got themselves into financial difficulties because they didn't properly plan and budget at the start. At best, this means the job takes a lot longer, because they have to stop halfway through and find the additional money. Or it never gets finished – a real nightmare when they come to sell. If you run short of dosh there is also a temptation to scrimp on the more important elements which can cause big problems when you come to get your building regs signed off (something you'll need to do when you come to put the property on the market).

So, get to grips with Excel, build yourself a spreadsheet and stay in control of your money.

Whilst we're on the subject of finances, protect yourself and negotiate staged payments with your contractors – say, 40% on commencement, another 30% when you're halfway through and 20% on completion. With the remaining 10% paid once everything is completed to your satisfaction. *Never pay 100% upfront. Ever.*

USE PROFESSIONAL, QUALIFIED TRADESPEOPLE

I'm still amazed at the amount of people who get taken in by cowboy builders. Don't be one of them. Check to make sure your contractors are registered with the relevant trade body, and look on websites such as **www.ratedpeople.com** or **www.checkatrade.com**.

Best of all, go on personal recommendation. If a friend, neighbour or family member has recently had a project completed and had a good experience, ask for the contractor's details. Do remember that the best tradespeople are rarely short of work and get booked up months in advance, but it's always worth waiting to get the right people on the job.

Also, before you commit to anyone, ask to see their work – ideally visit the properties where they've completed work in the past. Check their terms and conditions and ask how they organise their project planning and management. Ask to see a project plan and job spec so you know everything has been considered, and that they are on the ball.

Consider achievable values and the Stamp Duty threshold

If you're spending money with the express intent of eventually making a profit, for goodness' sake do the maths first to make sure the numbers stack up.

Why? Well, you need to figure out how much profit you'll make *after* your costs versus what's achievable. This is based on a couple of factors:

Firstly, what other properties in the same area are currently selling for. So easy-peasy lemon squeezy, just go online and see what houses that have already got the attributes you're planning to add are selling or have sold for. Don't get all competitive and try to set the ceiling price for the road, just be realistic. You could also speak to your friendly estate agent and ask them what they would value your house at with the improvements made. They are at the coalface in your local area and know better than anyone what buyers are looking for, so that's great advice if you can get it.

The other element is that buyers are put off a property valued too close to a Stamp Duty threshold. For example, if your property is currently valued at £210,000 then I'd say spend a maximum of £20,000 on improvements with a view to potentially making up to £20,000 profit. At £250,000 you'll hit the Stamp Duty ceiling and it's unlikely you'd get £265,000 (you may want to read Chapter 4, 'Buying Your First Home' for more info on Stamp Duty and why it's such a key factor in property valuation).

Overextending

No, I'm not talking about your mortgage. Extending for the sake of it won't necessarily create additional value, it's more likely to just put people off. If you create a large house that sits on a disproportionately small plot, you're going to end up with something which is tough to sell. You. Have. Been. Warned.

Don't underestimate 'kerb appeal' and 'wow factor'

Electric gates, private gardens that aren't overlooked and a well-kept exterior are all things that will impress would-be buyers before they've even walked through the door. These things don't necessarily add value but they do add *desirability*.

Likewise, when you go inside, aim for a quality finish. Heavy internal doors and stylish handles make more of an impact than you realise. A well-specced kitchen and bathrooms really do turn heads. These are the things that make people fall in love with a property within the first few minutes of their viewing. The devil is in the detail, as they say. But a word of caution on bathrooms and kitchens...

Don't over-personalise big ticket items

If you're spending money on a big ticket item like a kitchen, don't make it too personal unless you're going to be there for a long time.

A few years ago, I was helping a professional sportsman and his girlfriend find their first home together. They were a lovely couple to work with, dream clients in fact, and as you can imagine they had a rather generous budget – so the properties we were viewing were stunning.

However, there was one fairly unique element that I had to factor in: the lady in question had extracted a rather unusual promise from her other half. Regardless of what they bought, she wanted a pink kitchen. Yes, that's right, pink.

The house I eventually found for them was magnificent, as it should have been for a couple of million, and it had already been redeveloped to an exceptional standard. My buyers could have picked up their personal possessions and moved straight in – I would have done, that's for sure. But the designer kitchen, brand new and worth tens of thousands in its own right, was the wrong colour. It had to go.

In its place went a strawberry-milkshake hued confection of painted units and bespoke composite worktops colour-matched to her favourite nail varnish (yes, really), even a cerise cooker. To be fair, whilst it wasn't my cup of tea, it was pretty amazing and it certainly had the 'wow' factor.

I don't think the guy ever cooked or made a cup of tea (by his own admission) so it didn't bother him in the slightest. Until a couple of years later when they wanted to sell.

Then I got the phone call to pop round. The girlfriend, now his wife, tearfully explained that the property had been on the market for a few months with no takers. They'd already dropped the price once, but the agent was still struggling and they couldn't understand what the problem was, particularly given the buoyant market in the area and the fact that everything else was selling very quickly.

It's not going to take you too long to work out what my answer was. As tactfully as I could, I gently explained that the kitchen, along with some of the other more 'imaginative' interior design choices, possibly wasn't everyone's cup of tea and that it might be wise to revisit a few rooms and introduce a more 'diffused' palette.

I packed them off on holiday for a few weeks and told them to leave it with me and I'd see what I could do.

One month, one updated kitchen and a tribe of painters and decorators later, we listed the property via another agent and quickly secured an offer at the asking price. My clients were delighted. I was relieved.

The moral of the tale? Even at that level, buyers just couldn't see past the couple's taste. They didn't want to spend what they thought would be another couple of hundred thousand to get the place looking, well, normal. It didn't cost my clients anywhere near that to make the changes needed, but perception is everything. That's what was holding the property back.

Of course, this is an extreme example, but the point is relevant regardless of how much you're spending. Redecorating to make a property feel like your own is one thing. Upgrading the kitchen is a great way to add desirability. But never, *ever* invest a lot of money making something so personal that the only person it will ever appeal to is you.

Conclusion

Before I leave you to consider all I've said, one final word on improving a property to add value. Do it well or don't bother.

Unless your finish is spot on, you've got guarantees for the works, proof of your permissions and your building regs are signed off, you will have issues when you come to sell. If you take nothing else I've said in this chapter on board, please remember this one thing.

Oh, and no pink cookers either, eh?

10.
Moving
Stories

I don't know about you, but when I move house, as soon as I've got the keys and I'm through the door, the first thing I do is clean…everything.

Maybe it's some weird, inbuilt nesting instinct, or an addiction to the smell of Mr Muscle. Whatever it signifies, it's only once I've finished polishing, hoovering and disinfecting that I can begin to even think about unpacking. And I've moved house a lot. At the last count, eleven times in the last fifteen years.

I'd like to think that makes me qualified enough to:

a) Know better than to do it again anytime in the near future, and

b) Pass on a few pearls of wisdom I've learned the hard way.

It never gets any easier – you just get more organised and able to foresee problems before they happen because you've been through the pain before. These days, I pride myself on being able to do a total move, with all boxes emptied and everything put away and organised, within seventy-two hours.

How do I do that? Well, for me, moving house is akin to a military operation. The more planning you put into it, the smoother the process. I've got a spreadsheet that I adhere to religiously, a list for everything (and I do mean *everything*), and all boxes receive the colour-coded sticker treatment. I've got a removal company that I've used for my last six moves (they don't do loyalty points, more's the pity) who patiently allow me my foibles and do a magnificent job.

OK, so my approach might not be everyone's cup of tea, but you know, it works for me, and even if you only pick up a couple of tips from my ramblings, hopefully it'll make your life a bit easier. If not, at least I might be able to entertain you with tales of my neurotic behaviour.

Now, other than spreadsheets, the other thing I love is a good list. I adore lists. In fact, I'm so addicted to them, I thought I'd make a couple for you as well so that you can tick away to your heart's content.

Seriously, with so much going on in your life, I thought it might help to give you my top five questions to ask the previous tenant or owner before they move out. If you can, email these to the letting agent or your estate agent, and then get the response by email so that it's one less piece of paper to lose:

1. Where are the gas and electricity meters?

2. Where is the thermostat and do you have any written instructions on how to reset the timing on the central heating?

3. Where are the main stopcock and fuse box?

4. What day are the bins collected? Are there particular rules about recycling? What sort of bin bags are required?

5. Which company currently supplies the energy, broadband and home phone?

If you can at least get the answers to these questions before moving day, it's going to really help you get your phone and broadband transferred, your utility bills set up for the new place and, most importantly, make sure you've got heating and hot water for when you just need to sit in the bath for a while.

Next up, get your post redirection in place. This is so easy to do, and can be sorted very quickly either online at **www.royalmail.com** or in person at your nearest Post Office.

Once you've exchanged and got your move date confirmed, get it all sorted out a minimum of five working days before you move. This gives Royal Mail a chance to get the service in place in time. Not only will this ensure that your 'Happy New Home' cards all arrive, it will help to protect you against identity theft, which is rather handy.

The next task is quite daunting, but it's an administrational chore not digging a ditch, so build a bridge and get over it. Yes lovely people, you need to confirm you're moving with a whole host of companies, organisations and individuals. There are no quick fixes to this. It's just about being methodical and crossing them off as you go. At least there's one less thing to do because I've made the list you'll need for that as well:

Financial

- Bank/building society
- Credit card
- Finance agreements and loans
- Pensions and investments
- Store cards
- Buildings and contents insurance
- Life insurance

Car

- Motor insurance
- DVLA (car registration and driver's licence)
- Breakdown service
- Car finance

Government

- Electoral Commission
- Council Tax
- Benefit providers
- HMRC

Utilities

- Gas
- Electricity
- Water
- Landline phone
- Mobile phone
- Internet service provider
- Cable/satellite/digital TV provider
- TV licence

Health

- Doctor
- Dentist
- Optician
- Donor card
- Medical insurance

Kids

- Nursery
- School
- College
- University
- Private tutors
- Babysitter
- Sports teams/after school clubs

Pets

- Pet insurance
- Vet
- Dog walker
- Microchip registration
- Name tag on collar (if you're changing the number)

Others

- Gym
- Loyalty cards
- Magazine subscriptions
- Newspaper deliveries
- Place of work

Do not put doing this off – make sure that you contact any and all of the relevant folk before you move and give them at least seven working days to make the necessary changes to your records. Don't forget, with important stuff like your bank account, you are going to have to present yourself at a branch with ID and proof of your old address (normally two utilities bills).

Also, boring but important, if you don't tell DVLA that you've moved, you are liable to incur points and a fine because both your vehicle records and driving licence will be incorrect. If you are registered with the Government Gateway, then there is a miracle tool that means you can update your address for HMRC *and* your driving licence online, and it's almost painless. Yes, really. I promise you, I've used it the last couple of times I've moved house and it rocks. Worth a go anyway. You can find out more and register by going to **www.gateway.gov.uk**.

So, the paperwork is out of the way. Now the real fun starts. Well, fun *is* a relative term, of course.

1. *Declutter in advance*

My mother once said:

"If we ever move, we'll need one van for all the furniture, and two articulated lorries for all the rubbish in the loft I've collected over the years."

Unsurprisingly, she hasn't moved house since Thatcher was in power.

Now, I really do believe there is a little bit of my Mum in all of us. That 'I'll just keep it because you never know when you might need it' philosophy is as germane to guys as it is to gals. You don't think so? OK, tick any or all of the following that apply:

• Clothes that were once favourites that you can't bear to throw out because of the great memories they hold.

• That pile of vinyl that you haven't played in years because you don't have a turntable, but which you simply can't part with on nostalgic grounds. Even though you've downloaded the same tracks from iTunes.

• Proper photos that are a bit creased around the edges; like pictures of you and your Uni mates (who you've not seen for years) gurning your way round fresher's week.

• Tat that you've bought as you've travelled the various continents, reminding you of a time when you were free and had no responsibilities. Extra points scored for carved wooden animals/men/masks/pictures painted by elephants with their trunks or any kind of musical instrument you carried onto a plane against the wishes of the air hostess.

• Ski gear that you bought in a sale five years ago but that you've never actually got round to using, which is now slightly dated so chances are it will never get an airing.

Come on, you know what I'm talking about. When you think about it, the real pain of moving house isn't the big stuff, like sofas and beds. It's packing up all the little objects that are effectively your life. It's impossible not to have to look at *everything*, reminisce a bit, then spend ages working out where it's all going to go when you reach the other end.

Over the years (and eleven house moves) I've become almost Spartan-like in my approach to possessions. Yes, it's lovely to have a few treasured keepsakes, but try and keep it to one or two boxes' worth. As for the rest of it, employ the six-month rule:

> *"If you've not worn it, used it or looked at it in more than six months, you don't need it. End of."*

That means it can either go to the charity shop, on eBay, or in the (recycling) bin. You choose, just do it. The more you streamline your life with regard to clutter, the easier you'll find your move and the tidier your new pad will be from the outset.

Start the de-junking exercise at least a month or so before you move, to give you time to sort through stuff and get it all packed up in good time. Otherwise, you'll find the bags that were destined for Oxfam will somehow magically end up in the removal van, then in your new home, and then sit in the spare room until you move house again. Not what we're looking to achieve.

2. Book your new phone line or broadband connection

Ask anyone who has moved house in the last few years what their biggest nightmare was, and I reckon you'll come back with the same answer: getting the broadband sorted. They should start a survivors' club, you know.

But out of pain and frustration is born nerves of steel, and these days, having been burned before, I know the drill. It's all about meticulous planning and constant nagging. Trust me – it works, but you have to be determined.

As soon as you have your moving date confirmed, ring that horrific, automated customer service line. Once you've eventually navigated your way through the whole "Key one for enquiries about your current line, key two for technical faults... key forty-six to arrange your own funeral because you've died of boredom" routine, you will eventually get to speak to an advisor.

If the property you're moving to already has a live phone line and broadband connection installed, this is relatively straightforward. You'll need to ring your provider again the week before to make sure they're awake, that all the arrangements are in place and that they will switch you off at one gaff and switch you on at the other on the right day, and send you a final bill. They should also be able to give you your new landline number. Then it's just a question of ringing yet again the day before to make sure they are still awake, that they haven't forgotten and fingers crossed, all will be well.

Plug in your router as soon as you can on the day that the switchover should take place (see Section 7, 'My tried and tested two-day move plan'). If your little green light is on and you've got tinterweb, then stand back and pat yourself on the back. Mission accomplished.

However, if you're moving into a brand-new pad or where there currently isn't a live line going into the property and you need to be connected to the exchange and get broadband plumbed in, then welcome to hell my friend.

You're going to have to deal with making an appointment for an engineer to come out, as well as keeping on top of your order to make sure they haven't forgotten you. Whatever you're doing, always have your customer reference number to hand – this ensures that they can find your file quickly; when you're speaking to a call centre operative for the eighteenth time that day, it will be a bonus. (Quoting a telephone number isn't as efficient due to the way most call centre systems are set up. Ask me how I know this. I dare you…)

Make notes of who you spoke to and when, and if they have a department, take a note of that for good measure, so that when it goes wrong – and it probably will – you've got a record of who said they would do what, by when. Always, always, always ring the day before an engineer is due to come to visit to confirm that he really will be there. Yes, I realise that you'll probably be given one of those 'it will either be between 8am and 1pm or 1pm and 5pm' time slots, but at least stay on their case to make sure someone is turning up. Do not leave it to chance.

If you want a hope of getting broadband relatively quickly after you've moved in, you generally need to book this ten days *after* you've had your new line installed, or not more than seven days in *advance* if you've had an existing line reconnected – but different providers vary, so do check. Again, it's a question of being organised, putting in the call and continuing to chase. Assume that it's all in hand at your peril. The more you ring and pester, the higher the odds that you will, actually, get what you want, when you want it.

Whilst we're on the subject of broadband, it's always handy to find out what speeds you'll be able to expect at your new place. Uswitch (**www.uswitch.com**) has a great tool that allows you to check broadband speeds and see what providers are offering in your area. All you'll need is the postcode of your new property. It's also worth doing to make sure your current provider (should you wish to stick with them) can continue to supply you at the new place. I'm not going to go into detail here about how to switch to another supplier – suffice to say it's up to you to change to a different company, but for the purposes of this chapter, I'm assuming that it's your main priority just to get in and get online.

If you want to take your current provider with you to your new property, I strongly suggest you talk to them a few weeks before you move, just so you can find out what you need to do. Courage, mon brave.

3. DIY vs The Professionals

Sounds obvious, but moving is not a job to do single-handedly – even if you're flitting from one flatshare to another and don't have much in the way of furniture or big stuff to shift. What appears to be not a lot – clothes, TV and a few boxes – never all fits in the boot of your car in one go. It's going to take at least three trips (it always does, I don't know why) so to be more efficient, rope in friends or family to assist – anyone with an estate or 4×4 is especially welcome.

Alternatively, hire yourself a van and bribe some mates to help with the heavy lifting. But do think about how far you're actually moving. If it's just around the corner or 20 minutes up the road, and you don't have that much stuff, you'll probably get away with a DIY job. I would always recommend hiring a bigger van than you think you'll need, because for the extra ten or twenty pounds, it normally turns out to be money well spent. The fewer trips you need to make, the less fraught you'll be.

Also, unless your spatial awareness is excellent, it's actually quite hard to visualise how much cubic capacity you will require just from looking at a load of stuff strewn around a room.

If you have a few bits of bulky furniture to contend with, if at all possible try and get something with a tail lift (that's a sort of mini Stannah stairlift to the rear of your truck). It will really save your back when you're trying to get large, heavy and awkward items into and out of it. Also make sure you've got plenty of blankets or towels to wrap around furniture to stop it getting scratched, as well as plenty of rope or ties to secure things to the inside of the truck to stop them from moving around whilst you're in transit.

It's worth asking about these sorts of things when you ring the van-hire place to see if they can throw a few in for you. Also see if you can get yourself a couple of sack trucks as well; they will come in handy for lugging heavy boxes and other items, and really do help to avoid putting too much pressure on your back if used correctly. Again, ask your van-hire company if they have any you can hire, or if they come included in your rental price.

The other thing to consider if you're self-moving is insurance. Unfortunately, accidents do happen, and you may not be covered under your contents insurance policy automatically, so it's worth checking what the deal is. Some policies include cover for house moves free of charge, whilst some only allow a percentage or capped amount of cover, so look into this before you start.

If, however, you're moving a *lot* of furniture along with the rest of your worldly possessions, it really is a task for the experts – particularly if you're moving some distance, as you'll need to do it all in one trip. I realise that hiring a removal company isn't a cheap exercise; according to Pickfords, the average cost of using professional movers is £900, and of course the larger your property and/or more stuff you have, the more expensive it gets. But trust me, if you can possibly find the money to do it, your move will go a whole lot smoother and you will find yourself less stressed and exhausted. These guys do it all day, every day. Trust me, there really is a knack to getting a three-seater sofa into a second floor apartment.

To find a good removal company, either ask around and get one on recommendation or take a look at the **British Association of Removers** website (**www.bar.co.uk**) for registered companies in your area. Members of BAR will have signed up to a strict code of practice, offer pre-payment protection and there's also an independent alternative dispute resolution service, just in case things go wrong. Get three companies round to quote for the job, and don't forget to ask about things like:

- **Goods in Transit insurance**: how much are they covered for in case of any accidents? What's the excess and is there a limit per item you can claim for?

- **What's included in the price**: for example, some companies charge extra to completely pack the contents of your kitchen cupboards for you, as it's fiddly and takes longer.

- Do they offer **cancellation insurance** in case your move falls through? (Handy if you're buying and booking your removals before you've exchanged.) And do they offer late key waiver in case your move date is postponed?

- Whether they will lend you **mobile wardrobes**: these are massive cardboard boxes with hanging rails in them, so you just load your clothes from the wardrobe in at one end, then take them out and hang them straight up at the new place... assuming you've got wardrobes to put them into, that is.

- **How many people** they are actually going to send round to help you on the day.

Most removal companies will include dismantling and reassembling beds in their fees, though again it's worth checking. They will usually provide specialist packing materials for delicate items like electrical equipment, china and glass.

Once you've selected your removal company, get them to put their quote in writing, so you know exactly what it's all going to cost and to eliminate any surprises on the day. Most removal companies will expect you to box up your things before they arrive on moving day, so that when they pitch up the majority of packing is done and they can get on with loading up the lorry. They may help you with the odd box or two, but unless you've ordered the full monty service, expect to have to do some things yourself in advance.

On the day there will probably be a team leader – he's the guy in charge of the crew and who you need to talk to about any items that need special care. Although I find sticking big labels on stuff marked 'Fragile – Don't Move Without Telling Me' works quite effectively. Spend five minutes before you get started running through everything with whoever's in charge. If, like me, you've made a list that relies on colour-coded stickers on boxes, explain this to the nice man *before* they start loading.

Any personal items that you wouldn't feel comfortable having anyone else handling should be packed before the removal men arrive and put safely out of the way. I'd also recommend that any small valuables, such as jewellery, laptops etc. are packed by you in your car and not put in with everything else. It's too easy to lose stuff, and there's nothing worse than panicking because you think you've misplaced something and spending weeks trying to find your grandmother's pearl necklace or the PS4 because you know you 'put it in a safe place so you could find it later'. You may also find that some removal companies refuse to move very valuable or specific items, such as jewellery, so do ask the question when you get your quotes. It's best to know upfront should you need to make alternative arrangements for certain bits and pieces.

4. Labelling boxes

This is my favourite part, but then I am a bit obsessive. To maximise efficiency on moving day, get a few sheets of A4, a lot of coloured stickers (the biggest you can find) and a few thick, black marker pens. Create a list (in effect, an inventory of what you're packing) on a separate sheet for each room. As you pack your boxes, clearly number each one on the side with a big black marker pen and make a note of the box number on the sheet for that room.

Next, allocate a coloured sticker for each room in the new place – so red sticker for lounge, green sticker for kitchen, blue for bedroom, etc. – and affix the appropriately coloured sticker on the side of the labelled boxes. This system achieves three things:

1. You'll know how many boxes should be in each room, so it's easy to see if anything is missing or forgotten once you get to your new place.

2. It quickly organises your new home, because stuff goes into the right room first time. Then it's just a question of unpacking boxes and putting your stuff away.

3. If other people are helping you, everyone will know where things belong – providing you make them aware of the system before they start. Clear instructions (particularly if you are using a removal company) will help everyone.

This process does involve a bit of prior consideration; you'll need to know what storage you have in your new home in order to make a call on what boxes should go where. What you want to avoid is everything being dumped in one room, and you then having to work it all out after everyone's gone.

5. *Packing tips from the pros*

If you want to minimise breakages, you need to have the right tools for the job. This invariably involves strong boxes, bubble wrap, brown tape and a lot of paper. I'm not going to insult your intelligence here by explaining how to wrap things in plastic, but I do just want to give you a few nuggets of advice.

• Don't use newspaper to wrap things. Although modern newsprint is better than it used to be, you'll still get smudges of ink on stuff. Use plain white lining paper or sheets of proper packing paper, which you can buy from any DIY store. Or if you're self-moving you can buy packing materials from storage facilities such as Safe Store or Big Yellow Storage. Both of these offer the option of ordering online, so no excuses. If you can, order more than you think you'll need. If you have employed a removal company, check to see if packing materials are included in your price and ask them to drop off everything you'll need a week before so you can get cracking.

• Double tape the base of boxes or risk a 'comedy' moment when you pick it up and everything you've carefully crammed inside falls through the bottom. Not amusing and guaranteed to cause a sense of humour failure. Don't be tempted to skimp on this bit – you need strong cartons, rather than any old cardboard box you can get from the back of a supermarket. Again, you can order cartons online. Get three different sizes – small, medium and large.

• Try to mix light things in with heavier stuff, so you don't end up with boxes so heavy no one can lift them.

• If you've packed a crate full of glasses then write 'GLASS' on at least two sides of the box in big letters. Better to be Ronseal with these sorts of things I find.

- Once you've wrapped them in paper, pack plates on their side, rather than flat. They can withstand more pressure this way, and are less likely to crack if, for example, a heavier box is mistakenly put on top.

- If you run out of bubble wrap, tea towels or pillowcases make good emergency alternatives for wrapping fragile items. If you can find them, that is...

6. Avoiding kitchen nightmares

I can't settle until I've got my kitchen sorted. There's nothing worse than waking up the day after you've moved house and having to open numerous boxes to find a toaster or bowls, just so you can have a bit of breakfast.

If you've followed my advice and labelled your boxes as you pack them, it's going to make this job a whole heap easier, as they will be in the right room to start with. After you've cleaned the insides of the cupboards, you can start to stack things away. Try to replicate how you organised your last kitchen in the new place (e.g. cutlery drawer at the top if that's where it was before) so that you aren't playing 'hunt the crockery' for at least a week.

To help speed up the organisation process in the new place, I pack my kitchen boxes with big letters on the side.

'A' means the box contains essentials, such as mugs, plates or glasses.

'B' means stuff that needs to go somewhere it can easily be got to – such as pots and pans – but can wait a day or so to be unpacked.

'C' means the box has stuff in it I don't use that often – cake tins, serving plates, salad bowls, recipe books etc. – which go in a top cupboard and can be unpacked last.

Yeah, yeah, I know, it sounds OTT, but actually, when you put it into practice, you'd be amazed at how much it helps.

Other jobs to tackle in your kitchen, ideally the day before your main move if you can get access to your new pad (as per Section 7, 'My tried and tested two-day move plan') are:

- Check the taps are running and the sink isn't blocked. If you do have a slow draining situation, you can buy bottles of chemicals from most supermarkets that you slosh down the plughole to nuke things like fat, food and any other nasties that are causing the problem, which in most cases sort it out pretty well. It's a good idea to do this now, so that your sink is usable over the next couple of days when you go to make tea and coffee as sustenance for yourself and those helping you move.

- If the dishwasher has been left by the previous occupiers, consider giving it a spruce up with one of those packs of special cleaner you can buy which you put in an empty machine and run through on a normal cycle. Before you do that, pop out the filter and give it a good scrub under the tap to get rid of any food or debris that may be lodged in there. Also, check the salt level and rinse-aid situation and get everything topped up.

- Likewise, if you've inherited a washing machine, put it through a heavy-duty cycle using some towels just to give it a good freshen up, then wash out the fabric softener compartment and hook out all the lint that gathers around the drum.

- Musty smells emanating from the fridge are easily dealt with by spritzing with hard surface cleaner, followed by a wipe down with a solution of water and bicarbonate of soda. To tackle a really strong stench, pop half a lemon in there overnight; it usually does the trick.

- If the oven needs a bit of TLC, you have a couple of options, although I'd recommend you leave both until you've finished your unpacking. You can either buy an oven-cleaning pack from somewhere like Robert Dyas, Wilkos or most supermarkets. This comes with those plastic bags that you squirt really putrid smelling chemicals into, before popping the oven racks in, leaving and rinsing off a while later (the one I use is called Oven Pride). Or, you can pay a nice man to come in and steam clean your oven for you. The DIY option will cost around a fiver and some elbow grease – it's very satisfying though, even quite therapeutic. To get a man in, expect to pay between £30 to £60, depending on where you are in the country and how big your oven is. It's easy to find someone in your local area online, or look on **www.checkatrade.com** or **www.ratedpeople.com** for recommendations.

7. *My tried and tested two-day move plan*

As I said earlier, I've moved a few times in the last few years, so I've now got my very own moving methodology. And you know what? Out of the goodness of my heart, I'm going to share it with you so that you too can enjoy a less stressful move.

The way I work is to move over a two-day period, doing the 'fiddly' stuff on the first day and the heavy stuff on the second. I always try to arrange my move dates to accommodate this – it just takes a bit of choreography and jiggling, but it really does help you get settled quickly. Of course, if you're in a chain it might be more difficult to organise, but it's always worth asking to see if you can get the extra day. If you're a first time buyer or moving between rented properties, it's pretty straightforward to arrange.

There are a couple of caveats:

- You will need to have packed up your kitchen cupboards and got your clothes sorted before you start. And you will need to have everything ready to go *before* you get your keys on day one for this operation to run smoothly. (I've not allowed time on day one for you to be putting stuff in boxes.)

- You're going to be looking at two very long days, with early mornings and late nights, to complete the schedule. Of course, the more people you've got helping you, the quicker things will get done, so perhaps look at allocating jobs to make the most efficient use of time.

As far as packing up your kitchen goes, this is where reading through Section 5, 'Packing tips from the pros' and the previous section, 'Avoiding kitchen nightmares', may come in handy. It takes a while to wrap fragile items properly and this isn't a job you can rush. Start two or three days before you move so you can take your time and get everything boxed up.

In terms of your clothes, ideally hire some mobile wardrobes. You can literally take everything still on hangers, put them on the hanging rails in the cartons then when you get to the other end they can go straight into your new wardrobes. They are awesome and will save you so much time (and creases). If not, another idea is to use black bin liners as impromptu garment covers. Use sticky tape to fold up and secure the bottoms (you know, like they do when you pick stuff up from the dry cleaners) so that items don't fall out and you can prevent longer clothes dragging on the floor. Just poke your hangers through the bottom of the bags and *voila*! All good to go. You can normally get about five or six hangers into one bin liner – any more than that and things end up crumpled, which is exactly what you're trying to avoid.

Another thing is to pack up your airing cupboard in advance. So towels, bedding, and any clean clothes you've got in there: get it all boxed or bagged up and sorted out because all of that is going over with you on day one as well.

OK, the following plan is all predicated around you getting the keys to your new property on a Thursday lunchtime, and needing to be out of your old place on a Friday afternoon. Obviously it will vary a bit depending on how much cleaning and faffing you have to do, but generally speaking this approach works for most moves:

Thursday lunchtime

Pick up keys to new property as early as possible (the easy bit). Check new property throughout and make a list of all the cleaning jobs. Priorities are:

- Kitchen cupboards.

- Wardrobes in bedrooms.

- Airing cupboard (if there is one).

- Bathroom sink and loo (the shower can wait for now).

Clean through your kitchen cupboards with hard surface cleaner/ bleach/weapon of choice, and slosh a bit of bleach down the sink. Work through the wardrobes to remove any dust and cobwebs and, if you feel the need, spritz with hard surface cleaner also. Dust and clean the airing cupboard, and go over the bathroom sink and toilet to ensure it's clean and ready to use.

Unpack your kitchen boxes. Put everything away as near to where it was located in your old kitchen as you can. Replicate the order of your drawers, where you put your food, plates, glasses etc. As you work through and empty them, pile your boxes in a corner; you'll be taking them back to your old property later on to reuse when packing more stuff for the next day.

If they're in situ, check to see if the fridge and freezer are turned on – if not, get them going now so that they are ready to put food in tomorrow. You may want to give them a bit of a clean now as well (see Section 6, 'Avoiding kitchen nightmares').

THURSDAY AFTERNOON

If today is the day you booked for your existing telephone and broadband line to be switched over (see Section 2, 'Book your new phone line or broadband connection') then it's worth spending a few minutes now to plug in a handset and check your line is working. If you get that longed-for dial tone, connect your router – when the green light flashes, give thanks to the telecommunication gods and and congratulate yourself on a job well done. If not, don't spend (more) time on the phone to your provider today; leave that Herculean task until Monday. Remember, on the day your line is switched over, it can take up to midnight for the change to take effect. So maybe give it another go tomorrow morning before you completely lose the plot.

If you're not using a removal company and have hired a truck, go and pick up it up now so that you can make an early start in the morning. Resist the urge to pack your furniture and rest of your stuff this evening – leaving the van full overnight on your drive or in the road. It's likely that would invalidate your contents insurance, and I'd hate to think that all your worldly possessions would get nicked. If a removal company is doing a two-stage move for you – for example, you're moving a long way away so it can't all be done in one day – they will be locking a full van or lorry away in a secure compound overnight, and will be correctly insured for the procedure.

THURSDAY EVENING

Get yourself something to eat, have a quick break and then get back on the job.

Move your clothes to your new place and get everything hung up. Don't worry so much about hanging everything in colour groups right now (or is that just me?). Just get your things put away so that you can move on to the next job. Unpack anything else that you stored in your wardrobes (shoes, bags, sports equipment etc.) into their new home.

Unpack your airing cupboard. Get your towels, clean bedding and anything else that lives in there neatly stacked and sorted.

Make that the last job for tonight – it's been a long day and you've got an early start tomorrow.

FRIDAY MORNING

If you've got a removal company assisting you, chances are that you will have spent the last few days packing boxes to get everything ready. You *have* been getting everything ready in advance, haven't you? Your team are likely to arrive around 8am, so make sure you're ready to go the minute they get there.

If you're moving yourself, start as early as you can. Things generally take longer than you expect. And if the new owners or tenants are moving into your old house today, you need to allow yourself plenty of time so that you're clear of the property before they arrive. Remember to load the van so that the items you want out first at the other end are packed on the truck last.

Once the whole place is packed up and you're ready to go, take a photo of the meters (see Section 10, 'A couple of other important things to remember…').

Do one last final check of cupboards, wardrobes, garden shed and garage. You'd be amazed how easy it is to forget stuff. Then shut the door for the last time and get on the road to your new pad.

FRIDAY AFTERNOON

Hopefully you're almost there.

By now, if you've followed my plan, your kitchen will be sorted, your clothes will be hanging up, your phone and internet connection will be working – hopefully – and you'll have milk (or wine) in the fridge. The end is in sight.

As you're moving the furniture into your new place, get your bed(s) made as soon as you can. I know that sounds a bit weird, but if you have them ready, later on tonight, at the precise moment that it all gets a bit much, you can just throw in the towel and get some much needed sleep. Rather than having to muck about with mattresses and bed-frames at midnight.

Keep all your bedding handy and put it straight into the bedroom it's destined for on arrival. Likewise, put dressing gowns, PJs and a couple of clean towels in with the bedding so you can find it all easily when you need them most, e.g. when you're knackered, and all you want is a hot shower and bed.

FRIDAY EVENING

In theory, you should be pretty much done. Yes, there may be (colour-coded) boxes in a few rooms but any you can't face unpacking now, you've at least got the weekend to sort.

Of course, don't forget to order yourself pizza, crack open the wine and celebrate. It's a tough job moving, no matter how much help you have, but you've done it.

You do know where the bottle opener is, don't you...?

8. Plug in the TV (and other appliances)

There are practical reasons for doing this as soon as you can. No, it's not so you can take a sneaky breather and catch up on your *Breaking Bad* box set.

Televisions are quite fragile; it only takes a bit of a knock to render your lovely LCD out of action.

If you have used a professional removal company, you need to photograph and report any damage to the team leader as soon as you can. If you've taken **Goods in Transit insurance**, you will have a *limited* time to make a claim in the event of any damage. So it makes sense to check that the telly and any other major electrical appliances that you may have moved are working correctly shortly after you arrive. Make the team leader aware of any problems, so that he can document it the same day.

If you've moved a fridge or freezer, you should leave it stood upright in your new place for at least six hours (24 is preferable) before you turn it on. This allows the coolant gasses inside to settle. Some removal companies will even set your appliances up for you – check with yours to see if this service is included in your quote.

9. Your essentials box

Regardless of how laissez-faire your approach is to moving, and you ignore all my other advice, you should at least do *this*:

Pack one box with the kettle, some teaspoons, tea, coffee, sugar and UHT milk along with a few mugs and plates, some kitchen roll and toilet roll. Throw in a bottle of all-purpose surface cleaner, along with a Stanley knife (and spare blades) and a couple of rolls of bin bags – the ones for garden rubbish are the best, as they are stronger.

Keep your essentials box in your car, *not* the removal van, so you can get to it easily when you arrive. Then at least you can make yourself and anyone else a hot drink throughout the day without the need to ferret around, and you've got most things on hand that you'll need to get you through the first twenty-four hours. Other useful items to have to hand are your mobile phone charger, some painkillers, some plasters and a pair of kitchen scissors.

Also pack yourself an overnight bag with a change of clothes and your toiletries so you don't have to start wading through boxes just to get yourself clean the next morning. Yeah, I know it sounds like one more thing to have to do, but you'll thank me for this one day. Honestly.

10. A couple of other important things to remember...

Reading the meters is my least favourite thing to do (I seem to have a mental block with it) and it's such a chore, but it *is* important.

If you're moving out of a rented place, you might get lucky and the inventory clerk will do it for you. If not, once everything is in the car/van/lorry, give the place a once-over to make sure you've not forgotten anything (pets and children included). Then check your meters and take a note of the readings (do this at the new place when you get there as well). These days, I just take a picture of the meter readings on my mobile – it means I can't lose the bit of paper I've scribbled it on.

Once you've had a couple of days to recover, you can be terribly efficient and ring the utilities companies to arrange your final bills. Better that you do it this way round than wait for the new occupants to get things sorted out, which can lead to confusion and you potentially paying more than you need to.

Check how many sets of keys you've got for your new home – if you've only got one, then it may be a good idea to get a spare set cut asap to avoid any danger of getting distracted and locking yourself and everyone out. You really don't need to be breaking and entering or trying to find a locksmith the day you move house. That said, you may want to book a locksmith for the day *after* you've moved to change the locks and make sure you're as secure as possible. You don't know who else has got a spare key, so this is a smart thing to do, especially if you're living on your own. For the handy amongst you, it's actually relatively straightforward to change the barrel of a lock yourself, and you can pick them up at most DIY stores for twenty to thirty pounds.

If you've moved into an area where you have to display a parking permit on your car, make sure you get it sorted asap. The local traffic warden isn't going to realise that you only moved house a couple of days ago; all he's going to see is the fact that the required sticker isn't on your windscreen.

See, there's a hundred quid or so on a parking fine I've just saved you.

Conclusion

Moving house is, mostly, a positive and exciting time. I wouldn't exactly say it's a pleasure, but there are ways you can make it easier on yourself and reduce some of the stress involved.

The golden rule is: *the more you can do in advance, the better.* Your buyer waiting on the driveway on a hot summer's day with their kids, dog, cat and everything they own sweating in a lorry without air conditioning whilst you frantically throw china into any receptacle you can find is never going to end well.

However with planning, preparation and patience you will triumph. But before you head off down the pub, there's one last thing you *might* want to do.

You see, I thought that this was just my little foible. But, after extensive research, it seems that practically every other female (and some guys) I know will only settle for a box-fresh place to perch their posterior in their new home.

Changing a toilet seat is normally a very quick and easy thing to do – most loos have a standard seat fitting – and it's something that even the most DIY-phobic person can achieve. A word of caution – make sure it's on securely. The first time I changed a toilet seat I thought I'd done a great job, only to fall off it in the most spectacular fashion after a couple of celebratory glasses of wine later in the evening. Enjoy!

Au revoir

If you made it this far, I really hope that this book has:

- Been (slightly) helpful.

- Made you laugh, or at least hasn't been too boring.

- Not offended anyone (if so, please accept my profuse apologies, it certainly wasn't intentional).

As I said at the beginning, this has all been about making information that I believe should be available to everyone easy to understand, accessible and (where possible) light-hearted. Fingers crossed, this compendium gets close, because that means I will have done an alright job and you will feel that buying it wasn't a complete waste of money.

All constructive comments and feedback are always welcome, so if you fancy getting in touch, you can find me on the tinterweb at **www.louisafletcher.com** or **@louisafletcher** on Twitter.

OK then, who's for another cuppa?

Index

315